CONTEMPORARY AMERICAN-JEWISH LITERATURE

Critical Essays

CONTEMPORARY AMERICAN-JEWISH LITERATURE

Critical Essays

Edited by

IRVING MALIN

Indiana University Press

BLOOMINGTON　　　　　　LONDON

Contents

Acknowledgments

"Philip Roth and the Jewish Moralists," by Theodore Solotaroff, appeared in *Chicago Review*, Vol. XIII, no. 4 (Winter, 1959); it is reprinted by permission of the editor.

"Breakthrough?" by David Daiches appeared in *Commentary*, August, 1964. It is reprinted from *Commentary* by permission; copyright © 1964 by the American Jewish Committee.

"The Conversions of the Jews" is from Allen Guttmann's article, "The Conversions of the Jews," *Wisconsin Studies in Contemporary Literature*, Vol. VI, no. 2 (copyright © 1965 by the Regents of the University of Wisconsin), pp. 161–76.

"Jewish Dreams and Nightmares." From the book *After the Tradition* by Robert Alter. Copyright © 1969, 1968, 1967, 1966, 1965, 1964, 1962, 1961 by Robert Alter. Dutton paperback edition, published by E. P. Dutton and Co., Inc., and reprinted with their permission.

The authors gratefully acknowledge permission to quote selections from the writings of Bellow, Malamud, and Shapiro as noted below.

Saul Bellow, *Mr. Sammler's Planet*, copyright © 1969, 1970, by Saul Bellow. All rights reserved. Reprinted by permission of The Viking Press, Inc., and Weidenfeld & Nicolson.

Bernard Malamud, *The Assistant*, copyright © 1957, Farrar, Straus and Cudahy, Inc., and Eyre and Spottiswoode (Publishers) Ltd.; *The Fixer*, copyright © 1966 Farrar, Straus and Giroux, Inc., and Eyre and Spottiswoode (Publishers) Ltd.; *The Magic Barrel*, copyright © 1958, Farrar, Straus and Cudahy, Inc., and Eyre and Spottiswoode (Publishers) Ltd.; *A New Life*, copyright © 1961, Farrar, Straus and Cudahy, Inc., and Eyre and Spottiswoode (Publishers) Ltd.; *Pictures of Fidelman*, copyright © 1969, Farrar, Straus and Giroux, Inc., and Eyre and Spottiswoode (Publishers) Ltd.

Karl Shapiro, *The Bourgeois Poet*, copyright © 1964; *Poems of a Jew*, copyright © 1958; "The Alphabet," copyright 1953 by Karl Shapiro;

"The Dirty Word," copyright 1947 by Karl Shapiro; "The First Time," copyright © 1957 by Karl Shapiro; "The Leg," copyright 1944 by Karl Shapiro; "Exile," copyright 1951 by Karl Shapiro; "The Kiss," copyright 1951 by Karl Shapiro; "The Synagogue," copyright 1943 by Karl Shapiro; "The University," copyright 1940 and renewed 1968 by Karl Shapiro. All reprinted with the permission of Random House, Inc.

Portions of the Introduction are reprinted by permission of the editors of *Studies in Short Fiction*, *Reconstructionist*, and *Commonweal*.

CONTEMPORARY AMERICAN-JEWISH LITERATURE

Critical Essays

Introduction

In 1964 Irwin Stark and I edited an anthology of contemporary American-Jewish literature entitled *Breakthrough*. We included selections from the poetry, essays, and fiction of more than twenty writers. Our collection was widely reviewed by critics, who invariably questioned the choice of selections—why this story? why that writer?—or the idea of a literary *movement*. They assumed that they knew the real definitions of "Jew" and "American"— that our schematic introduction missed the point!

In 1965 I wrote *Jews and Americans*. I tried to clarify and complete the interpretation presented in the anthology. Again there were many reviews—including a lengthy "non-review" by Stanley Kauffmann on the front page of the *New York Times Book Review* (May 30, 1965)—and these were once more the "launching pads" for speculations about the movement.

I have not bothered to reread either of the two books—which I now realize were surely "breakthroughs"—or the different reviews they received. I know, however, that American-Jewish literature continues to flourish. (I have learned that Irving Howe and Sheldon Norman Grebstein are working on critical studies. Their approaches will be different from mine.) It is the only movement in twentieth century American literature as important as the "Southern Renaissance."

I do not want to repeat here my book-length interpretation of the subject. I continue to insist that it can and should be approached from a "theological" framework. Malamud, Bellow, Shapiro, Philip Roth—to name a few writers—give us new read-

ings of American-Jewish experience, but they consciously or unconsciously celebrate traditional religious moments (exile, covenant, transcendence, etc.). Even when they are most "modern,"
they dramatize the heritage they cannot escape.

I hear the objections. *Portnoy's Complaint, Pictures of Fidelman, The
Bourgeois Poet* are not "theological"! They are even anti-Jewish!
There is no doubt that some of our writers are celebrating rebellion against the religions they once learned, and they have
reached the point of being as "sexy" as *Playboy*. But they still
retain their sense of irony and "sacred rage"; they know that their
"complaints" are not merely physical or neurotic. The more they
write about "exotic" Italy (Malamud) or Protestant America
(Roth in *When She Was Good*), the more they affirm the source of
their creative ambivalence. That source is not Middle America or
Mother and Father; rather, it is the search for new images of
divinity in the absence of orthodox belief. Our best writers are
"mad crusaders," hoping for a transcendent ideal—art, potency?
—to replace the tarnished ones they embraced in their youth.

I find that various critics who have written about American-
Jewish literature do not deal completely with the search for new
images of divinity. Perhaps I can clarify my position, while exploring the validity of their views.

Gerda Charles has brought together in *Modern Jewish Stories*
(1965) fifteen stories. In her introduction she continually uses the
word "Jewish," but she never defines it. Is a story Jewish because
it contains Jews? Can a Catholic write a Jewish story? Does the
story have to adhere to, or rebel against, orthodox doctrine? Miss
Charles avoids such questions; she apparently believes that such
phrases as "strong delicacy of feeling" for goodness or "tender
sophistication" will explain things.

I disagree. I would try to isolate "Jewish" stories as those that
witness, even in disorted or inverted ways, traditional religious
and literary moments. "The Conversion of the Jews," "Angel
Levine," "The Hand that Fed Me," and "Gimpel the Fool"—to

mention the best stories in Miss Charles' collection—are examples. They demonstrate that their creators seek to escape from exile, to break old covenants, and to embrace transcendent ideals. They are ironic, otherworldly, odd, and biting parables which are written in a state of "mad crusade."

Although Robert Alter is interested in the "theological" approach in his *After the Tradition* (1969), he would probably argue with my previous remarks. He tends to take a dim view of so-called American-Jewish writers as "only peripherally or vestigially Jewish." He notes the "ersatz touches of Jewish local color" in a Wallant or Faust, but he offers little justification for his attacks upon "fakery" in much of American-Jewish literature.

I agree with Mr. Alter's praise of *A Pile of Stones* as a "genuinely religious" book, but I am not sure of his underlying definitions. Surely Hugh Nissenson is trying to do the same thing as the writers I have mentioned; unlike Malamud and Roth, he is a "mad crusader" for a return to orthodoxy. It would, however, be dangerous to say that one crusade is *more* religious than another.

I can illustrate my disagreement with Mr. Alter's approach by quoting the following sentence from his preface: "It would never have occurred to me, for example, to write an essay on Norman Mailer while involved with the concerns of this book because Mailer's Jewish origins have only the most marginal bearing on his work as a writer." Mailer is said to have "Jewish origins." The phrase is ambiguous; we are not told why they are Jewish (we guess that they are a matter of descent). These origins are then called "marginal" to his fiction. Mr. Alter does not leap imaginatively. I find it revealing that Mailer has written on Hassidic tales for *Commentary*, has worshipped the devil in *An American Dream*, and has concerned himself obsessively with new Messiahs throughout his career. I have included an essay on Mailer here which tries to grasp the Jewish activism (actually a search for images of divinity) in his recent work.

Mr. Alter and I read post-traditional American-Jewish litera-

ture in different ways, but we share the assumption that at its best
it ambivalently and powerfully informs us, in his words, "of the
precarious, though stubborn, experiment in the possibilities of
historical continuity, when most of the grounds for continuity
have been cut away." Perhaps this assumption also lies behind
Philip Roth's fascinating statements: "The circumstance of being
born a Jew in America was a very special one in that it announced
not only the specialness of being born, but a kind of extra specialness, the specialness of having been a Jew or being a Jew. This,
however, remained a mysterious thing: one did not know exactly
what it was and so one had to invent being a Jew."

"Invent being a Jew." The phrase captures the central point
that I have been making. Only when unsure of one's heritage
(that is, of the *complete acceptance of one's heritage*) can our writers,
including Roth, try to create disturbing religious fictions.

I believe that Max F. Schulz joins me. In *Radical Sophistication*
(1969) he refuses to chart literary history. He assumes that he
must select important writers (or, better yet, important works by
these writers) and study these in depth. By plunging into the
fictional worlds of Singer, West, Malamud, Mailer, and Salinger,
he convinces us that American-Jewish writers are "radically sophisticated"—they "balance between polarities, too honest to
human experience as they witnessed it either to drop out or
falsify, either to opt for absolution of a personal decision or to
claim the ultimate harmony of contraries."

I think that Mr. Schulz is on safe ground in his insistence upon
dialectics, but at times he uses the phrase "radical sophistication"
in a loose way. Perhaps he should look at Jewish theology for the
real understanding of such sophistication. The theologian,
Abraham J. Heschel, for example, has emphasized that dualities
(exemplified best by exile and Israel) are at the core of Judaism.
The awareness of dualities leads a believer (and even a non-
believer) to an ironic, skeptical view of life. Theology helps to
create psychology. Although Mr. Schulz does not pursue this

point at length, he is right in affirming that techniques of opposition incarnate the vision of life's "uncertainties, mysteries, doubts," which is crucial to the "invention of the Jew."

I am especially impressed by his chapters on Mailer and Salinger, two writers not usually described as Jewish. He demonstrates that they are primarily concerned with their religious heritage. Unable to accept orthodox doctrine or relinquish the need to believe in transcendence, they are uncertain Jews—but aren't all Jews uncertain?—who search desperately for inventive ways to battle and/or accept their heritage. In their heretical, dialectical, and extreme works they present modern equivalents of traditional belief. Mr. Schulz perceives that Mailer defines "power in terms of religious and psychological growth. A conventional release of spirit, a going out of self with its resultant joy—an existential control over self, not a totalitarian authority over others —is what ultimately fascinates Mailer in the mystique of sex and death." The use of religious-sexual imagery in *An American Dream* affirms his contention that only a "radical sophistication" would enable a writer to be open to the Hasidic possibility of marrying body and soul. Salinger's case is also instructive. *Seymour: An Introduction* is for Mr. Schulz a brave, unsuccessful attempt to convey religious contemplation ("mystical" is really a better adjective) through fictional technique. Mysticism does not discriminate; words do. When the two marry, incompletion and boredom result. Salinger is less successful than Mailer in creating the proper dramatic tensions to contain and express religious views.

Obviously my definition of American-Jewish literature is limited. I do not hope to embrace any work containing Jews as necessarily "Jewish," nor do I certify any work by a Jewish writer (that is, one born a Jew) as "Jewish." *Only when a Jewish (by birth) writer, moved by religious tensions, shows "ultimate concern" in creating a new structure of belief, can he be said to create "Jewish" literature.* Certainly such structures will appear heretical, violent, and obsessive. I think of "The Conversion of the Jews," "Eli, the Fanatic," "Seize

the Day," "King Solomon" by Isaac Rosenfeld, *The Assistant,*
many of Karl Shapiro's poems, Fiedler's essays about Simone
Weil or American-Jewish literature, *The Tenants of Moonbloom,* and
An American Dream. Although these works are strikingly different
in form, they capture the dialectics of Jewish thinking or, better
yet, they "invent being a Jew."

In the further attempt to "invent being a Jew"—yes, even an
anthology can try to accomplish such a task!—I am pleased to
present this collection of essays. I have reprinted four overviews
in the first section. It would be difficult to get Solotaroff, Daiches,
Alter, and Guttmann to agree on first (or second) principles—let
alone the achievement of our writers. Guttmann stresses a sociological approach; Alter dislikes "grand mythic plots" and wants
to save art from archetypal criticism; Solotaroff and Daiches deal
with the significance of a literary breakthrough. Of course, no
overview wins. Each critic, however, tries to define Jewishness in
an exciting, complex manner.

Contradictions abound in the second section of nine original
essays. We have studies of individual writers (Malamud, Mailer,
Singer); studies of literary structures (Pinsker on autobiography);
studies of single works *(Mr. Sammler's Planet, Poems of a Jew);*
studies of an archetypal figure (the "Jewish Mother"). I will not
attempt to restate or even quarrel with the interpretations the
various critics offer, but I stress that these contributions are en-
lightening (especially on such relatively undiscussed, new works
as *The Dick, Starting Out in the Thirties,* and *Pictures of Fidelman* and
on such usually slighted forms as literary criticsm and autobiography). They continue the noisy discussion; they leave us with no
"final solutions" about the true achievement of American-Jewish
literature. In the hope of continuing the discussion beyond this
collection, I have included Jackson R. Bryer's rewarding, comprehensive bibliography.

I have tried to speak softly in this introduction because I do not
want to impose my pattern upon what follows. I regard this

collection as a "group encounter." The critical approaches vary; so do the specific subjects—the important point is that all the contributors attempt to capture the essence of American-Jewish, literature. Do the critics succeed? Are they fair or one-sided? Are some closer to the "truth" than others? I leave such questions unanswered. I think that the reader will profit from the communal experience represented here and begin his own search for new images and, therefore, also "invent being a Jew."

March, 1972   IRVING MALIN
                                                          City College
                                            City University of New York

OVERVIEWS

Philip Roth and
the Jewish Moralists*

THEODORE SOLOTAROFF

Goodbye, Columbus, a novella and five stories by Philip Roth, has been widely reviewed and has already stirred up considerable enthusiasm and some acrimony. Neither is surprising. Roth, who is only twenty-six, writes mainly of contemporary Jewish life and does so with special color, freshness, and honesty. The first two qualities are what have pleased most of the reviewers, and the third is what has gotten him into trouble, in a depressingly predictable way, with a number of Jews and liberals. However, the really surprising and elating achievement of Roth's work, at least for this reader, is the way he has triumphed over the major disabilities of his subject.

For one thing, Jewish life seems so self-contained and peculiar, so drenched with nearly invariable shades of local color, that it can become almost inaccessible to the imagination. The writer simply begins to remember and details of character and milieu come by the bucket, along with their own directives for the story's tone and contours; and usually the material is long since played out, overly nostalgic or bitter, and only half true. Also, the Jewish writer's judgment as well as his imagination is likely to find itself

Originally published in Chicago Review, Vol. XIII, no. 4 (Winter, 1959); reprinted by permission of the editor.

being dictated to by his world, which makes so much of morality
as well as the main chance that the writer begins to worry about
the Jewish heritage, the need for good public relations, the fate
of the six million; or if he has shaken that, he can fall into lambast-
ing the goats and ignoring the sheep. In either case, Jewish
material can be as intractable morally as it is imaginatively: one
result is that until fairly recently American-Jewish fiction has been
mainly a vehicle for either reverence or outrage but seldom for
both; the other is that it has been usually very literal, claustral,
repetitive, and rather dull.

All of which makes *Goodbye, Columbus* seem so remarkable. The
consistent vitality of Roth's stories and their full emotional range
give one the sense of a writer who has somehow broken through,
who is really in touch with both the American-Jewish scene and
with himself. Like Wallace Markfield, Roth appears to have
managed it by making the energy and color of his stories flow in
from direct connections to his own wit and feelings and observations, and by an almost aggressive frankness about Jewish experience. In any case, he deals with his situations and characters in
the rare, right way—without piety or apology or vindictiveness,
and by combining a first-rate eye for surfaces with a sense of
depth. All of which sharply distinguishes his Jews from the bland,
sentimentalized robots that Herman Wouk assembles in *Marjorie
Morningstar*. Roth really sees—sees through the Jewish types,
which takes some doing—and his reports are wonderfully candid.
Beneath a more or less "typical" character such as the aging
Epstein—harassed by the lack of a son to inherit his business as
well as by the springtime and the sexuality of the young people
around him—you find a man. And along with the man, you find
again in his strife and griefs something fundamentally Jewish—
for example when he is defending himself for having had an
affair:

"But what! But *this?*" He was pointing at his crotch. "You're a boy, you don't understand. When they start taking things away from you, you reach out, you *grab*—maybe like a pig even, but you grab. And right, wrong, who knows! With tears in your eyes, who can even see the difference!" His voice dropped now, but in a minor key the scolding grew more fierce. "Don't call *me* names. I didn't see you with Ida's girl, there's not a man for that? For *you* it's right?"

Roth does it equally as well and as truly with his unsavory characters. Here is one of his contemporary rabbis—an Army Chaplain —illustrating a contemporary and a probably timeless characteristic:

"It is about the food that I want to speak to you for a moment. I know, I know, I know," he intoned, wearily, "how in the mouths of most of you the *trafe* food tastes like ashes. I know how you gag, some of you, and how your parents suffer to think of their children eating foods unclean and offensive to the palate. What can I tell you? I can only say close your eyes and swallow as best you can. Eat what you must to live and throw away the rest. I wish I could help more. For those of you who find this impossible, may I ask you that you try and try, but then come to see me in private where, if your revulsion is such, we will have to seek aid from those higher up."

Throughout *Goodbye, Columbus* Roth works into his stories what he has seen and felt, fortifying it with his sense of traditional Jewish values and conduct that shows up, for example, in the contrast between the chaplain and the impressive figure of Leo Tzuref in "Eli, the Fanatic." And whether angered or touched or amused by his Grossbarts and Tzurefs and Patimkins, Roth is so obviously attached to Jewish life that the charge of his being anti-semitic or a "self-hater" is the more absurd. The directness of his attack against arrogance, smugness, finagling, and acquisitiveness should not obscure the perfectly obvious fact that he does so flying a traditional Jewish banner of sentiment and humaneness and personal responsibility—all of which makes the accusation have some further melancholy implications.

Most of the reviewers of *Goodbye, Columbus,* however, have been content with reading it as a penetrating social commentary on present-day Jewish life, particularly on the rearrangements of its middle class—whose more prosperous members are drifting out of their urban neighborhoods and parochial culture and into the suburban mainstream of modern American life. Roth's short novel, which tells the story of a sharp-eyed boy caught between these two classes in a love affair, is a particularly well-illuminated picture of the new suburban family, whose home, bursting with food and sporting goods, rather resembles a ZBT house at one of the Big-Ten schools. "Eli" provides some equally telling observations of a Jewish group who are nervously assimilating with a formerly Christian community in Westchester. However, the focus of "Eli" is not on social questions but moral ones, and generally this is true of Roth's work as a whole, including the other published stories that are not in this collection. In fact, what gives real depth to Roth's notation of the social and ethnic changes that assimilation has produced is that he fixes them not only by their external signs (country club membership, horseshows, the schools the children go to, the "right" synagogue, and so forth), but also by their subtle effects upon the individual's sense of his personal, moral identity as a Jew. The boy in "The Conversion of the Jews" struggles to get out from under the shadow of the old, unreasonable dogmas, but the characteristic problem is rather that of Sergeant Marx in "Defender of the Faith" or of Eli Peck, both of whose Jewishness has become merely a vague feeling and requires both a direct challenge from the outside and an act of moral imagination to come alive and identify them and their basic values. Even "Goodbye, Columbus," for all its thick social and cultural reference, turns out to be really a story about the fatal moral demands that Neil Klugman has made on Brenda Patimkin and (as Neil's aunt puts it) on her "fancy-schmancy" world, and involves, though in different terms and with more ambiguous results, the same problem of identity, the same moral question of "What am I?" that lies at the center of Roth's other stories.

For, at bottom, what directs and defines his stories are a few brave values that connect human feeling with human conscience. In stories such as "Eli" and "Defender of the Faith" he associates these values with Jewish tradition; and even the criticism of the Orthodox dogma in "The Conversion" is one that the early Hassidim would have had no trouble understanding. However, as these stories make clear, Roth tries to put his values through the fire—working from the impulses, strains, and solutions of a modern Jew outward to the traditional morality of sentiment, suffering, and rectitude that a writer such as Sholom Aleichem more or less takes for granted. At the same time, Roth's hard, clear comedies of Jews who discover in their hearts that they are neither more nor less than human, suggest by the comic mode of his moral analysis, as well as by its terms and its firmness, Roth's affiliations with other contemporary Jewish writers, led by Malamud and Bellow, and in its own way, *Goodbye, Columbus* helps to make their particular imprint on American fiction more visible and significant.

Despite sharp differences, Roth seems closest in his general moral intentions to Malamud. His characters and situations are usually quite different: Roth's emerge from the Jewish here and now in America while the life of most of Malamud's Eastern-European Jews runs in lonely, isolated channels in New York that make it seem folk-like and almost timeless. While Roth is clearly writing about the modern Jew in America, Malamud appears to be writing mainly about Jewishness itself as it survives from age to age and from place to place. Also Roth's style, which is open, voluble, and contemporary, is in striking contrast to Malamud's prose, which is as terse and sternly restrained as Babel's, for all of the same magic and feeling he gets into the stories themselves. However, both Roth and Malamud seem involved in a similar effort to feel and think with their Jewishness and to use the thick concreteness of Jewish moral experience to get at the dilemmas and decisions of the heart generally. Writing from the struggle to illuminate and assess and extend the fading meaning of being a Jew, they write from their hearts—sophisticated, witty, tough-minded as they may be—and usually it is back to the heart that their work leads us: to its suffering and its trials and, particularly, to its deep moral potency.

This underlying affinity between Roth and Malamud can be seen by comparing *The Assistant* and "Eli, the Fanatic." In Malamud's novel, a young Italian drifter, Frank Alpine, takes part in robbing and beating up a poor Jew, who keeps a rundown grocery store in the Bronx. But still destitute, and bothered by his conscience, Alpine continues to hang around the neighborhood and, in little ways, to help out his victim, Morris Bober. In time he becomes Bober's assistant, chases after his lonely daughter, Helen—who earnestly tries to make him like Dostoevsky, Tolstoy, and Flaubert—and works hard to build up Bober's pitiful trade. But at the same time that Alpine is lusting after Helen, he is stealing from Bober. Eventually Bober catches him and sternly casts him out, and on the same evening, Alpine loses the girl when, after saving her from a rape, he rapes her himself. Deeply suffering now from this double rejection, Alpine is also horrified, as Malamud tells us, by a recognition that underneath he is himself a man of stern morality. He continues to stay in the vicinity, hiding in the basement of the store where at one point he prevents Bober—the honest man—from setting fire to the property to collect the insurance. Twice after Bober falls ill, the haunted assistant comes back to run the failing business again and even takes a night job in a diner to keep it going. He wastes away himself from these labors to prove to the Bobers, mainly to the girl, that his heart has changed; but they ignore him as much as possible. Meanwhile his antics as well as his serious striving become more grotesque and meaningful; for example, he takes to wearing his version of a *yarmulke* in the store, and after Bober dies he stumbles into his open grave at the funeral. At the funeral the rabbi defines Bober, who had been indifferent in his religion, as a Jew by his suffering and by his hopeful sacrifices for the higher ambition he had for his daughter, and here the point behind Alpine's behavior begins to emerge. He continues the ordeal of holding both his jobs, doing so finally to send Helen to college. And as the cycle of his days begins to run in the grooves of the dead grocer's former routine, the conversion of the young Italian into the elderly Jew comes clear, even before Alpine gets himself circumcized and becomes a Jew.

In "Eli, the Fanatic" much of the same inner pattern and much of the same fusion of the comic form and the suffering hero are compressed and pointed to much the same moral. Alpine's role of the aggressor who through suffering and sacrifice becomes his victim, is played here by an assimilated Jew, an unstable lawyer named Eli Peck, who has been commissioned by his fellow Jewish townsmen to get an Orthodox school for refugees evicted from their pink and chrome, Scarsdale-like community. Starting out as their agent against the orphans and the elders—Leo Tzuref, the Patriarch-like director and his assistant, who is particularly obnoxious to the "Jewish community" of Woodenton because he wears the long gabardine and beard of the fanatical Hassidim—Peck soon comes to the point of helping the refugees by trying to work out a compromise. He first sacrifices his best suit (a good deal is made of this in the story) to the offensive assistant so that the latter will be less so to the aroused and nervous Jews of Woodenton. The "greenie" does put on the suit and shaves his beard and sidelocks, and everyone is delighted and satisfied— except Peck, for by now he has become involved in deeper issues with himself. Moved, despite his reason, by Tzuref's appeal to the heart instead of to the law ("the heart is law! God!"), by the suffering that the Yeshiva people represent (the assistant, for example, has had a "medical experiment" performed on him by the Nazis), and by Tzuref's question of which of the two communities Peck really belongs to, the lawyer has become vaguely aware that his best suit is not enough. When the assistant leaves his Hassidic outfit on Peck's doorstep, he slowly tries on the black clothes and then walks outside. He wanders up to the Yeshiva but the assistant, still wearing Peck's suit, casts him out by pointing in the direction of the town. Their appearances and roles reversed, pondering on who is who, Peck walks down into the town. He stops traffic along its main street by his appearance and then goes to the hospital where his first child has just been born. And as he goes, Eli silently recognizes and endures what Tzuref has had the black clothes sent to him for. His friends think that he is having another of his nervous breakdowns but as Roth tells us —"he knew who he was down to his marrow," and standing before his new son, Peck swears aloud that the child will always know, too.

Thus, in both works, there is the similar conversion into the essential Jew, achieved by acts of striving, sacrificing, and suffering for the sake of some fundamental goodness and truth in one's self that has been lost and buried. Further, both Roth and Malamud emphasize the vague, semiconscious character of the decision, proceeding not from any clear idea but rather from awakening feelings of sympathy, love, identification, and guilt which, becoming more and more powerful, finally indicate their purpose —to produce the suffering and sacrifice that lead to purification and to a discovery of one's true identity. And in both Alpine's and Peck's cases, this "consummation of his heart's "ultimate need" is represented by becoming thoroughly a Jew, which is apparently Malamud's and Roth's composite symbol, into which the separate terms are knitted—striving, sacrifice, and suffering;

purification and true identity. But, more importantly, becoming and being a Jew refers beyond this definition of its morality to the moral role and power of the human heart and will discover and recreate the self, and this is what Malamud seems to mean by his frequently quoted statement that "all men are Jews."

Roth probably wrote "Eli" with *The Assistant* in mind; however, the theme of conversion is a familiar one in Jewish literature and "Eli" is much more than a reworking of Malamud's novel with a new twist. It is more just to say that Roth is drawing upon the same idea, embedded in the same traditional morality, and like Malamud he has provided a different, contemporary context in which to display its power. Also a comic action of suffering that leads to the truths of the heart is a familiar one to readers of Saul Bellow or Herbert Gold or the late Isaac Rosenfeld. "Seize the Day," "The Heart of the Artichoke," "The Hand That Fed Me," are stories that come to mind as clear examples of it and as having some sort of Jewish background upon which it focuses.

The phrase I quoted above—"the consummation of his heart's ultimate need"—is from Bellow's comic and shattering "Seize the Day," and a consideration of it may help to make these connections clearer. The "day" that Tommy Wilhelm (originally named William Adler) seizes is the day of his Gethsemane. In the course of it Wilhelm, a forty-year-old failure, has his last eight hundred dollars swept away in a crazy speculation in lard; his partner in the investment, a quack psychologist named Tamkin, swindles and deserts him; his father, a retired doctor whose help and blessing Wilhelm desperately needs, curses him; and his wife continues to torture him by refusing Wilhelm the divorce he needs to hold onto a girl he loves, and by refusing to let him reduce his extravagant payments to her and their two children. Without a job and—though he has been a successful salesman until recently—without prospects, his health shattered, Wilhelm takes these blows one after another. However, as Bellow writes:

since there were depths in Wilhelm not unsuspected by himself,
he received a suggestion from some remote element in his
thoughts that the business of life, the real business—to carry his
peculiar burden, to feel shame and impotence, to taste these
quelled tears—the only important business, the highest business was being done. Maybe the making of mistakes expressed
the very purpose of his life and the essence of his being here.
Maybe he was supposed to make them and suffer from them on
this earth . . .

The point of Wilhelm's suffering begins to emerge when Tamkin—another of Bellow's fascinating mixtures of hokum and insight—tells Wilhelm of the two souls inside each man. There is
the "pretender soul" and the "true soul"—the former the instru-
ment of "egotism" and "social control," and the latter the
searcher for love and truth that "pays the price" for the pretender's ways, that "suffers and gets sick." Wilhelm is moved by this
description, for there are two distinct sides to him that he believes correspond to his two names. Or at least he knows that
Tommy is the pretender soul but is unsure who is the true soul,
thinking it might be named "Velvel," his grandfather's name for
him. But whatever its name, Wilhelm's "true soul" rises powerfully at the end of all his antics and suffering to define itself and
him. But now "stripped and kicked out," Wilhelm finds his way
into a funeral parlor and, for no apparent reason, falls in with the
mourners passing before the bier of an important Jew. He begins
to weep for the man, "a fellow human creature . . . so fallen in
the eyes," then for himself, and then beyond any reason and
control. As Bellow puts it, "the great knot of ill and grief swelled
upward," and the story ends:

> The flowers and lights fused ecstatically in Wilhelm's blind,
> wet eyes; the heavy sea-like music came up to his ears. It poured
> into him where he had hidden himself in the center of a crowd
> by the great happy oblivion of tears. He heard it and sank

deeper than sorrow, through torn sobs and cries toward the consummation of his heart's ultimate need.

"Seize the Day," then, moves, though more obliquely and negatively, in the same general direction as do the two works I have been considering. There is the same drama of the heart under its burden of baffled love, aspiration, and guilt, the same stern payment for confusions and mistakes, the same brutal suffering that leads to the indication of the hero's true identity—for the suffering of Wilhelm's "true soul" and his "heart's ultimate need" are one and the same. Of course, unlike Alpine's or Eli Peck's, the fulfillment of Tommy Wilhelm is the doom of a man whose fate, as well as his need, is to suffer; he is Henderson without Henderson's strength or his millions. However, there is a different moral grain to these two works by Bellow and partly it has something to do, I think, with the Jewish background of "Seize the Day." Bellow does not identify its implications explicitly with Jewishness, though the points about "Velvel," about Wilhelm's recognition that it is the Tommy Wilhelm in him who is the pretender, and about the final "consummation" taking place at a Jewish funeral—all suggest this connection.

At any rate, what is definite is the preoccupation with the griefs and potencies of the heart that Bellow shares with Roth and Malamud (it is also worth noting that they use the term "heart" repeatedly), and with a tough, realistic morality that develops out of it. Thus, the Yiddish proverb that Roth uses as the epigraph to *Goodbye, Columbus*—"The heart is half a prophet"—illuminates much of Malamud's work and much of Bellow's (even showing the links between such very different novels as *The Victim* and *Augie March*) as well as Roth's own stories. Moreover, it illuminates the work of such otherwise ill-assorted writers as Rosenfeld and Gold and the underrated novelist Leonard Bishop. For at least two things are suggested by Roth's epigraph that one keeps finding among their stories and novels. First, there is the intense

concern with situations in which the blood feelings become powerfully engaged—pity, love, guilt, hate. What almost always generates them is the hero's involvement in some basic, human relationship—sometimes sought by him but, as often as not, inflicted
upon him, with the distinction tending to become lost as a relationship develops: the seeker becoming the victim or vice versa.
Often, too, a complicated moral problem is involved, some radical question of right and wrong. However, what lies at the center
of the tale are the feelings that direct the hero finally to a truer
recognition of himself, or at least direct the reader to a truer
recognition of him, and often produce a solution to his personal
moral problem. Sometimes the recognition comes from strong,
new feelings of love or pity but often these are mixed with a
recognition of personal guilt as in Bellow's *The Victim*, or Malamud's "The Last Mohican" and "The Mourners," or Rosenfeld's
"The Colony" or "Coney Island Revisited" or Bishop's *Days of
My Love*. And sometimes, too, the recognition is produced by an
act of hatred as in Malamud's "Take Pity," or Roth's "Defender
of the Faith," or Gold's "The Heart of the Artichoke." Nonetheless, whatever the feelings or combination of them, it is the trust
in the strong, instinctive impulses of the heart that is one of the
things that characterizes this fiction. It is also characterized, as
Roth's epigraph suggests, by its moral rectitude that is flexible
and searching but firmly centered too. Definite concepts of right
and wrong reinforce these writers' moral analyses as well as a
tough-minded realism. Nothing of real value is easily won in their
fiction; moral development tends to be a very painful process and
mistakes and failures, as well as sins, are paid for, often at an
appalling price. Thus, though these writers often deal with life's
losers and victims with deep compassion, they do so with a
firmness and intelligence that guards their pity from the sentimentality that keeps leaking into the fiction of a writer like Nelson
Algren.

In Roth's story "Defender of the Faith," a sergeant named

Nathan Marx, who fought through the German campaigns and is now training a company of recruits, has the orders of a wheedling Jewish private changed so that he is sent to fight in the Pacific theater along with the rest of the company. Marx does so, as he says himself, out of a feeling of vindictiveness, for Grossbart, the private, has been cynically using him for weeks by trading on the fact that both are Jews. Out of vindictiveness, then, comes Marx's righteous act to "defend the faith," but his final act is that of accepting the consequences of what he has had to do to defend it. At the same time, these are the culminating happenings in a story which has also been explicitly about Marx's regaining his identity as a Jew and about the "softening" of his "infantryman's heart," which like his feet, had grown "horny enough for him to travel the weirdest paths without feeling a thing." The terms of the moral analysis here, as well as its subtlety, complexity, and rigor, sum up the general moral position I have been trying to suggest. Moreover, Roth's story suggests a final generalization: that the values placed on free-flowing feeling on the one hand, and on moral firmness, even toughness, on the other—fortifying, testing, correcting each other—is what comes from the peculiar heritage of the modern Jew (who has kept himself aware of it) into the fiction I have been mentioning. It is what he carries and preserves within the larger, more immediate experience of being an American today, and it is what helps to direct these writers in their search for values that men can still live by and remain human. Exploring and affirming the potency of the heart to make men better and truer and to help them survive as men, they indicate a course through our shifting sands of determinism and nihilism. And given the moral evasiveness, rootlessness, and blankness that characterizes so much modern literature, this is a considerable contribution.

At the same time, it would be mistaken to view these writers only as moralists and their stories and books as preachments. On the contrary, Roth—like Malamud, Bellow, and Isaac Rosenfeld

—is a shrewd craftsman, and like them, he appears to be involved in a deliberate attempt to restore and broaden the base of the novelist's and story writer's special interest—the tale or action itself—and to move serious fiction out of the *longeurs* of technique and literary decorum that often mark it today in America. Along with the intelligence, concreteness, and roughened texture of their writing, one of its noticeable features is the presence usually of a clear, explicit action. As a rule, their tales are strongly and carefully plotted; they write of happenings rather than of coolly objectified states of mind. Thus one follows their stories and novels through visible conflicts, complications, crises, climaxes, instead of from sets of veiled coordinates which require that the reader detect them and draw the lines in order to find the story. The Chekhov-Joyce-Mansfield story—the story of low dramatic pressures, of impersonality, indirection, and implication—is still the influential one today: it is canonized in the anthologies, taught determinedly in the colleges to illustrate "the art of the short story," and becomes more and more bloodless and vague by its development, as Harry Levin remarks, into "an industry."

Similarly in the novel: Flaubert remains "our Penelope" as much as he was Pound's. "Do you have feelings? There are correct and incorrect ways of indicating them. Do you have an inner life? It is nobody's business but your own. Do you have emotions? Strangle them." So, early in his career, Saul Bellow phrased the position that he was rebelling against in *Dangling Man*—the position of detachment and impersonality that goes back to Flaubert. In his best work Bellow has continued to do so, though after *Dangling Man* be began to experiment with actions that would translate his inner life into viable fiction. Moreover, his rebellion against Flaubert has continued and he has publicly asked for a re-evaluation of Flaubert's tremendously influential literary method, which he believes cuts the writer off from the real conditions of life and makes his content thin and pessimistic. In a lecture at The University of Chicago, Bellow made clear the grounds of his opposition to the Flaubertian image of the alienated writer and, more importantly, to the lack of moral circumspection and artistic vitality that his method has produced.

Bellow, Malamud, and Roth are anything but alienated men and their attempt to confront the human situation as they see and live it, and to make moral sense out of it, is bound up, it seems to me, with their concern for constructing definite actions and characterizations. The esthetic that they share at these points (the kind of double life Bellow leads in his fiction makes generalizations here rather shaky) is close to that of Gogol and Dostoevsky, both committed moralists and first-rate story tellers, who, as Malamud has defined his own "moral-esthetic," "keep the moral invisible, locked in the tale, the fabric one might say, of the human action, being, feeling." It is the primacy of the "tale" that seems to be important here—the return to a reliance upon a visible, strongly developed story in which the other elements—all given considerable force—cohere and are illuminated. All of which is what gives such dramatic power and clarity of meaning to *The Victim* and "Seize the Day," to *The Assistant* and such stories as "The Magic Barrel," "Take Pity," and "Angel Levine," as well as to their more introspective stories as "Looking for Mr. Green" and "The Last Mohican." And it is where their hold upon the "story" is weak and where sheer invention and "ideas" take over —as in *The Natural* and *Augie March*—that their fiction loses both dramatic strength and moral clarity. And this is equally true of Roth's work.

Roth seems at his best where the current of his imagination is guided by a strong, clear action—where, in other words, the story comes closest to telling itself, to defining its characters and feeling, and to making its point. This is true of "Epstein" and "Defender of the Faith," and the last forty pages or so of *Goodbye, Columbus*. For all the impact of its concluding pages, "Eli" doesn't quite come off, I think; nor does "You Can't Tell a Man by the Song He Sings," though this, too, has some of Roth's best writing in it. In both stories, as in "The Conversion of the Jews," the moral or idea is heavier than the story itself. Eli Peck's conversion seems to me the material for a much longer story; it is prepared for by clever details as much as by happenings and it comes too quickly; the result is that the character and the conversion itself become less real beside the concrete actuality of Woodenton and beside the massive and beautifully executed figure of Tzuref. In "You Can't Tell a Man" and in "The Conversion" one finds a compact and sensitive story suddenly being inflated to get in the message: in the former, the action trails off into a discussion of its implications; in "The Conversion," it becomes flabby with its bravura, jokes, and symbolism. Also, where Roth's plot lapses, his tendency to overwrite emerges to get between the reader and the story, and his general weakness for tags (most of his minor characters are tagged rather than rendered) and for gags seems particularly marked.

Similarly "Goodbye, Columbus," though it flows resonantly between its feeling and its satire, seems to lack the fusion of its materials, the sense of being really "done," that one finds in "Epstein" and "Defender of the Faith." Again, I think the trouble is with the action and one sign of it is the kind of abstractness that Neil Klugman takes on. He is seen too much as an observer and he is too far along the path he is supposed to be traveling in the story. One could wish, for example, that he were more his aunt's nephew, more troubled and attracted by the life of the Patimkins and more willing to test it and himself. As is, already classless, fixed vaguely by his job in a library and by his degree in philosophy, he seems less genuinely involved with the Patimkins, including the girl (who, too, isn't dramatized enough), than he is with the Negro boy that he takes risks and tells lies for. For two-thirds of the story, then, Neil's social ambitions and moral problems connected with Short Hills are too often stated rather than made visible to the reader by the action and it is only when he forces the situation by demanding that Brenda get a diaphragm that the story takes on complexity and force. But until this point, the faint overtones of Scott Fitzgerald in "Goodbye, Columbus" make it seem a little like *The Great Gatsby* with a single hero being both Carroway and Gatsby.

All of which is not to take away from Roth's remarkable eye and ear, his strong narrative sense, and the verve and sparkle of his prose. These are what keep his stories going and also what keep even the weakest of them, "The Conversion of the Jews," from being clearly second-rate. Also, too, the faults I have been mentioning are those of a story-teller learning his art, not weaknesses in his basic equipment, with which Roth is as well endowed as any young writer that has appeared in recent years. On the whole, then, *Goodbye, Columbus* is a more than promising beginning. At an age when most writers are still looking for their own voice, Roth already has one that rings out with a live, personal, and commanding tone. And at this stage of his career, that is probably as important as his other virtues and more important than his present limitations.

Breakthrough?*

DAVID DAICHES

"With the coming of age of the children of Jewish immigrants, we find that quite a few of them are taking their place in the front ranks of American literature. They function in every sphere of literary creation—as poets, novelists, playwrights, and critics. Their work is part and parcel of the national literary product, and this is clear evidence of the fact that the American Jews have reached the stage of integration with the native environment. They are spectators no longer but full participants in the cultural life of the country."

These words appeared in the *Contemporary Jewish Record* (*Commentary*'s predecessor) of February 1944 as part of an introduction to a symposium on "American Literature and the Younger Generation of American Jews." The writers who contributed—all of them then under forty—gave various accounts of the influence on their writing of their Jewish background, but the majority minimized these influences and suggested that they were rather escaping from a Jewish background than using it. "I do not think of myself as a 'Jewish writer,' " wrote Lionel Trilling. "In what I might call my life as a citizen my being Jewish exists as a point of honor. . . . I can have no pride in seeing a long tradition, often great and heroic, reduced to this small status in me, for I give only a limited respect to points of honor: they are usually mortu-

*Originally published in Commentary, August, 1964; reprinted by permission. Copyright © 1964 the American Jewish Committee.

ary and monumental, they have being without desire. . . . Surely it is clear at once how minimal such a position is." Many of the contributors to the symposium seemed to think that their Americanism had subsumed their Judaism. One writer went so far as to equate the Declaration of Independence with certain Jewish prayers, and Lincoln with Hillel.

Twenty years later the situation has changed. American Jewish writers are no longer concerned to prove that "they are spectators no longer but full participants in the cultural life of their country." They take that for granted, and go on (many of them, at least) to explore aspects of their own past which can provide something special to their vision as modern American writers. The change is interesting, and has more than one cause. Even in the 1944 symposium the late Isaac Rosenfeld had noted that the Jew, being an expert in alienation, could speak to the condition of the artist and intellectual of his time, who was inevitably alienated. The Jewish writer today does not want to fly from his parents' or grandparents' status as unadapted or only partially adapted immigrants to a cozy, all-embracing, interfaith Americanism. He is aware that there is never anything cozy about being a writer and that there is a sense in which, in the modern world, all sensitive men are Jews. Joyce's Leopold Bloom, both citizen and outsider in Dublin, both member of a community and rejected by it, is not only a Jew in Ireland: he is Man in Society. Thus not only is the artist alienated; all men are, if not alienated, at least torn between isolation and communion. The individual self can never wholly communicate with other selves: Bloom in a Dublin pub engaging in one of the oldest of all ritual gestures of companionship (compotation or drinking together) is at the same time cut off from his fellows, dwelling in a unique and lonely consciousness. To be a Jew is part of the human condition.

But to realize this is hardly an invitation to an American Jewish writer to emphasize, or even to use, his Jewishness. If all sensitive men are Jews, he can be a Jew simply by being a sensitive man.

(Isn't that the theme of Malamud's *The Assistant?*) There is more to it than this, however. To emphasize one's Jewishness may be, in this environment, to emphasize one's sensitivity, one's awareness of the intractability of human destiny, one's refusal to subscribe to any facile optimism about the rapid movement of modern industrial democratic society to Utopia, one's involvement in the contradictions and paradoxes of human nature. Twenty years ago there was still enough vitality in the left-wing traditions of the 1930's to enable many American Jewish writers to feel that human problems were soluble through the cultivation of sympathy and intelligence, and thus they used their Jewishness only if they could in some way equate it with a tradition of sympathy or a tradition of intelligence. And in so equating it, they lost it. Today we know that both sympathy and intelligence, though admirable qualities, can be merely ways of avoiding a genuine confrontation of the deepest truths of experience. What is needed by the artist in our time is an inwardness with suffering, a genuine personal recognition not only of what Hitler did to European Jews but also of how this throws light on, say, the Negro problem in America and how American Jews regard Negroes, and an awareness of what all of it means for an ethical and psychological understanding of man. On this view, the Jewish artist has the advantage over his Gentile neighbor: he can draw on his own traditions of alienation, of suffering, of being on the *other* side of a dividing line, and use his knowledge to investigate and to project the nature of man.

Is modern American literary Jewishness, then, simply a stance of the sensitive man? To some extent it is; but this is far from the whole story. The characteristic critical activity of the 1930's and 1940's was intellectual and anti-emotional; it emphasized the ability to discriminate, to analyze, rather than the capacity to feel. The "New Criticism" (as Norman Podhoretz has so well explained in his essay, "Jewish Culture and the Intellectuals," included in *Breakthrough,* an anthology of contemporary American

Jewish literature*) was no more hospitable to the claims of feeling than traditional Jewish teaching of Hebrew literature was hospitable to the claims of dispassionate critical analysis. But some time in the late 1940's the pendulum began to swing in the other direction. Mr. Podhoretz records what happened at Columbia: "Meanwhile something was happening in the world of Columbia that seemed too good to be true. Hasidism, ushered in by Martin Buber and Gershom Scholem, like a surprise witness in a sensational murder trial, exploded on the intellectual consciousness of New York. One suddenly found a rash of articles not only on Hasidism, but also on Maimonides, written by people who only yesterday were deep in Eliot, Original Sin, and Kierkegaard. . . . I remember too with what a sense of personal triumph I first heard that Lionel Trilling was writing an essay on Wordsworth and the Rabbis."

As I write this, I reach out to my bookshelves and take down a copy of Martin Buber's *Tales of the Hasidim* presented to me by Norman Pearson of Yale in 1950 with the inscription: "This past for the present." Yes; writers—and not only Jewish writers—were discovering a "useable past" in Jewish traditions (or in some selected Jewish traditions) and this corresponded to something interesting that was happening all along the American literary front. Is it an accident that at the same time American writers on history and civilization were discovering Edmund Burke and dropping Tom Paine? And that myths, symbols, archetypes were replacing paradox and ambivalence in the language of criticism? It became academically and critically respectable to discover an organic relation to your past rather than to believe that the American destiny was to reject the past and build a future free of the errors and tyrannies of Old World history (though of course some American critics, from the South especially, had done this all along). Now the Jews are the people with a past *par*

*Edited by Irving Malin and Irwin Stark, McGraw-Hill, 1964, 376 pp., $7.50.

excellence; as Philip Rahv explains in his admirable introduction to
Discovery of Europe (also reprinted in *Breakthrough*), America sees
her share in the older European civilization as "now fully equal
to that of the Europeans," and as Leslie Fiedler puts it in another
valuable essay ("Negro and Jew: Encounter in America") in the
collection: "The Jew . . . is the gateway into Europe for America;
for he has carried with him, almost against his will, his own
history, two thousand years of which is European." In the nineteenth century it was the New England prophets of high culture
who preserved the links with Europe; in the first half of the
twentieth century, with some significant exceptions, the most
"progressive" of American writers tended to turn their eyes away
from Europe; in the beginning of the second half of the twentieth
century a new kind of emotional implication in Europe was discovered—a kind that made American Jewish writers its natural
mediators. Whether this is related to America's political involvement in Europe since the end of World War II, I shall refrain
from trying to guess. I should think that it was at least as much
related to the growing sense that it is not only a "complex fate"
being an American, as Henry James had maintained, but that it
is a complex fate being human, that the deepest human problems
are not easily and perhaps never fully soluble, and that the
dilemma of being a Jew is therefore worth exploring as a paradigm of the general dilemma of being human.

There were obviously other and less easily definable impulses
at work. It would be impertinent of me to speculate on what led
Lionel Trilling to write the essay, news of which so excited Mr.
Podhoretz in his undergraduate days, but it was presumably
some desire to associate his Jewish heritage with his interest in
English literature, a desire sharply at variance with what he said
in the 1944 symposium. It is not, in my opinion, a good essay;
the analogies are forced and the whole argument strained; it
reads to me like something Trilling wanted to make himself believe rather than something he really discovered. But Trilling is

represented in *Breakthrough* by his brilliant essay on Isaac Babel, which is the record of genuine, excited discovery associated with shock and disturbance. The Jew as Cossack—and Babel served for a time as a supply officer in a Cossack regiment—is absurd, counter to all our expectations; the Jew forcing himself to violence outrages our notions of the Jew as passive sufferer. "It is not easy for us—and it is not easy for Babel. Not easy, but we must make the effort to comprehend that for Babel it is not violence in itself that is at issue in his relation to the Cossacks, but something else, some quality with which violence does indeed go along, but which is not in itself merely violent. This quality, whatever it is to be called, is of the greatest importance in Babel's conception of himself as an intellectual and an artist, in his conception of himself as a Jew." These conceptions are not as simple as we once thought. To accept the self-contradictory varieties of Jewish consciousness is one way of responding to the realization that experience is more intractable than had been dreamt of in our philosophy. The rediscovered Jewish consciousness of American Jewish writers is thus not a religious thing and not a national thing; it has something to do with Keats's "Negative Capability, that is, when a man is capable of being in uncertainties, mysteries, doubts, without any irritable reaching after fact and reason." Dwelling among the uncertainties and mysteries of Jewish experience, the modern American Jewish critic is dwelling in the world that the modern American imagination, sadly awakened at last from the dream of the *Aufklärung,* has recognized.

Is the same true of the modern American Jewish novelist and poet? Is there really a "breakthrough" in American Jewish creative writing? I find it less easy to answer this question with respect to creative writing than with respect to criticism, where the achievement is evident and formidable. The selection here provides uncertain evidence. Philip Roth's "Eli, the Fanatic"—about the respectable, assimilated Jew in a prosperous Westchester community who adopts the dress and pose of a pious Old World immigrant out of a sense of guilt—falls uneasily between story and parable; the hero's change is not sufficiently probed or presented with enough specificity to carry imaginative conviction. The description of the Einhorn family from Saul Bellow's *Adventures of Augie March* is sociologically and psychologically observant but adds up to no real Jewish insight. (The working of a Jewish consciousness in Saul Bellow's work as a whole presents a much more complex question; but I do not see how it can be said to be part of a general Jewish breakthrough.) Many writers represented in *Breakthrough* do little more than present neatly etched (and sometimes moving) documentaries of the tensions between the older, immigrant generation and the younger American one; some give examples of the contradictions involved when, say, a Jewish child has to participate in a Gentile environment at school (Christmas is the standard theme here). Isaac Rosenfeld is represented by a strange and oddly powerful symbolic story about Solomon and Sheba, but the level of probability keeps wavering; Ivan Gold has an impressive story of a Jew carrying his persecution with him to Japan; Paul Goodman has a beautifully drawn little sketch of a rabbi conducting an auction for the honor of opening the Ark for *T'filas Tal*, the prayer for rain, with a thunder storm raging outside; there is an extract from Norman Mailer's *The Naked and the Dead* giving a sketch of Joey Goldstein's life until he joins the army; Bernard Malamud (perhaps the most deliberately Jewish of all American writers of his generation) is represented by a sad little story of pity, pride, and despair which comes straight out of the Yiddish tradition and, though extremely effective, lacks the teasing, exploratory dimension of his best work. As for the poetry, there are a few interesting poems on biblical themes, or on the symbolic role played by the Jew in our time and always; and there is Allen Ginsberg's self-pityingly exclamatory *Howl*, which I cannot take seriously as poetry or as anything else. (Ginsberg's images of revolt, suffering, defiance, despair, lunacy,

bad luck, persecution, exhibitionism, and distortion are so hopelessly jumbled and so slackly expressed that the poem in the end
means nothing at all.)

The editors in their discursive introduction to the anthology
try to trace themes and find unity, with doubtful success in spite
of some illuminating observations by the way. "The overriding
problem," they conclude, "is not God but self-identification, the
problem of locating the self within the community of other men."
I suppose the question "Who am I?" does recur in this literature,
and I suppose, too, that it is a question always likely to be asked
by a Jew in Western society. To ask the question, however, is not
enough; it must be answered in such a way as to illuminate both
the Jewish and the general human situation if it is to be taken
seriously as literature. There is a kind of great documentary like
Zangwill's *Children of the Ghetto,* which brilliantly fixed a moment
in the history of English Jewry; and there is the Yiddish tradition
(most ably discussed by Irving Howe and Eliezer Greenberg in
their "Introduction to Yiddish Literature," reprinted here) which
plays with resigned irony—an irony born of too much knowing-
ness, too much experience—amid the tensions set up by religious
pride and optimism on the one hand and suffering on the other,
and by the interpenetration of Yiddish and Hebrew, of pilpulistic
argument and daily life, of the lost Temple and Holy Land and
the facts of the Ghetto, of messianic hope and present despair.
The American Jewish writer today is reaching out beyond the
Zangwillian documentary and beyond the dated and restricted
(for all its glories) ghetto literature in Yiddish. Yet there is still
a lot of the sociological documentary in this recent work, and, in
a few writers, still much of the Yiddish tradition. There is some
very good and much interesting writing. Does it add up to a
movement, a real comprehensive breakthrough into new art
forms, higher literary achievements? I should say rather that the
American Jewish writer has been liberated to use his Jewishness
in a great variety of ways, to use it not aggressively or apologeti-

cally, but imaginatively as a writer probing the human condition (one cannot avoid using clichés here), and that we have recently had some exciting evidence of this. But, in spite of some admirable individual works, an achieved literature based on this liberation is something we must still wait for. The paradox is that if and when it comes, it may well not be recognized for what it is, for literature has a knack of transcending origins and categories. Perhaps so long as we can talk of a "breakthrough," the achievement is incomplete.

The Conversions
of the Jews*

ALLEN GUTTMANN

When the builders of Bay Colony likened themselves to the Israelites of the Old Testament, when they spoke of their settlements
at Boston and Salem as a "wilderness Zion," they could not have
known that the Jews of the Diaspora would come, within a generation, to complicate the metaphor that made America the promised land. But come they did, only to discover that acceptance in
the new world undid them as persecution in the old had not.
Many became Christians. More became converts to the American
Way, to the religion of Americanism.

As early as 1825, Jews in Charleston rejected the Orthodoxy
of Congregation Beth Elohim and organized the Reformed Society of Israelites. Their statement of principles repudiated rabbinical interpretations and accepted the laws of Moses only as far,
in their words, "as they can be adapted to the institutions of the
Society in which [we] live and enjoy the blessings of liberty."
Their slogan was simple: "America is our Zion and Washington
is our Jerusalem." Reform Judaism, the intellectual consequence
of Jewish Emancipation, flourished in America under the leader-

*This paper was read at the English Institute, Columbia University, September, 1964. First
published in Wisconsin Studies in Contemporary Literature, Vol. VI, no. 2 (© 1965
by the Regents of the University of Wisconsin), pp. 161–176; reprinted by permission.

ship of David Einhorn, Kaufmann Kohler, and Isaac Mayer Wise. The Pittsburgh Platform of 1885, the basic document of Reform Judaism in America, was a manifesto that might almost have won the support of William Ellery Channing and Ralph Waldo Emerson: "We recognize in every religion an attempt to grasp the Infinite One, and in every mode . . . of revelation held sacred in any religious system the consciousness of the indwelling of God in man." The Mosaic and rabbinical laws of diet and dress, and even of morals, were rejected insofar as they did not conform "to the views and habits of modern civilization."

Even as the Reformers extended the "hand of fellowship to all who co-operate with us in the establishment of the reign of truth and righteousness among men," they must have realized that the "views and habits of modern civilization" are often ignoble. Historians and sociologists—Nathan Glazer, Oscar Handlin, Will Herberg, Moses Rischin, Marshall Sklare—have shown that Jews converted to the Age of Enterprise as well as to the Ideals of the Enlightenment. At their best, American Jews have contributed immensely to the institutionalization of liberty, equality, and fraternity. At their worst, American Jews have been late-comers to the "great barbecue" of American capitalism, scramblers after the scraps left by Carnegie and Rockefeller and Vanderbilt, greedy greenhorns of the Gilded Age. Many a reformer of traditional Judaism must have wondered—in the din of the marketplace—if the baggage left behind at Ellis Island wasn't better stuff than the shoddy goods bought and sold in Brookline and in Brownsville. But very few have recanted from their metaphoric conversion to America.

As the words of Emma Lazarus on the State of Liberty suggest, the story of Americanization is the first great theme of Jewish literature in the new world. The first great name, after Emma Lazarus herself, is Abraham Cahan, whose novel, *The Rise of David Levinsky*, was published in 1917. When David Levinsky, a pious student of the Talmud, confides in Reb Sender his decision to emigrate, the Rabbi is dismayed: "To America! Lord of the World! But one becomes a Gentile there!" Reb Sender was right. David shears off his earlocks and abandons one by one the 613 commandments by which the pious Jew regulates his life. "If you are a Jew of the type to which I belonged when I came to New York and you attempt to bend your religion to the spirit of your new surroundings, it breaks. It falls to pieces. The very clothes I wore and the very food I ate had a fatal effect on my religious habits." David rises, becomes a millionaire in the garment industry, a freethinker from whom Spencer's Unknowable replaces the Living God of Sinai. His deepest loyalty is to America. David describes a concert where the audience sat apathetically, unmoved by themes from *Aida* and by Yiddish songs; the national anthem brought the Jews enthusiastically to their feet: "It was as if they were saying: 'We are not persecuted under this flag. At last we have found a home.' " Like Silas Lapham, whom he very much resembles, David remembers the old ways: "I can never forget the days of my misery. I cannot escape from my old self. My past and my present do not comport well. David, the poor lad swinging over a Talmud volume at the Preacher's Synagogue, seems to have more in common with my inner identity than David Levinsky, the well-known cloak-manufacturer." Despite nostalgia and regret, there is no return. Abraham Cahan, whose editorship of the *Jewish Daily Forward* made him the foremost figure in Yiddish journalism, wrote his *Meisterwerk* in English.

A generation later, Meyer Levin, in the book that insures him a place in our literary history, chronicled the rise of the second-generation Jews of Chicago's West Side. *The Old Bunch,* published in 1937, moves from 1921 to 1934—the years of *The Jazz Singer* and *Show Boat* and Leopold and Loeb and the Lindbergh Flight and Samuel Insull and Al Capone and the magnificent mid-depression symbol of hope, Chicago's Century of Progress World's Fair. The older generation speaks Yiddish and fears that bobbed hair is the short cut to prostitution. The younger generation leaves the old ways behind as it climbs into the middle class. Doctors, lawyers, dentists, artists, teachers, dry-cleaners, realtors, and part-time bicycle-racers, yes; rabbis and Talmudic scholars, no. *Mitzvot*—God's commandments—are as little regarded as the Volstead Act. Passover becomes a drunken brawl, with paper hats, comic place cards, and a layer cake topped with an effigy of Moses: "Manny picked up a curled streamer that lay near his plate and blew noisily. The red crepe paper shot across the table and dropped over Sam's ear. . . . The maid brought in an immense, sugar-baked ham." The idealistic lawyer, soon to become a defender of labor-leaders and rent-strikers, rushes in disgust from those who have sold their birthright for a mess of *trefa* (non-kosher food). No one can imagine what bothers him. Isn't he, after all, an atheist?

A generation later, in 1963, Burt Blechman writes of the War of Camp Omongo and charts the erosion of Jewish values in the great out-of-doors. The camp is, of course, run for financial profit and sexual exploration. The boys at the camp are wise in the ways of the Age of Eisenhower: "Nobody believes in God. But you still gotta have a religion." When the camp's rabbi misunderstands his decorative role and begins to speak of Jehovah, the camp's owner drowns him out with a tape-recorded rendition, by the Marine Corps Band, of "The Stars and Stripes Forever." The creed of Camp Omongo is a parody of Sinai's: "All graven images shall be as follows: Gold for 1st; Silver for 2nd; Bronze for 3rd; and Strontium 90 for the rest. . . . Thou shalt kill for God and country on demand. . . . Thou shalt adulterate the water, pollute the land, and poison the air for the sake of our fathers' pride." Burt Blechman, like Philip Roth and Bruce Jay Friedman, seems to disbelieve—and to be appalled by those who disbelieve.

Philip Roth's collection of stories, *Goodbye, Columbus*, appeared in 1960. The Patimkins have risen on kitchen sinks. Business was, during the war-years, phenomenally good. Is not cleanliness more profitable than godliness? Their refrigerators burst with fruit; their trees bear sporting goods. Brenda Patimkin is a paragon of Olympic virtues: she plays tennis, she runs, she rides, she swims. In the pool, she is a long way from the Yiddishe Momma of yesteryear. "I went," says her boy-friend,

> to pull her towards me just as she started fluttering up; my hand hooked on to the front of her suit and the cloth pulled away from her. Her breasts swam towards me like two pink-nosed fish and she let me hold them. Then, in a moment, it was the sun who kissed us both, and we were out of the water, too pleased with each other to smile.

And, as Leonard Baskin laments in a recent symposium, "For every poor and huddled *mikvah* [the ritual bath] there is a tenhundred of swimming pools." In this suburban world, the past seems passé indeed. In another of Roth's stories, the father who attempts to affirm a heritage he never inherited is shocked to discover what that heritage includes:

> Sundays mornings I have to drive my kid all the way to Scarsdale to learn Bible stories. And you know what she comes up with . . . —that this Abraham in the Bible was going to kill his own kid for a *sacrifice!* You call that religion? I call it sick. Today a guy like that they'd lock him up.

When the hero of the story becomes "a guy like that," he is, indeed, locked up. The suburban Jew, for better and for worse, is far closer to his Gentile neighbors than to the vanished world of the East European *shtetl.*

Theoretically, the ultimate consequence of *acculturation* is *assimilation;*[1] the penultimate step is intermarriage. What prevents the children of nominal Jews from intermarriage with the children of nominal Protestants and Catholics? Very little. Sociologists, who once stated flatly that 5 percent was the natural limit of the rate of intermarriage, now chart rates three times as high.

And higher. Where today, in child-centered America, is the parent who will rend his garments and sit *shiva* for the son who marries a *shiksa*, who will say for his errant son the prayer for the dead? In his very language, the father of Myron Kaufmann's hero, Richard Amsterdam, betrays his inability to stay the course of Americanization: "All these generations, and now I'm the Last of the Mohicans."

Kaufmann's novel, *Remember Me to God* (1957), is one of many commended by sociologists for their insight into the last stages of assimilation. The rabbi of Richard Amsterdam's temple is beloved by his congregation because he *can't* speak Yiddish. Richard himself goes to Harvard, mends his manners, and becomes an unscrupulous aspirant to Hasty Pudding. He scorns a lovely Jewish girl in order to whore after a Jezebel from Beacon Hill. His father, an immigrant who worked himself through law school, is pathetic in his inarticulate efforts to stop his son from intermarriage and conversion to Christianity. No longer aware of the reason of his Jewishness, the father cannot persuade the son to remain a Jew: "I can't explain it. . . . It's sort of as if that word is me. When I hear the word 'Jew,' I know it means me." He is more dignified, even when striking his son and weeping in despair, than Rabbi Budapester, who tells Richard, "It's fun to be a Jew." Budapester borrows from those literary critics who have ignored the Revelation at Mount Sinai in their vision of the Jew as archetypal Victim or Marginal Man; "Jews are Man in the extreme," says Budapester; they "have been at once the most magnificent and the most wretched of peoples, and this is the essence of Man." Richard is unmoved; "I don't want to be anybody's legend. . . . The trouble with you guys is that you want me to act out your fairy-tale." Rabbi Budapester leaves in a huff—in a Cadillac.

Complications of the subplot prevent Richard Amsterdam's marriage. Paul Shiel, the hero of Neal Oxenhandler's *A Change of Gods* (1962), takes the final steps. Attracted by blonde Candy

Martin, he marries her in Florence. He is as free of Jewish traditions as she is of Catholic dogma. But motor-scooter and hotel room are false symbols of mobility and freedom. Families are real. Paul's family is vulgar and oppressive. Candy's grandfather —a philologist—is austere and devout and determined that Paul convert to Catholicism. Paul becomes a communicant, is denounced as an Eichmann and—the plot is complicated—sent to prison. Father and son are consequently reconciled, but the conversion to Christianity is for keeps. Paul has joined the ranks of those who pray on Good Friday, until the Vatican Council shall deem otherwise, for the conversion of the Jews.

There are not, in America, very many Paul Shiels. There are, moreover, Christians who become Jews. Bernard Malamud's assistant and Philip Roth's Libby Herz are fictional characters whose roads to Judaism parallel the improbable paths taken by Marilyn Monroe, Elizabeth Taylor, and Sammy Davis, Jr. As Mordecai Kaplan has insisted since 1934, as Nathan Glazer points out in his excellent history of American Judaism, the real threat to the survival of the Jewish community in America is the pervasive secularism of the modern world. The majority of American Jews are Jews only by the quirks of popular definition.[2] When asked about his heritage, Philip Roth spoke for many:

> I cannot find a true and honest place in the history of believers that begins with Abraham, Isaac, and Jacob on the basis of the heroism of these believers or of their humiliations and anguish. I can connect with them and with their descendents [only] as I apprehend their God. And until such time as I do apprehend him, there will continue to exist between myself and those others who seek his presence, a question, sometimes spoken, sometimes not, which for all the pain and longing it may engender, for all the disappointment and bewilderment it may produce, cannot be swept away by nostalgia or sentimentality or even by a blind and valiant effort of the will: how are you connected to me as another man is not?

American Jews who *have* apprehended the God of Abraham, Isaac, and Jacob have not ignored the threat of assimilation or been blind to the conversion of Jews to secularism. American Jews who have remained true to Torah and Talmud have struggled to win converts, and with some success.

In 1886, only one year after the Reformers' Pittsburgh Platform, Conservative Jews established the Jewish Theological Seminary, the point of departure in the quest for a traditional and historical compromise between Orthodoxy and Reform. The exodus of two million Jews from Eastern Europe saved the Conservative seminary from collapse and enabled the Orthodox to begin, in 1896, the first American Yeshiva, the Rabbi Isaac Elchanan Theological Seminary, now Yeshiva University. The Gordian rapidity with which secularized Jews severed the bonds that bound them to their tradition brought the leaders of Reform Judaism to Columbus, Ohio, in 1937, in order to restore to their creed the centrality of the Torah and a belief in the peoplehood of Israel. In Horace Kallen's philosophy of cultural pluralism, Jews anxious to avoid assimilation discovered a rationale by which they hoped to be good Americans and yet maintain the ways of their fathers. In the theology of Mordecai Kaplan, Will Herberg, and Abraham Joshua Heschel, many Jews have found a faith relevant to the twentieth century. Although the third and fourth generations continue to drift further and further from any knowledge of historical Judaism, their elders no longer encourage them.

Within the literary world, the campaign to win converts for Judaism has been three-fold: first, the attack on those who defect from or denigrate the Jewish community; second, continued emphasis on the dangers of anti-Semitism; third, an affirmation of the positive aspects of Judaism and of the Jewish community.

In 1937, Meyer Levin's work was, he writes in his autobiography, preached against in the temples and described in some of the Jewish press as a degradation of our people. I received a call from the secretary of the Anti-Defamation League who took me to lunch at one of the downtown Jewish clubs. . . . The general theme was: Why do you young Jewish writers feel impelled to describe your people in this disgusting manner?

More recently, Edward Adler, Jerome Charyn, Babette Deutsch, Leslie Fiedler, Norman Fruchter, Herbert Gold, Irving Howe, Alfred Kazin, Philip Roth, Muriel Rukeyser, L. S. Simckes, and Louis Untermeyer have been denounced as anti-Semitic or abused for their aloofness from the Jewish community. Even Norman Podhoretz, struggling to "do" the modern without undoing the traditional, has run into difficulty: "Once . . . I nearly caused a riot when I attacked the prosody of a minor Israeli poet by invoking E. E. Cummings as a standard. I was howled down with talk of the blood shed by the six million." A representative chastisement begins as follows: "The renegade Jew in the limbo of lost identity is a sad phenomenon of the West. He is a self-hating, self-created, ectoplasmic figure who, having renounced his origins, realizes from time to time that he has also deprived his own children of a history." The reference to "self-hating" derives from Theodor Lessing's book, *Der Jüdische Selbsthass*, imported into this country by the social psychologist Kurt Lewin. This immensely overworked theory holds that alienated Jews apparently committed to secularism or converted to Christianity are actually driven by self-hate. They seek neurotically to deny what they know to be their true identity. Meyer Levin has, for instance, accused Budd Schulberg of self-hate, written a novel that shows Leopold and Loeb murdering Bobbie Frank because of self-hate, and suggested in his latest novel that converts to Communism are exemplars of self-hate. Preachments against the "self-hate" of Philip Roth have become the missionary's *modus vivendi*. Roth too has been called up and taken to lunch and advised to be more positive. He too has been denounced in the synagogues. Stuart Rosenberg, for example, has noted that Roth is one of those hateful intellectuals who publish in *Commentary*, one of those whose "criticisms, exaggerated by the self-hate of their alienation, cannot serve as an adequate guide to the true condition of the American Jewish community today." Unlike most writers, Roth has braved the fury and answered back:

> The question really is: who is going to address men and women like men and women, and who like children? If there are Jews who have begun to find the stories the novelists tell more provocative and pertinent than the sermons of some of the rabbis, perhaps it is because there are regions of feeling and consciousness in them which cannot be reached by the oratory of self-congratulation and self-pity.

It is the threat of anti-Semitism and fate of European Jews under Hitler that make understandable the fanaticism of some of the attacks on allegedly "self-hating" young writers. For those who have lived through Auschwitz and Dachau, books that do *not* return us in imagination to the apocalyptic horror of the concentration camps must seem, at times, utterly irrelevant. John Hersey's novel of the Warsaw ghetto seems almost trivial when compared to the facts of history; most of the novels written about anti-Semitism in America seem trivial when compared to John Hersey's book.[3]

If one seeks arguments for the maintenance of the Jewish community, Arthur Miller's *Focus* and Laura Hobson's *Gentleman's Agreement* are worse than trivial. Both novels attempt to demonstrate that Jews and Gentiles are really indistinguishable. Only the name is different. But this argument weakens rather than strengthens the demand that Jews affirm their unique and distinctive faith. Moreover, the tendency of some to rely on anti-Semitism as the *raison d'être* for the community makes quixotic the fifty-year crusade of the Anti-Defamation League. Moreover, as

Nathan Glazer has noted, as Bruce Jay Friedman shows in his novel, *Stern,* as Ivan Gold suggests in his story, "Taub East," the defense against the evil of anti-Semitism can become disproportionately intense in the United States of Arthur Goldberg, Harry Golden, and Barry Goldwater.

The third form of response to the conversion to America is the presentation in literary form of a "positive" view of Judaism and Jewish life. There is, for instance, the case of Charles Angoff, whose multi-volume odyssey of the Polansky family has been hailed, in the Jewish press, as worthy of a Nobel Prize. "Charles Angoff looms head and shoulders above any Jewish writer in America today," says the reviewer in the *Boston Jewish Advocate;* "Angoff arises as a giant of Jewish literature," says the reviewer in the *Chicago Jewish Forum.* There is, for instance, the case of Karl Shapiro, whose poems for, by, and about Jews are a reproach to Joy Davidman, Muriel Rukeyser, Delmore Schwartz, Howard Nemerov, John Hollander, and all others who have forgotten from whence cometh their salvation.

There is, for instance, the case of Herman Wouk, the best-known of writers committed to Judaism. Although *Marjorie Morningstar* is an outraged polemic against assimilation, Wouk begins with an attempt at fairness. The attractions of Central Park West and Columbia University are real. Lobster and shrimp entice. Noel Airman is, despite the withered arm he inherited from Nathaniel Hawthorne, sexually irresistible. Marjorie sleeps with Noel: "There were shocks, ugly uncoverings, pain, incredible humiliation, shock, shock, and it was over." Sexuality without God is a matter of "nasty, squirming, writhing naked bodies." A kindly phychologist helps to restore Marjorie's peace of mind: "Food disciplines are a part of every great religion. Psychologically, they're almost inevitable, and extremely practical." Marjorie abandons Noel to his fate as a TV-writer and turns to a young lawyer who manfully survives the traumatic knowledge of Marjorie's sinful past. Majorie becomes Mrs. Milton Schwartz,

a regular synagogue-goer, active in the Jewish organization of
the town; apparently that takes up a lot of her time. . . . Her
husband is active too. . . . The only remarkable thing about Mrs.
Schwartz is that she ever hoped to be remarkable, that she ever
dreamed of being Marjorie Morningstar.

Sylvia Rothchild borrowed Wouk's formula for *Sushine and Salt.*
The heroine and her husband are suburbanites with only the
loosest connection to the Jewish community. Their false Eden is
destroyed by the arrival from Brooklyn of the heroine's mother.
Mama isn't acculturated. She fears the unnatural darkness of
nights in the country. Grass and flowers annoy her. Taken to the
kosher markets of a nearby city, Mama sees slums and is nostalgic. Mama brings the urban rabbi home and he nails a *mazuzeh* to
the doorpost and demands a list of the lapsed Jews of the suburb.
It is hard for the reader to love Mama, but Mama is right. The
goyish Jews of the suburb discover that the inner sanctum of the
Garden Club is closed to them. When Mama dies in a mysterious
accident, the Jewish community declares her a martyr. The heroine returns: "I forgot my fierce wish to be myself. I became more
involved in the [Jewish] community. . . . I couldn't help myself.
Everyone knew I was Celia Abrams' daughter."

Samuel Astrachan, Michael Blankfort, Miriam Bruce, Meyer
Levin, and Leon Uris are among those who have, since World
War II, dramatized conversions to Judaism and to Zionism, but
the best of the novels of return remains Ludwig Lewisohn's *The
Island Within,* published in 1928. Lewisohn himself came to
America at the age of seven and pledged his allegiance to his new
home. He taught Sunday School, labored in the Epworth League,
and described himself as "an American, a Southerner, and a
Christian." He took an M.A. at Columbia and discovered that
Jews, even converted ones, were not hired to teach English literature and that Americans with German names were roughly handled in 1917 and 1918. Lewisohn became convinced that the

American dream was an illusion and that survival was possible only in Palestine. The novel is the powerful expression of that conviction. Lewisohn shows that the migration of the Levy family from Lithuania to Germany to America is also a movement from Orthodoxy to the most tenuous kind of secularized attachment. American-born Arthur Levy, thinking the attachment to Judaism has completely vanished, marries the agnostic daughter of a Christian minister. "Couldn't one help to destroy all those remnants of man's barbarous past by living as though they had no real existence, by living in the light of reason?" The answer is an emphatic *No!* Ironically, Arthur Levy, a disciple of Freud, finds himself married to a sexually repressed woman who sublimates her energies into a career as a hack-writer. A distant cousin, Reb Moshe, gradually brings Arthur Levy back to the path he had strayed from. Reading ancestral documents almost a thousand years old, Arthur Levy realizes that Jews are destined to suffer. The Crusaders massacred the Jews of Speyer and Mainz in 1096; Jews die today in pogroms in Elizavetgrad and Kishinev. Arthur divorces his wife and returns to his people.

When Hitler came to power, Lewisohn reminded us that he had warned us. Lewisohn also understood and warned against the only category of conversion to rival in historical importance that of St. Paul—the conversion to Utopia.

> Escape, escape, anything on any irrelevant periphery. Anything but the center, the heart, the blood. Virgin Spain, the Soviet Fatherland. Anything but the real, the attainable, the given, that for which real work can be done in a world of reality and real sacrifices made and real tears shed and real blood; anything but that to which one is called by nature and unperverted instinct and tradition and where one is wanted and needed and where . . . one can give one's whole heart. Any place but home. Any people except one's own. Any God except the God of one's fathers. . . . Utopia is the opiate of . . . the Jewish people.

Utopia is the opiate of the Jewish people. . . . Or their truest vocation. When seen in perspective, the commitment to Marxism will be seen as part of a much more important movement of those alienated from the past and dedicated to the future. The history of political radicalism in America from the anarchism of Emma Goldman and Alexander Berkman through the socialism of Victor Berger and Abraham Cahan and Morris Hillquit to the Communism of Herbert Aptheker and Howard Fast and Joseph Freeman and John Gates and Benjamin Gitlow and Mike Gold and Jay Lovestone and Bertram Wolfe—the history of political radicalism in America has very largely been the history of Jews doubly alienated from Judaism and from Christendom, apostates from the Mosaic dispensation and from the gospel according to Adam Smith.

If assimilation means a world of Babbitts tenuously tied to the B'nai Brith, if assimilation means a transfer of loyalty from the faith of our fathers to that of our neighbors, if assimilation means removal from Brownsville to Miami Beach, if assimilation means a political lemming-drive led by Barry Goldwater, then assimilation is not enough. The task of the writer alienated from traditional Judaism is the secularization of Judaism's historic sense of mission. If the writer departed from the temple is not to lose himself in the lonely crowd, he must labor to bring about the transformation of society. He must create the Zion in which exile can be ended.

For half a century at least, the conversion to Utopia has been a major theme of Jewish writers in America. Israel Zangwill, the English novelist, rewrote *Romeo and Juliet* fifty years before Leonard Bernstein set it to music. David Quixano, the hero of *The Melting Pot*, composes an American symphony, an orchestration of all the ethnic strains of our nation of nations. He and Vera Revenal break through the barriers of hatred that separated them:

America is God's Crucible, the great Melting-Pot where all the races of Europe are melting and reforming! Here you stand, good folk, think I, when I see them at Ellis Island, here you stand in your fifty groups, with your fifty languages and histories, and your fifty blood hatreds and rivalries. But you won't be long like that, brothers, for these are the fires of God you've come to—these are the fires of God. A fig for your feuds and vendettas! Germans and Frenchmen, Irishmen and Englishmen, Jews and Russians—into the Crucible with you all! God is making the American!

A generation later, Mike Gold's autobiographical sketch of *Jews without money* ends with an equally millenial vision:

A man on an East Side soap-box, one night, proclaimed that out of the despair, melancholy and helpless rage of millions, a world movement had been born to abolish poverty. . . . I listened to him. . . . O workers' revolution, you brought hope to me, a lonely suicidal boy. You are the true Messiah. You will destroy the East Side when you come, and build there a garden for the human spirit.

Even Meyer Levin, whose deepest passion was Zionism rather than socialism, wrote in the thirties of poverty and injustice, of bribed judges and corrupt doctors and a tendency among policemen routinely to beat anyone suspected of Communism. When the police, on Memorial Day, 1937, killed ten strikers at the Republic Steel Plant in South Chicago, Meyer Levin wrote *Citizens*, a novel still alive with its author's passionate protest against justice denied in Illinois. In the novel, a doctor committed only to his family and his career accidentally witnesses the Memorial Day massacre. He treats the wounded and struggles to keep the police from dragging them from ambulances and hospital beds. He reads the Chicago papers: MOB ATTACKS POLICE, 200 INJURED AS STRIKERS CHARGE, STRIKERS DRUGGED TO ASSAULT POLICE. By the end of the novel, he marches in the procession to pay homage to the dead:

> As the people approached the wreath, the column narrowed to a single file, and passed slowly, one by one they dropped their dark red flowers, like great swollen drops of blood augmenting the spreading dark pool on the ground.

Marxism, as a mass movement, is finished in the United States. It is common among historians to say that the American consensus has always been too strong for the success of a radical movement. It is more correct to say that the progressive transformation of America has vindicated the few who prodded the many to radical reform. Abraham Cahan's decision to vote for F.D.R. was not the betrayal of socialism that it has sometimes been called, nor is Norman Thomas's faint praise for Lyndon Johnson the result of a loss of faith. Although the word "socialism" is political suicide, we *have* crept a long way.

What of those Americans for whom Fabian progress toward social justice is far too slow, for whom the CIA is the sinister symbol of invisible government, for whom the poverty of the "other America" is a national disgrace? It is obvious to all of us that Negroes have now begun to lead the fight for racial equality. It is obvious to readers of *Dissent, The Monthly Review, New America, New Politics,* and *Studies on the Left* that many of the most articulate spokesmen for American radicalism are drawn now, as they were a generation ago, from the ranks of men and women alienated from the Jewish community if not from the tradition of the prophets. The movement for Proletarian Literature is an almost forgotten episode in our history; we are waiting, it is said, for Godot rather than for Lefty. But novelists and poets continue to dissent. Saul Bellow, Norman Fruchter, Herbert Gold, Barbara Probst Solomon, and Harvey Swados support socialist journals today as writers on the left supported *New Masses* and *The Partisan Review* thirty years ago. "Socialism," wrote Irving Howe and Lewis Coser, "is the name of our desire."[4]

The strange career of Norman Mailer is one sign of the alienated Jewish intellectual's continued dedication to the radical transformation of society. "The sour truth," writes Mailer, "is that I am imprisoned with a perception which will settle for nothing less than making a revolution in the consciousness of our time." Mailer's quest is for the classless society in which the shits will no longer kill us, for the perfect orgasm that will give us the time of our time. *Barbary Shore* fails as a novel but who has better described what Trotsky meant to American Jews?

> There was a great man who led us, and I read almost every word he had written, and listened with the passion of the novitiate to each message he sent from the magical center in Mexico. . . . I lived more intensely in the past than I could ever in the present, until the sight of a policeman on his mount became the Petrograd proletariat crawling to fame between the legs of a Cossack's horde. . . . There never was a revolution to equal it, and never a city more glorious than Petrograd, and for all that period of my life I lived another and braved the ice of winter and the summer flies in Vyborg while across my adopted country of the past, winds of the revolution blew their flame, and all of us suffered hunger while we drank . . . the wine of equality.

Paul Goodman, another Utopian, castigates society's absurdity:

> [Our society] thwarts aptitude and creates stupidity. It corrupts ingenuous patriotism. It corrupts the fine arts. It shackles science. It dampens animal ardor. It discourages the religious convictions of Justification and Vocation, and it dims the sense that there is a Creation. It has no Honor. It has no Community.

No community. The United States today lacks the communal sense of a traditional society, lacks, for instance, the closeness and compassion of the world described by Alfred Kazin in his memoir, *A Walker in the City*. Goodman believes that the community can be recreated by the radical reconstruction of society. His book, *Communitas*, written with his brother Percival, is a blueprint of the new society. His novel, *Making Do*, is the dramatic revelation of the possibility of a reasonable love that transcends barriers of class, nation, religion, race, and sex. The novel contains violence and disappointment as well as love, but Goodman refuses to settle for the world as it is. "No," he concludes, " 'The Lord has yet more light and truth to break forth,' as John Robinson said to the Pilgrims embarking toward America."[5]

Goodman and Mailer are not alone. Herbert Gold's best novel, *The Prospect Before Us*, is the epitaph of a stubborn hotel-keeper who defies the prejudices of white America and rents a room to a Negro girl—and dies for love of her. Harvey Swados' stories and essays document the degradation of factory life and debunk the myth of the happy worker. Clancy Sigal's *Going Away* is perhaps the most minutely thorough criticism of American life since Dos Passos' *USA*. Driving from Los Angeles to New York, Sigal's anonymous hero seeks traces of that lost world of the thirties, where *unions* meant sit-down strikes rather than racial discrimination, where *Spain* meant the defense of Madrid rather than another article in *Holiday*. "I really wanted, while I was on the road, to look at America and try to figure out why it wasn't my country any more." Even Henderson the Rain King and Sergius O'Shaughnessy and Moses Herzog are restlessly radical in their refusal to affirm the status quo, in their active quest for a world more attractive.

I am sure—despite the affluence that fills the land with YWHAs—that traditional Judaism will not disappear from America. There will always be those for whom Abraham and Isaac and the Tables of the Law are more important than Danny Kaye and Leon Uris and ledgers in the black. There will always be those for whom the Utopian dream of the brotherhood of man means less than the historical reality of the peoplehood of Israel. I am also sure that these Jews will decline in numbers. They will also, if the descent from Ludwig Lewisohn to Herman Wouk is any indication, decline in literary importance. For the great majority of American Jews, the process of secularization seems certain to continue toward assimilation in a more secular, if not more attractive, America. The Jewish Book Club of the future will have fifty Edna Ferbers to choose from. The Communist Party will search unsuccessfully for a second Michael Gold. If present tendencies continue, Negroes are more likely than Jews disproportionately to fill the ranks of dissent and to imagine in novel and in poem another country better than the one we live in now. Paradoxically, the survival in America of a significant and identifiably *Jewish* literature depends on the unlikely conversion to Judaism of a stiff-necked intractable generation that no longer chooses to be chosen.

NOTES

1. These terms are used throughout as in Milton M. Gordon's book, *Assimilation in American Life* (New York, 1964).

2. For an explanation of this comment, see my article, "Jewish Radicals, Jewish Writers," *American Scholar*, XXXII (Autumn 1963), 563–75.

3. The exception, Saul Bellow's *The Victim*, is a book that suggests that Semite and anti-Semite are essentially the same man.

4. Ironically, dissenters like Irving Howe and Alfred Kazin and Norman Mailer have become highly conscious of their debts to Judaism in the very years that have seen the majority of American Jews covenant themselves under the New Deal and the New Frontier.

5. Bellow's *The Adventures of Augie March* ends with a very similar image: "Why, I am a sort of Columbus of those near-at-hand and believe you can come to them in this immediate *terra incognita* that spreads out in every gaze. I may well be a flop at this line of endeavor. Columbus too thought he was a flop, probably, when they sent him back in chains. Which didn't prove there was no America."

Jewish Dreams
and Nightmares*

ROBERT ALTER

What have I in common with Jews? I have hardly anything in common with myself and should stand very quietly in a corner, content
that I can breathe.—Franz Kafka, *Diaries*

There is something presumptuously proprietary about the whole
idea of sorting out writers according to national, ethnic, or religious origins, like so many potatoes whose essential characteristics can be determined by whether they come from Idaho or
Maine. Obviously enough, the primary focus for useful criticism
of any original writer must be on the stubbornly individual imagination that has sought to articulate a personal sense of self and
world through the literary medium, and this attention to individual peculiarities rather than shared characteristics is especially
necessary in understanding serious writers since the middle of
the last century, so many of whom have been alienated in one way
or another from their native social groups. Indeed, as Kafka's
chilling confession of self-estrangement reminds us, some of the

*From the book, After the Tradition *by Robert Alter. Copyright © *1969, 1968, 1967,
1966, 1965, 1964, 1962, 1961 by Robert Alter. Dutton Paperback edition. Published by
E. P. Dutton & Co., Inc., and reprinted with their permission.*

most troubled, and therefore representative, modern writers
have been alienated from themselves as well, haunted by the fear
that every affirmation or act of communication was a falsification,
a betrayal.

Nevertheless, the onerous question of the writer's background
persists. One justifiably speaks of Melville, Hawthorne, even Poe,
as essentially American writers, for their achievement cannot be
intelligently grasped without an awareness of its intimate relationship to the common social and cultural experience of nineteenth-century America. Even more strikingly, the Jewishness of
writers like Mendele, Peretz, and Sholom Aleichem obviously has
the greatest relevance to any serious assessment of their literary
enterprise because their fictional worlds are shaped out of the
stuff of East-European Jewish life, its language, its folklore, its
religious traditions, its social realia. With Jewish writers, however, the attempt to attribute literary qualities to ethnic origins
is in many instances acutely problematic. The Jews, in any case
a perplexing group to define, become almost perversely elusive
as the process of modernization spreads after the French Revolution. It is by no means clear what sense is to be made of the
Jewishness of a writer who neither uses a uniquely Jewish language, nor describes a distinctively Jewish milieu, nor draws
upon literary traditions that are recognizably Jewish. If one were
to compile an anthology of all the unabashed nonsense written
by literary critics over the past fifty years, a good many pages
would have to be devoted to what has been advanced about the
Jewish values, vision, and world view of a wide variety of apostates, supposed descendants of Jews, offspring of mixed marriages, or merely assimilated Jews, from St. Theresa and Heine
down to Proust and even J. D. Salinger.

One cannot, however, simply discount the possibility that some
essentially Jewish qualities may adhere to the writing of the most
thoroughly acculturated Jews. Most readers have sensed in at
least some of these "post-traditional" or "transitional" Jewish

writers certain modes of imagination or general orientations toward art and experience that seem characteristically Jewish, even
where the writer scrupulously avoids all references to his ethnic
origins. The difficulty, of course, is to translate such vague intui-
tions into clear descriptive statements about what actually goes
on in the literary works.

I was led to ponder again this intriguing but treacherous question of Jewish literary identity by an essay of Leslie Fiedler's,
"Master of Dreams," published in the summer, 1967, issue of
Partisan Review. What Fiedler sketches out in his essay might be
described as a single grand mythic plot which, in sundry variations, modifications, and reversals, is presumed to underlie all
Jewish literature, and, apparently, all Jewish cultural activity as
well. Fiedler's point of departure is the Joseph story in Genesis,
which he interestingly characterizes as a "dream of the dreamer,
a myth of myth itself." Joseph, whose troubles begin because of
his own seemingly grandiose dream, makes his way to power by
interpreting the dreams of others and so translates his original
dream into dazzling fact, his fathers and brothers—and virtually
the whole world besides—bowing down to him as viceroy of the
mightiest king on earth. In the light of this communal dream of
the Joseph story, Fiedler sees the Jew's characteristic cultural role
as a vendor of dreams and an interpreter of dreams to the world,
that is, as poet and therapist (in Fiedler's anecdotal English, "My
Son the Artist" and "My Son the Doctor"). The Jewish sons who
become poets, according to this account, continue to pursue the
original myth of myth: their fictions are about the attempt—what
some of them now recognize as a doomed attempt—to make the
splendid dream literal fact, and their fictional surrogates are even
frequently called upon to resist the temptations of a Potiphar's
wife in order to remain faithful to the dream they bear within
them. Fiedler concedes that there are wide differences in the
literary forms adopted by Jewish writers, but he suggests that
they all belong to a single tradition both because they all partici-

pate in a Joseph-like myth of myth, and because they share a distinctive purpose, which, in keeping with the double role of the biblical master of dreams, is "therapeutic and prophetic."

Before I speak to the issues raised by this interpretation—and the hasty account of it here hardly does justice to its athletic ingenuity—I would like to point out a general characteristic of Fiedler's critical enterprise which this essay makes particularly clear. Fiedler's criticism has a paradoxical doubleness of effect. On the one hand, because his favorite critical activity is the relentless pursuit of archetypes, an ill-considered literary fashion of the fifties that went out with the Eisenhower administration, there is often an odd hint of datedness in what he writes, despite the swinging, up-to-the-minute prose he affects. One senses in Fiedler, on the other hand, a peculiar venturesomeness and energy of imagination that set him off from the academic myth-mongers of the fifties, indeed, that endow his work with a perennial fascination. The main impulse of Fiedler's criticism is neither analytic nor evaluative but poetic:[1] the fidelity it most steadily preserves is not at all to the works or figures discussed but to its own inner coherence as a poetic invention.

The treatment of the biblical subject in "Master of Dreams" suggests a useful analogue for Fiedler's criticism—Midrash, the early rabbinic method of homiletic exegesis. One possible way of describing Midrash is as the art of imaginatively connecting things intrinsically unconnected, and the same could be said of much that Fiedler has written. Since for the creators of the Midrash the entire Bible, together with the Oral Law, exists in one eternal, divinely revealed present, everything is potentially an intricate commentary on everything else. One needs only the recurrence of, say, a verb-root in a verse in Genesis, in Isaiah, and in Psalms, to see the later statements as explications, developments, fuller revelations of the earlier one. When, for example, the Midrash Bereshit Rabba tells us that Abraham's "splitting" of wood for the sacrifice of Isaac was answered on a grand scale by God's "splitting" of the Red Sea for his descendants, our real knowledge of the relevant verses in Genesis and Exodus has not been augmented, but what we may enjoy is following the trajectory of the interpretative imagination from point to point, not unlike the delight we take in the linking of ostensible disparates that is effected through poetic metaphor. This procedure is not so far removed from that of modern archetypal criticism, which in just such an instance might easily speak not of verbal continuities but of "the recurrence of the cleavage motif," with or without Freudian innuendos.

Fiedler is more subtle and inventive than most mythopoeic critics in his articulation of archetypes, but he clearly shares with the medieval Midrash an indifference to historical perspective which allows him to speak of the varied literary productions of far-flung times and places as one eternal system, and he is thoroughly midrashic in his readiness to establish through the merest hint of an association a "real" connection between things. Thus, there is actually not the faintest suggestion in the biblical story that Joseph is either a poet or a therapist. He interprets dreams for purposes at once practical and divine, but surely not to cure anyone, while the common association between dreamer and poet which Fiedler invokes is not even vaguely intimated in the biblical account. Though Fiedler would have us think of Joseph as a prototype of both Freud and Kafka, it makes better sense on the grounds of the text itself to imagine Joseph rather as a sort of ancient Near Eastern RAND Corporation figure—the Jewish intellectual as government planner, manipulating that great Pharaonic power structure from the top, managing, through his two Seven-Year Plans, to centralize control of land and economic resources to a degree unprecedented in Egyptian history. If Fiedler's own bold anachronisms invite anachronistic response, this, too, is in the ahistorical spirit of midrashic interpretation: the rabbis did not hesitate to represent Joseph as an earlocked talmudist applying himself to the subtleties of the Law in the study-house of Shem, and by the same logic he can be given a Viennese beard, a passion for literary self-expression, or a knowledge of computer mathematics.

There is, then, a special fascination in Fiedler's criticism, but as in the case of the ancient Midrashim, we may sometimes want to qualify that fascination with an adjective like "quaint." The real question raised by his whole scheme of an archetypal Jewish myth of myth is not whether it is firmly anchored in the biblical story but whether it is really helpful in locating and identifying a distinctive Jewish movement in Western culture, and in this essential regard I cannot see that it has any utility at all. On the contrary, it seems to me to encourage a common error much in need of correction. For there has been a tacit conspiracy afoot in recent years to foist on the American public as peculiarly Jewish various admired characteristics which in fact belong to the common humanity of us all. The Jewish folk is imagined as possessing a kind of monopoly on vividness, compassion, humor, pathos, and the like; Jewish critics and novelists are thought to be unique in their preoccupation with questions of morality; and now we are asked to believe that the Jews have all along exercised a privileged control over the cultural market on dreams.

When Fiedler characterizes the Joseph story as "the dreamer's own dream of how, dreaming, he makes it in the waking world," and then goes on to represent modern Jewish writing as a varying account of the difficulties of "making it" through dreams in actuality, he is describing not a distinctively Jewish imaginative mode but the central tradition of the novel, from *Don Quixote* to *Lolita*. Cervantes had hit on a new set of literary terms to encompass a new, radically disorienting world (the one we still inhabit) by inventing a dreamer who madly and persistently tried to live out his shining dream in a gray existence stolidly resistant to dreams and intolerant of their perpetrators. The model of the heroically unhinged Don, progenitor of a genre, is followed by Stendhal's Julien Sorel, Flaubert's Emma Bovary, Dostoevski's Prince Mish-

kin and his Raskolnikov, Melville's Ahab, George Eliot's Doro-
thea Brooke, Gide's Lafcadio, Joyce's Stephen Daedalus as well
as his Leopold Bloom—in fact, by the protagonists of most of the
substantial novels written over the past two centuries. One might
of course seize on the conjecture of some literary historians that
Cervantes himself was a Marrano or the descendant of converts
from Judaism, but this would be to succumb to a kind of philose-
mitic version of the *Protocols of the Elders of Zion* as an explanation
of Western culture. According to such a theory, which seems to
be tacitly assumed by many critics, the main currents at least of
modern culture all derive from subterranean Jewish sources: a
tenuous connection through three Christian generations with
Jewish forebears is supposedly enough to infect the writer with
a uniquely Jewish imagination, and this in turn he passes on to
the Gentile world around him. (Fiedler applies much the same
logic to fictional characters in describing the hero of *An American
Dream* as an "essentially" Jewish figure by arbitrarily identifying
him as a compound of two projected characters in Mailer's unwritten long novel, one Gentile and the other one-quarter Jewish,
which then enables him blithely to assert that "Stephen Rojack
. . . is half-Jewish, since in the world of myth a quarter Jew plus
a full Gentile equals a half-Jew.") All this is undoubtedly somewhat less incredible than the obverse theory that the Jews have
secretly seized control of Western civilization in order to destroy
it from within, but it resembles the *Protocols* myth in reshaping
observable realities to fit the contours of collective fantasy.

It is not the Jewish dreamer in Exile but the writer at large who,
"thinking only of making his own dreams come true, ends by
deciphering the alien dreams of that world as well," and the
"prophetic" and "therapeutic" ends which Fiedler assigns to
Jewish writers are in fact the general aims of most serious European and American writers at least since the middle of the nineteenth century. The Joseph scheme works all too well in too many
cases, whether we apply it to the writer's life or to his literary

creations. Who, for example, could be closer to the archetype of Joseph than Charles Dickens, a master of dreams who determined from early youth to realize a great dream of worldly success and achieved it by creating and selling dreams to the millions —"the artist as tycoon," in F. W. Dupee's telling phrase—even to acquiring the very Gads Hill mansion he had envisaged from afar as a boy? The prophetic and therapeutic impulse in Dickens' novels hardly needs comment at this point in time, and it is equally clear that in the works of his maturity, by bodying forth in fiction his own dreams, he was interpreting the collective dreams of a culture to which part of him remained permanently alien, from his descent into the pit of the blacking warehouse as a child to his glorious assumption into the palaces of the great.

Or, using this same mythic touchstone to identify characteristically Jewish literary inventions, one might justifiably conclude that the most remarkable American Jewish novel is neither *Call It Sleep* nor *Herzog* but Ralph Ellison's *Invisible Man*. Ellison prefaces his book with a dedication to Morteza Sprague, "a dedicated dreamer in a land most strange," which is a neat description of the archetypal Joseph himself and also accurately characterizes Ellison's protagonist. The novel begins and ends with a dream and many of the intervening episodes are strikingly dreamlike, for the protagonist is at once attempting to escape a nightmare and realize a dream of worldly success, on the world's own meretricious terms. His slow recognition of who he really is—"I am your brother Joseph," one almost hears him saying in the poignant scene where he realizes his deep kinship with an evicted Harlem couple—involves a rejection of the false dream, a perception of the extent to which the nightmare is reality. In this version, it is at the end of his long journey from home that he is cast into a dark pit, Joseph-like, by those who should be his brothers, and he promises us that he will emerge from these depths with a new unillusioned strength. There are even Potiphar's wives to mislead this young man with a vision on his progress through a land most strange. In contrast to the three sexual partners of Steve Rojack—that highly supposititious "mythical" Jew—who are improbably seen by Fiedler as Potiphar's wives, the two white seductresses in *Invisible Man* are really imagined as alien women who, by using the hero for their own gratification, would thrust him into a false role, would unwittingly involve him in a symbolic betrayal of himself and his people. It is difficult, finally, to think of a novel written by a Jew that is as intent as this one to enunciate a prophecy and effect a kind of therapy. The young Negro, by working out the visions that haunt him, ends up deciphering the darker dreams of American society as well. It is entirely appropriate that the novel should conclude with a long dreamlike sequence charged with intimations of apocalypse, the nightmare now galloping across the waking world, and that this episode in turn should be followed by a formal, allegorical dream of apocalypse, prophesying doom to America if it does not act quickly to redeem its own humanity.

The tracing of archetypes is a pleasant enough pastime, but its value as a means of making useful literary identifications is dubious. Ellison himself has stated the matter succinctly in objecting to another archetypal interpretation of his novel: "archetypes are timeless, novels are time-haunted." If we are to discover any clue to the connection between a writer's origins in a particular group and the nature of his work, we must begin in time, which is to say, we must take history seriously into account. The case of Kafka, whom Fiedler cites as the great modern paradigm of Joseph as artist, the Jewish son as dreamer, takes us to the heart of this whole issue. No other Jew who has contributed significantly to European literature appears so intensely, perhaps disturbingly, Jewish in the quality of his imagination as Kafka. Though he never introduces explicitly Jewish materials into his work, though he never really writes "about" Jews (even symbolically, I would argue), most readers of *The Trial, The Castle, Amerika,* and the shorter parables and fables, have sensed that this peculiar mode of fiction would never have occurred to a Christian imagination. One is struck by the emphatic difference of Kafka's work from the various kinds of fiction that have been predominant in the European novel, but it is not so easy to determine whether or how that difference is Jewish.

To think of Kafka as a Joseph-figure will not really help us, for reasons which I hope I have already made clear. The invocation of that archetype does not, for example, enable us to distinguish between Kafka and Dickens, a writer whom he admired and imitated, and who shared with him a "Jewish" preoccupation with failed relationships between fathers and sons. Critics have made a variety of other suggestions about the Jewishness of Kafka's fiction, some of them comical, some interesting, some perhaps even credible. To begin with, there has been a general rush to align Kafka with various Jewish cultural traditions, without regard to the degree of familiarity he may actually have had with them. The fact that Kafka is both a Jewish writer and an arcane one has invited a certain degree of loose talk about the "kabbalistic" elements in his work, though he had no direct knowledge of the Kabbalah, and the Germanized home in which he grew up was hardly the sort where he could have picked up very much of it through oral tradition. More plausibly, comparisons have been drawn between the Hasidic folktale and the parable form Kafka favored in which the order of action is so often inscrutably miraculous. The biographical evidence, however, suggests affinity rather than influence. Kafka was fascinated by whatever he learned of Hasidic lore, but the better part of his acquaintance with it took place toward the end of his life, through his friendship with Georg Langer and then from his reading of Buber's early compilations, especially *Der grosse Maggid,* which did not appear until 1922. Again, a good many critics who have never studied a page of the Talmud have not hesitated to describe the peculiar questioning movement of Kafka's prose as "talmudic," but there is virtually no real similarity, and in any case Kafka's knowledge of the Talmud, until his last years, was confined to quotations passed on to him by those of his friends who had once studied in the East-European *yeshivot.* One is free to suppose, of course, that Westernized Jews as a rule simply continue to talk and think in talmudic fashion, but such a supposition can be made only out of ignorance of both the Talmud itself and the way modern Jews actually talk and think.

Heinz Politzer, in his book, *Franz Kafka: Parable and Paradox,* links Kafka's fiction somewhat more probably with a still older mode of Jewish literature. Politzer compares Kafka's spare, taut tales, which repeatedly generate a sense of fatal significance in the events narrated, to the narrative method of the Hebrew Bible. Picking up the notion developed by Erich Auerbach of the biblical story as a tale "fraught with background," Politzer argues that in Kafka's enigmatic fictions one can observe this same general effect of starkly drawn surfaces which suggest a heavy pressure of dark meanings behind them that are never spelled out by the narrator. In Kafka, he goes on to say, as in the ancient Hebrew stories, the characters are at once impersonal and more than personal, uncannily representative in their very distance and peculiarity, inviting multiple interpretation by leading us to think of them as our surrogates in a cosmic drama. Kafka certainly read the Hebrew Bible in translation intently, occasionally even alluded to aspects of his own experience in biblical terms, and at the end of his life he was learning to read it in its original language. It is at least plausible that his familiarity with the Bible helped him work out his own characteristic narrative art; in any case, he must have discovered in it a compelling imaginative kinship. Such notions of kinship, however, can be adopted for the needs of precise literary analysis only with great caution, for they are but a step away from assuming a Hebrew Imagination over against a Greek Imagination as timeless categories, which, of course, would bring us back through another door into the wide-and-woolly realm of myths of culture.

Critics less interested in Kafka's treament of literary form than in his moral, philosophical, and theological concerns have associated him not with Jewish literary traditions but with the distinctive values and assumptions of historical Judaism. Thus, the absence of any radical disjuncture in Kafka between spirit and flesh, this world and the next, even between the prosaic and the miraculous, has been attributed to his Jewish background, which, it must be admitted, is a suggestive idea if not altogether a demonstrable one. The fact, on the other hand, that moral or spiritual obligations in Kafka so often take the form of commandments from an unreachable authority and frequently necessitate torturous interpretation, can obviously be connected with Kafka's personal awareness of rabbinic Judaism, and represents a particularly Jewish formulation of a general spiritual predicament. Still clearer is the condition of exile—for Jews, a theological category as well as a historical experience—which underlies all of Kafka's major fiction. It is this, above all else, that commentators have quite properly stressed in identifying the distinctively Jewish note in Kafka: if modern literature in general is a literature that adopts the viewpoint of the outsider, Kafka, as the alienated member of an exiled people, is the paradigmatic modernist precisely because he is a paradigmatic Jew.

The general validity of this familiar idea is, I suppose, unassailable, but its usefulness is limited because of the very fact that in its usual formulation it remains so general. "Exile" tends to be applied to Kafka and to other Jewish writers as an evocative but unexamined abstraction with a supposedly fixed meaning, when in fact exile meant different things to different Jews at various times and places, and for most of them, at least until fairly recently, it was quite distinct from alienation, a concept with which many literary critics automatically identify it. It makes sense, therefore, to try to state in concrete terms how this particular writer seems to have encountered the experience of exile and then how that encounter enters into the substance of his imaginative work.

Living in Prague, Kafka of course belonged to a very special kind of double exile—a Jew in the Austro-Hungarian Empire and a German writer in a Czech city. His position, moreover, as an employee in a state-sponsored insurance agency extended his initial sense of himself as a suspect intruder: at his office he was, as he pointedly phrased it, the single "display-Jew" in a "dark nest of bureaucrats," and so every workday forced upon him at least the negative awareness of Jewishness as a condition of being unwanted, mistrusted, transparently dependent on the favor of others. At the same time, Kafka was acutely conscious of Jewish history and Jewish peoplehood, even without any deep knowledge of the former or very much external involvement in the latter, until the Zionism of his last years. He was inclined to view the Jews of his own generation as in fact transitional, standing uncertainly at the irrevocable end of a long process of Jewish history, but this sense of belonging to a twilight period seems to have had the effect of sharpening his interest in the history and culture of his people. The Yiddish theater in Prague, for example, held a fascination for Kafka out of all proportion to the artistic merit of the plays it presented because he saw in it the living manifestation of an uninhibited, self-sufficient folk culture, unlike anything he had known personally. The very idea of Yiddish literature continued to attract him—he carefully read and took notes in his diary on Pine's *Histoire de la littérature Judéo-Allemande*—because with its obvious stress on "an uninterrupted tradition of national struggle that determines every work," he envisaged it as an alluring antithesis to that anguished exploration of a private world which writing inevitably was for him.

The case of Kafka, the acculturated Jew, shows how a man may feel his way into a body of collective history through his very consciousness of being outside it: Kafka brooded over the experience of the people from whom he derived, and I would argue that certain key images and states of awareness that were the product of European Jewish history exerted continual pressure on his imagination as he wrote. In this connection, there is one passage in his recorded conversations with the Czech writer Gustav Janouch that is especially revealing. Janouch had asked him if he still remembered the old Jewish quarter of Prague, largely destroyed before Kafka could have known it; this, according to Janouch, is the reply he received:

> In us it still lives—the dark corners, the secret alleys, shuttered windows, squalid courtyards, rowdy pubs, and sinister inns. We walk through the broad streets of the newly built town. But our steps and our glances are uncertain. Inside we tremble just as before in the ancient streets of our misery. Our heart knows nothing of the slum clearance which has been achieved. The unhealthy old Jewish town within us is far more real than the new hygienic town around us. With our eyes open we walk through a dream: ourselves only a ghost of a vanished age.

This remarkable statement is a kind of spiritual autobiography, a summary of what the awareness of being a Jew meant in Kafka's inner life; at the same time, it might be observed that what he has in effect described here is the imaginative landscape of all three of his novels—the hidden alleys and sinister attics of *The Trial*, the medieval squalor and confusion of the courtyards, the dubious inns and devious byways in *The Castle*, and even the new-world landscape of *Amerika*, which begins with skyscrapers but breaks off in a dark and filthy garret where the protagonist is held prisoner. The world of Kafka's novels incorporates the maddening impersonality and inscrutability of modern bureaucracy in an image of an insecure medieval community derived from a ghetto Kafka remembered obsessively without ever having known it. Let me emphasize that the recognition of such a connection may tell us something about the genesis of Kafka's enigmatic fictions but it is by no mans a key to their meaning. What Kafka's imaginative intimacy with the Jewish past did was to give a special shape to the imagery and a particular sharpness to the edge of feeling in his work, but the work is surely not intended as a representation of Jewish experience. It is, for example, a serious misplacement of emphasis to describe *The Castle*, as a few critics have done, as a Zionist myth of an outcast in search of a land, though the novel would not have been conceived in the terms it was and would not carry the conviction it does without Kafka's concrete imagination of uncertain steps and glances along the ancient streets of Jewish misery. Or again, to insist that the eternally exiled hero of "The Hunter Gracchus" is an avatar of the Wandering Jew would be to force a hauntingly elusive tale into the predictable contours of allegory. It seems wiser to say that Kafka's general and untranslatable fable of a wanderer through awesome eternity is imagined with such disturbing intensity because of the presence in the writer of Jewish memories, personal and collective, out of which he could create this particular "ghost of a vanished age" walking open-eyed through a dream of damnation. It is not as an archetypal Jew that Gracchus speaks at the end of the story, but the words and images his inventor chooses for him resonate with the experience of rejection and exclusion of many generations: "Nobody will read what I say here, no one will come to help me; even if all the people were commanded to help me, every door and window would remain shut, everybody would take to bed and draw the bedclothes over his head, the whole earth would become an inn for a night." It is one of those unsettling moments in Kafka when, in the retrospectively ironic light of history, we see the recollection of the past as a grimly accurate prophecy of the future, too.

Another major theme of Kafka's, which he often connects with the situation of the outsider or pariah, is the irruption of the inhuman into the human, or, more generally, the radical ambiguity of what seems to be human. While this movement of his imagination was obviously energized by the tensions and fears of his own private neuroses, it seems to me that his notion of a convergence of inhuman and human frequently draws on his hallucinated memory of the Jewish past. Even in a bizarre story like "A Report to an Academy," which is so far removed from any overt reference to Jews, I would contend that Kafka's fictional invention is formed on a kind of "analogical matrix" of his experience as a transitional Jew. The scientific report, one recalls, is that of a gifted ape who has managed "with an effort which up till now has never been repeated . . . to reach the cultural level of an average European." In the torturous confinement of a cage so small that he could neither stand nor sit in it, the idea had dawned on the ape of getting out by imitating his captors, and he began, most appropriately, by learning to spit, and then to drink schnapps by the bottle, an act which at first violently repelled him. In retrospect, the ape stresses again and again that he finds no intrinsic advantage in being human: "there was no attraction for me in imitating human beings; I imitated them because I needed a way out, and for no other reason . . . ah, one learns when one has to; one learns when one needs a way out." Conversely, the ape makes no special plea for apehood; there may be nothing especially admirable in being an ape rather than a human, but, if one begins as an ape, it is at least an authentic condition, what one would naturally prefer to remain, other things being equal. When at the end of the report the ape adjures his audience, "Do not tell me that it was not worth the trouble," there is a quaver of doubt in his voice: cages are admittedly maddening to live in, but has he not lost a great deal by betraying his native self for a way out, selling his birthright, so to speak, for a mess of lentils?

Now, one of the distinctive qualities of a Kafka parable is that it has no paraphrasable "moral," and I would not want to transform "A Report to an Academy" into an allegory of assimilation. I suspect, however, that this fable which calls into question the whole status of humanity was initially shaped around Kafka's awareness of himself as part of the modern movement of Jews who had emerged from the confinement of ghetto life to join European culture, and that the ape's disquieting ambiguity about his own achievement flows from Kafka's insight into how much of themselves Jews had left behind in their former existence without even the compensation of genuine acceptance in the "human" world outside the cage. The very contrast between human and Jew was one that modernizing Jews themselves implicitly accepted in their desperation for a way out. The poet Y. L. Gordon's famous line, "Be a man outside and a Jew at home," summed up this whole self-negating mentality as it was articulated in the Hebrew Enlightenment, and Kafka himself must have been particularly struck by Gordon's formulation, for he copied it into his diary when he ran across it in Pines's history.

Typically, however, confusions between human and inhuman in Kafka terrify more than they perplex, and the imaginative core of that terror is often Jewish for this writer who lived so intensely with the fear and trembling of a vanished ghetto. The nightmarish little tale entitled "An Old Manuscript" is paradigmatic in this respect. Again, the terms of reference of the story are as universal as those of some ancient myth. A nameless town in a nameless empire has been taken over by fierce, implacable nomads who speak no recognizably human tongue. The Emperor remains a powerless spectator, shut up in his palace, a little like the symbolic King of banished sons in many of the midrashic parables, while the townspeople, in the person of the cobbler who is the narrator, confess their incapacity to cope with the terrible strangers:

> From my stock, too, they have taken many good articles. But I cannot complain when I see how the butcher, for instance, suffers across the street. As soon as he brings in any meat the nomads snatch it all from him and gobble it up. Even their

horses devour flesh; often enough a horseman and his horse
are lying side by side, both of them gnawing at the same joint,
one at either end. The butcher is nervous and does not dare to
stop his deliveries of meat. We understand that, however, and
subscribe money to keep him going. If the nomads got no meat,
who knows what they might think of doing; who knows anyhow
what they may think of, even though they get meat every day.

One does not have to invoke mythic archetypes to feel the bone
and blood of Jewish memories in these ghastly images. Behind
the nameless nomadic horsemen are dark hordes of Cossacks,
Haidameks, pogromists of every breed—the alien and menacing
goy in his most violent embodiments, speaking no intelligible
language, obeying no human laws, even eagerly violating, as we
learn in the next paragraph, the Noahide injunction against con-
suming the flesh of an animal while it is still alive. To the Jew
trembling before the torch and ax and sword of the attacker, it
seemed that the enemy quite literally could not belong to the
same species, and so here the ironic displacement of inhuman
and human of "A Report to an Academy" is reversed, the Jew,
in the analogical matrix of this story, associated with vulnerable
humanity, and the Gentile with inhuman otherness.

What should also be noted is that the story pronounces judgment on the passivity of the townspeople as well as on the stark
bestiality of the nomads. Edmund Wilson has accused Kafka of
"meaching compliance" with the brutal and unreasonable forces
he means to expose in his fiction, but I think this misses the point,
for the object of Kafka's "satire" (the term is applied by Wilson)
is not only the inhuman powers but also man's pathetic inade-
quacy of response to them. To put this in terms of the ethnic
background of Kafka's imaginings, he never sentimentalized Jewish history; though he was intrigued by the lore of his forebears
and their unusual sense of community, he remained ruthlessly
honest about the way Jews were. In the passage quoted, one can
see a distinctly familiar response of Jews to violence and impend-

ing disaster—the attempt to buy off calamity, to temporize with it. (How sadly characteristic that the tradesmen of the community should answer the terrible challenge only by pooling resources to subsidize the principal victim of the invaders!) The story makes clear that this response represents a failure of courage and of imagination as well: in the face of imminent and hideous destruction, where bold, perhaps violent, action is required, the townspeople can muster no more than a piously impotent wringing of hands, a collection of donations, and the grotesquely timid understatement that "This is a misunderstanding of some kind; and it will be the ruin of us."

Kafka, in sum, addressed himself to the broadest questions of human nature and spiritual existence working with images, actions, and situations that were by design universal in character; but his self-awareness as a Jew and his consciousness of Jewish history impelled his imagination in a particular direction and imparted a peculiar intensity to much of what he wrote, where the abstractness or generality of the parable is strangely wedded to the most concrete sense of actual experience felt and recollected. He could envision the ultimate ambiguities of human life in general with a hyperlucidity because he had experienced them in poignant particularity as a Jew. Out of the stuff of a Jewish experience which he himself thought of as marginal, he was able to create fiction at once universal and hauntingly Jewish.

All this is far from exhausting the question of how Kafka's antecedents enter into his writing, but it should at least suggest that there is no simple formulaic key for identifying the Jewish character of all Jewish writers. As I have tried to illustrate in the case of Kafka, one must always attend to the particular ways in which Jewish experience impinges on the individual, and this impingement is bound to differ in small things and large from one writer to the next. The varied materials of art itself, with their confusingly various connections with reality, are more recalcitrant, less pleasingly symmetrical, than the neat designs of archetypal criticism, but, in the final analysis, they are a good deal more interesting.

NOTE

1. In his essay, "My First Gothic Novel" (*Novel*, fall, 1967), Fiedler has, while modestly claiming for himself a place with the great critics of the ages, asserted, "I am, almost above all else, an evaluating critic." What this means, though, is that he expresses emphatic opinions about the writers he discusses, not that he offers, in the manner of serious evaluative criticism, reasoned and persuasive criteria for assessing literature.

CLOSE VIEWS

The Activist Norman Mailer

HELEN A. WEINBERG

> And is not . . . the Jew of the generation of Auschwitz required to do what, since Abraham, Jeremiah, and Job, Jews have always done in times of darkness—contend with the silent God, and bear witness to him by this very contention?
>
> —Emil Fackenheim in "The State of Jewish Belief," *Commentary*, August, 1966.

> In his courtroom speech, Mailer said, "They are burning the body and blood of Christ in Vietnam."
>
> "Today is Sunday," he said, "and while I am not a Christian I happen to be married to one. And there are times when I think the loveliest thing about my dear wife is her unspoken love for Jesus Christ. . . ."
>
> Mailer said he believed that the war in Vietnam "will destroy the foundation of this republic, which is its love and trust in Christ." Mailer is a Jew.
>
> —A news story from *The Washington Post*, quoted by Norman Mailer in *The Armies of the Night*.

The continuing and abundant writing of Norman Mailer more than the writing of any other single serious writer in contemporary American letters presents the reader with an opportunity to trace the development of a writer's character in process and permits a view of the conflict between writing and action, literature and politics, which writers other than Mailer may experience while never embodying the conflict in their work. Beyond this, Mailer's consciousness of writing as an act, and as an act of serious consequences not only in the political and social world but also in the theological, metaphysical world of thought about the universe and God, is striking and unique in contemporary American literature. Norman Mailer intends to change things, to make things happen, to affect his readers, to revolutionize the way they see the world, to leave his mark on their consciousness so that they will not be the same after their encounter with his work. Whether or not Mailer succeeds in raising the consciousness of his time, he is often successful in effecting a change in the way the individual reader sees his world, if I may judge from my own experience. But even the minor success of so large an ambition is noteworthy. That the ambition itself seems peculiarly Jewish is a phenomenon I wish to examine after looking, rather sweepingly, at the strategies of the writer-who-would-be-an-activist.

Norman Mailer is an activist in the guise of a writer, and from his early career as a novelist to his present career as a journalist —that is, as a writer of *reportage,* his own blend of extremely subjective personal perception and the reporting of the external, actual, historical event—one sees the demands the activist makes on the writer and the demands the writer makes on the activist. The activist's demands upon the novelist are most clearly seen in what I have elsewhere (in my book, *The New Novel in America: The Kafkan Mode in Contemporary Fiction*) called the spiritual activism of the heroes of the three middle novels, *Barbary Shore, The Deer Park,* and *An American Dream.* Mailer's first novel, *The Naked and the Dead* (1948), is a work of narrower ambition—the desire to achieve fame and fortune—and was written, according to Mailer's own admission, with the use of cautious charts to plan character encounters and "significant" scenes. Such novel-writing was partly the product of his training as an engineer during his four undergraduate years at Harvard College. (Curiously, in his most recent book of *reportage*, *Of a Fire on the Moon*, his engineer's education is again of service: this time it serves as his credentials for an investigation of the Space Program—an investigation which he expands to include the metaphysical meaning of man's invasion of the heavens.) His last novel, *Why Are We in Vietnam?* (1967) is hardly novelistic at all and suggests the breakdown (into manic verbality) of any real impulse toward fiction under the pressure of the world, which is too much with him and which he urgently seems to feel is waiting for his participation in it, waiting for him to make a speech, or to run for mayor.

The three middle novels, then, represent his clearest and most individualized achievement as a novelist, and they are marked by his signature in their attempt to contain in a central fictive figure his own increasingly apparent inner promptings toward a seemingly social and political but really spiritual (metaphysical?) activism that by its deeds will plumb the mysteries in a universe felt to be full of signification and meaning but stubbornly withholding its answers.

Barbary Shore (1951) is perhaps too explicitly political to yield this interpretation; however, *Barbary Shore* is really the story of a post-political hero who lives in a vacuum, literally in a barren boarding house, seeking a message for the future out of another's socialist past and his own empty present. What is absent more than what is present in the novel pushes us to the conclusion that the hero's acts are "spiritual" and toward the definition of a transcendant self—the self beyond political and social givens, the self that will create the new, freer world of ideas and values after the failure of the old world in the concentration camps of Europe. *The Deer Park* enunciates much the same theme through a triad of central figures: Charles Eitel, Sergius O'Shaugnessy, and Marion Faye. Charles Eitel is the father-figure—the ex-Communist sympathizer and artist turned Hollywood writer: he represents the old world of politics, power, and enslavement. The two "sons" of Eitel are Sergius, the narrator and the true center-of-consciousness in the novel, and Marion Faye; they represent two sides of spiritual activism in a secular world. Each wills a better self and a better world outside of politics, but Sergius, the innocent, wills it through his hope for goodness, which comes to be seen as residing finally in the freeing possibilities of art, of writing, of the writer Sergius will become, while Marion Faye, the dark *alter ego* of Sergius, wills it through his belief in the power of personal evil to destroy the corruption of the world and to permit a new, free man to triumph over the petty machinations of gangsters as well as over the false compassion of weak men. The task Sergius has set for himself is later fictively elaborated in a short story, "Of the Time of Her Time"; Marion's philosophy is fully expounded in Mailer's notorious hipster essay, "The White Negro"—both of these were written after *The Deer Park* (1955) and published in *Advertisements for Myself* (1959). Will—the will toward personal transcendence—is the key to their activism.

Finally, the complete embodiment of this theme in the novels is realized in *An American Dream* (1965) through Stephen Rojack, a super-activist, who follows the imperatives of self to mythic extremes, shedding, often in fantastic circumstances, his given social and political roles or functions (Harvard graduate, war-hero, congressman, husband, husband-of-an-heiress, television talk-man, writer, existential-psychologist, and professor) to become more and more pure and naked—a cipher of existential self. It should be remarked that in *An American Dream* the discovery of self relies heavily on a primitivist return to the senses—to touch, smell, sight, taste, to sex, and to the special sense of intuition, which is a mixture of the others and itself magical.

An American Dream was written as an answer to a challenge Mailer gave himself as a novelist to write rapidly, month by month, a novel that would appear in serialized form in *Esquire* magazine. As this sort of project it culminates the impatience (first apparent in *Advertisements for Myself*, and then in the two other collections of essays, stories, and poems, *The Presidential*

Papers (1963) and *Cannibals and Christians* (1966)) that Mailer seems to have long felt with novel-writing as a way of being in the world. At the same time, it culminates his attempt to transform his own strong activist will—essentially social, political, secular in himself—to a spiritual activism in his novelistic hero with the successful creation of a Pop Art super-activist in the spiritual mode, Stephen Rojack.

Advertisements for Myself indicates by its very title the need Mailer felt at that time to combine his art and his life in some meaningful, effective, *public* way. The writer's art and life are always privately interwoven and the writer makes what he will of his experience from life when he uses it in his work, whether he is a "pure" artist, such as Flaubert and Joyce, or an artist-teacher, such as Saul Bellow, who says, quoting Whitman for his own purposes: "Touch me and you touch a man." But Mailer has a special, urgent quality about him as a man who will no longer remain even partially hidden behind his work. In *The Presidential Papers*, he often addresses himself as an advice-giver to John F. Kennedy, then President, directly, taking the position that he was responsible for having created an existential and dynamic image of Kennedy in his essay, "Superman Comes to the Supermarket" (which first appeared in *Esquire* just before Kennedy's election in 1960), and thereby partly responsible for Kennedy's successful election. (I was myself persuaded by that essay in 1960 and am more inclined to accept Mailer's view of its importance than I might have been if I had only his seemingly exaggerated word for its influence.) *Cannibals and Christians* stands out among the collections as the most unified group of short pieces, though unified in a curious way. Rather than making cursory, and often arbitrary, connections between one piece and another, as he does in *Advertisements for Myself* and *The Presidential Papers*, Mailer here seems inspired by an idea of himself as a writer working in the manner of an Action painter: each piece is the stroke of the brush which is itself a confrontation of the painter's mysterious will with the canvas. *Cannibals and Christians* read rapidly through gives the impression of a totality of personal vision, the parts of which viewed, or read, separately, are perhaps too abstract or too amorphous to contain clear sense. Reading *Cannibals and Christians* in 1966, after having read *An American Dream* in 1965, one recognized the various kinds of culmination apparent in Mailer's writing and wondered if he were not *done* in the sense of having achieved as much as he could with the combined impulses of his life and his work. Reading *Why Are We in Vietnam?* in 1967 seemed to confirm the suspicion that if Mailer did not repeat his obvious achievements he would have to be "original" in outlandish ways.

At this point Norman Mailer became a reporter and opened a whole new vein of interaction between the writer and the activist for his own exploration. As the novel-writer had felt the pressures of the activist, now the reporter-activist would feel the pressures of the artist's sensibility: the writer's demands on the activist are transparent in the latest books of *reportage*. In *The Armies of the Night* (1968) he labors to make an aesthetic for each part of that book which describes his own participation in the 1967 march on the Pentagon in Washington. Part One thus becomes "History as a Novel: The Steps of the Pentagon" and the second part becomes "The Novel as History: The Battle of the Pentagon."

In *Miami and the Siege of Chicago* (1968), he speaks of the constraint he feels because he has a deadline to meet—he must write his report on this 1968 Chicago convention and so cannot join freely in the protest marches of the Yippies: he wonders if he is really protecting his writing self or if he is a victim of a more basic fear of bodily confrontation with the Chicago police. He broods over the thought that he may have lost his courage—and since courage is, in Mailer's hierarchy of virtues, primary (it is that through which a man is enabled to change and move forward), this suspected loss of it makes dark thoughts which in their turn compel Mailer to dispel them with reckless and foolish action.

(Yet also in *Miami and the Siege of Chicago* it is sometimes not the writing self that constrains him but the activist self—in this passage, tinged with longing for the creativity of the novelist, he seems to see the novelist's art as freeing and actuality as restrictive: "And yes, he thought, Chicago was a great city. Finally it brought everyone into the sort of ratiocinated confrontation which could end a novel about a week in this big city" [p. 222]. He seems here to be regretting the loss of the novelist's freedom to make Chicago more Chicago than Chicago.)

In *Of a Fire on the Moon* (1971), he sees the writer's task as secondary to that of the man of action:

> Well, Aquarius [Mailer's third-person name for his reporter-*personna* here] was in no Command Module preparing to go around the limb of the moon, burn his rocket motors and break into orbit, no. Aquarius was installed in the act of writing about the efforts of other men, his attempts to decipher some first clues to the unvoiced messages of the moon obtained from no more than photographs. . . . (p. 293).

In his article-review of *Making It* (by his friend, Norman Podhoretz), Mailer attests to the difficulties in writing directly about one's own experience—the risks of such an undertaking are stressed, and Mailer's emphasis on the dangers of self-examination may be a clue to a limited but real sense of "courageous" self in the world provided by his new autobiographical writing as a reporter.

> If a man is writing an accurate narrative about himself with real people and their real names, and this narrative arises because some imbalance or pressure or obsession or theme persists in dogging the man through all his aesthetic or moral nature until he sets to work then he is willy-nilly caught in the act of writing into the unexplored depths of himself, into those regions which are as mysterious to him as other people. So he can comprehend, no, rather he can deal with himself as a literary object,

as the name of that man who goes through his pages, only by
creating himself as a *literary* character, fully so much as any
literary character in a work of undisputed fiction. That is the
only way a man in mid-career can begin to approach the mysterious forces which push him to write about these matters in
the first place. He is off on a search. Like Theseus he will
encounter his experience on the point of his walkingstick; here,
his pencil. To the extent that he succeeds in making a viable
character who will attract literary experience metaphorically
equal to the ambiguous experience in his life which impelled
him to write in the first place, so he will set out on that recon-
naissance into the potentialities of an overpowering work.
(*Partisan Review*, Spring, 1968, pp. 240–241).

The references here to career, ambition, and self-interest seem
weighted with special meaning from the Podhoretz book, but
otherwise this description of the perils of examining oneself existentially and perceiving oneself in the act of perceiving seems
adequate to what must have been Mailer's experience when he
made himself the hero-reporter of his books on the Pentagon
march, the 1968 political conventions, and the flight to the moon.

Leaving Norman Mailer, the juggler of two kinds of existential
experience, art-making and living, I wish to return to my second
premise—that Mailer's ostensible purpose, to bring the consequence and power of action in the world to writing, to his own
writing, is peculiarly Jewish. The premise is a difficult one, for
Mailer, while immediately recognizeable as a Jew—even as "the
nice Jewish boy from Brooklyn" (*Armies of the Night*, p. 134) from
which personality he declares his wish to disassociate himself—
is not immediately definable as a Jew.

The Brooklyn boy's obvious and simple Jewish characteristics
are easy enough to list out of the evidence Mailer supplies in his
books and even in the dedications of their title-pages: he is good
to his mother and father; concerned about his children; over-
rebellious toward Jewish laws, especially the codes of chastity and
kashrut, which he systematically goes out of his way to break

(consider "The Metaphysics of the Belly": "Only a few people want bulls' balls at any one time. The existential gamble is too fine, it leads to greater seriousness, greater commitment in one's life, or to greater danger" [*Cannibals and Christians*, p. 294]— could anyone but a rebel against Jewish codes make so much of bulls' balls?); overconcerned with the superiority of the condition of being male rather than female (here Mailer is not rebellious: one easily imagines him saying the Orthodox Jewish man's morning prayer, "Thank you, God, for not making me a woman"); given to considering *chutzpah* a form of courage; etc.

Also, there are in his work three motifs that seem to grow, either directly or perversely, out of his personal life as a Jew and his consciousness of himself as a Jew in history: they are his repeated reference to the Nazis and their concentration camps as the central evil from which other, more recent evils—in politics, gangsterism, war, and technology—inevitably receive their sinister resonance; his almost aesthetic interest in watching and categorizing Gentiles, who appear to have a variety of religion-affiliated lifestyles—the Quaker, the Roman Catholic, and especially, of course, the WASP (all these seem strangely intriguing to him, almost as if they were exotics); and, finally, his attempt to create what Leslie Fiedler has called "super-Gentiles" as fictive characters with whom he may identify—this last characteristic a product of a new Jewish anti-intellectualism, according to Fiedler (*Waiting for the End*, pp. 97–98).

Of all the above characteristics the most poignant to me is Mailer's view of the Holocaust as the signal event in modern history. Of all the above characteristics the most aesthetically interesting is his conversion of himself into what might be called an "anti-Jew" in the same way we often call the central figure in a modern novel the anti-hero. The anti-hero retains the same location in the modern novel held by the hero of the traditional novel; however, he has lost the conventional "heroic" attributes. We know the anti-hero by what he is not, but to know what he is not we must know what he was. Hence we may know the anti-Jew by what he deliberately avoids in the tradition: one might say Mailer has found a negative mode for being a Jew. Philosophically, his avoidance of Jewish laws and customs may not be so formal as to permit a name, even anti-Jew, for the semi-fictive self he creates for his essayist and reporter. One suspects that being Jewish—or being anti-Jewish in the way described—would be still too essentialist a mode for Mailer's existentialist propensities. More than anything else, he seems to yearn for freedom, for himself and his art, from all preconceived categories and laws.

It is this yearning that no doubt draws him, when he does look for meaning in Judaism, to the tales of the Hasidim and their glorification of the sanctity of life in, according to Gershom Scholem, "the experience of an inner revival, in the spontaneity of feeling generated in sensitive minds by the encounter with the living incarnations of mysticism" (*Major Trends in Jewish Mysticism*, p. 338). It is in his attraction to this Hasidic mystical celebration of life; in his deep God-consciousness; in his often-noticed prophetic stance; and finally and most importantly in his activist willfulness that one finally sees what is profoundly—not sociologically or aesthetically—Jewish in Norman Mailer's writing.

Mailer at one point undertook to explore a number of Hasidic tales from Martin Buber's *Tales of the Hasidim* for a series called "Responses and Reactions," first published in *Commentary* magazine and subsequently in *The Presidential Papers* and *Cannibals and Christians*. In an introduction to this material in *The Presidential Papers*, Mailer voices his admiration for the Hasidim, who "embodied the most passionate and individual expression of Jewish life in many centuries" (p. 189), and his alarm over Jewish assimilation into the "muted unimaginative level of present-day American life" (p. 188). In "Responses and Reactions I" he speaks of Jewish greatness as residing in "the devil of [Jewish] dialectic, which places madness next to practicality, illumination side by side with duty, and arrogance in bed with humility" (p. 191). This is reminiscent of Scholem's description of the charismatic irrationality of the Hasidim as well as Buber's interpretation of the Hasidic way as that which sees the profane and the sacred inextricably mixed in all life. And later Mailer speaks of the modern assimilated Jew who has lost this spark of greatness, perhaps because "no Messiah was brought forth from the concentration camps" (p. 192), and because it may be that "the Jews will never recover from the woe that no miracle visited the world in that time" (p. 192).

> Perhaps that is why we are now so interested in housing, in social planning, interfaith councils, and the improvement of the PTA in the suburbs. Perhaps that is why half of the American Jews have fallen in love with a super delicatessen called Miami, and much of the other half have developed a subtly overbearing and all but totalitarian passion for the particular sallow doctor who is their analyst. Perhaps that is why we have lost the root (p. 192).

Such Hasidic tales as "Before the Coming of the Messiah," "From the Look-Out of Heaven," "With the Evil Urge," "Knowledge," "Upsetting the Bowl," and "The Fear of God"—all of which are from Volume I, *The Early Masters*, of *The Tales of the Hasidim*—serve as a basis not only for Mailer's praise of an older Jewish passion and for his prophetlike exhortation of the modern Jew to refuse to become a dull part of a technological, mechanistic, conventional society and to begin instead, as one of the quoted tales suggests, "the labor which will bring forth the Messiah," but also for the exhibition of Mailer's special obsessions: with dread, with magic, with an existential God and His adversary Devil.

The God-consciousness which is everywhere present in Mai-

ler's work, leading sometimes to obscure and convoluted theological and metaphysical hypotheses, is found in his exegesis of
the Hasidic tales at its purest:

> The Jews first saw God in the desert. . . . In the desert, man may
> flee before God, in terror of the apocalyptic voice of *His* light-
> ening, *His* thunder; or, as dramatically, in a style that no Chris-
> tian would ever attempt, man dares to speak directly to God,
> bargains with Him, upbraids Him, rises to scold Him, stares
> into God's eye like a proud furious stony-eyed child" (p. 191).

To this is added Mailer's own perception of God's nature as
existential and of an existential Devil:

> If God is not all-powerful but existential, discovering the pos-
> sibilities and limitations of His creative powers in the form of
> the history which is made by His creatures, then one must
> postulate an existential equal to God, an antagonist, the Devil,
> a principle of Evil whose signature was the concentration
> camps, whose joy is to waste substance, whose intent is to
> prevent God's conception of Being from reaching its mysteri-
> ous goal" (p. 193).

This view of God is partially adopted in order to accommodate
the fact of the concentration camps:

> It is not so comforting a postulation as the notion of God
> Omnipotent. . . , but it must also be seen that if God is all-
> powerful, the Jews cannot escape the bitter recognition that He
> considered one of His inscrutable purposes to be worth more
> than the lives of half His chosen people (p. 193).

Having somewhat justified the idea of an existential God,
Mailer, in "Responses and Reactions V," reprinted in *Cannibals
and Christians,* gives the existential attribute of fear to God Himself in an analysis of the familiar tale of Zusya, the Hasid, and his
love and fear of God:

Or is the fear which comes over Zusya a part of the profound
love God feels Himself, a fear that His conception of Being
(that noble conception of man as a creature of courage and
compassion, art, tenderness, skill, stamina, and imagination,
exactly the imagination to carry this conception of Being out
into the dark emptiness of the universe. . . .) yes, precisely this
noble conception will not prevail, and instead a wasteful . . .
monotonous conception of Being will become the future of
man. . . . What a fear is this fear in God that He may lose
eventually to the Devil! (p. 377).

In this passage it is clear that man as God's vehicle for His
conception of Being has a special task in the battle against an evil
conception of Being.

The dualistic vision of a universe divided between forces of
good and evil, which Mailer's metaphysical speculation here em-
braces, is familiar from the Kabbalah, the particular medieval
mystical movement which was influential in the development of
subsequent Jewish mysticism. Hasidism, the latest phase in Jewish mysticism, an eighteenth century Eastern European movement, takes much of its flavor from Kabbalah. Yet, the Hasidim,
and other rabbinic sources, replace this radical dualism with the
notion of the *yetzer ha'ra*, the evil urge, and the *yetzer tov*, the good
urge, both of which may be found in all men. The evil urge which
tempts men to evil must be resisted, primarily with the help of
the Mosaic Law, or may, according to the Hasidim—and to
Buber, obviously much influenced by Hasidic mysticism—be "included" for the greater benefit of the whole man. In *Good and Evil*,
Buber refuses to see the good and evil urges as diametrically
opposed and interprets them instead as "similar in nature"—

the evil "urge" as passion, that is, the power peculiar to man,
without which he can neither beget nor bring forth, but which,
left to itself, remains without direction and leads astray, and the
"good urge" as pure direction, in other words, as an uncondi-
tional direction, that towards God. To unite the two urges

implies: to equip the absolute potency of passion with the one
direction that renders it capable of great love and of great
service. Thus and not otherwise can man become whole (p. 97).

When Mailer, in *The Presidential Papers*, quotes a Hasidic tale
called "With the Evil Urge" at the end of a discussion of the
nature of God and the Devil, in which the Devil is characterized
as "a monumental bureaucrat of repetition," the particular tale
about the evil urge that he selects is the one in which Rabbi
Pinhas assures his students they need not fear that the evil urge
pursues them, for they have not gotten high enough for it to
pursue them. " 'For the time being,' " he assures them, " 'you are
still pursuing it.' " Mailer's selection of this tale suggests that in
spite of his dualistic premise of an existential God and Devil to
explain good and evil in the world while avoiding the Christian
theology of "original sin" which involves all men in congenital
sinfulness, he knows the less radical rabbinical explanation of evil
in the world which relies on the theory of the *yetzer ha'ra*.
Throughout Mailer's ideological arguments the idea that views
the evil urge as the passion which gives energy to man's direction
and makes him whole is always eminently present.

Mailer asserts—in a *Paris Review* interview, reprinted in *Cannibals and Christians*—that he is obsessed "with how God exists" and
thinks the theme of God as "an embattled existential creature
who may succeed or fail in His vision" might "become more
apparent as the novels go on" (p. 214). This theme is readily
apparent in *An American Dream*, where the hero Rojack seems
intended as a knight of the good conception of Being, fighting
against evil incarnate in the Nazis, his own father-in-law who
represents the military-industrial complex in American society,
as well as other life killers, and again in *Why Are We in Vietnam?*
When he admits the theme of an embattled God to the narrative
of his novels, Mailer espouses the cause and adopts in the novels
the prophetic voice, most distinctly heard in the essays where he

chastizes the evils of modern society, and the style of the prophet, most visible in his creation of himself as activist-reporter in *Armies of the Night.* It is a commonplace to consider the prophet's way the Jewish way. I. F. Stone says in an interview published recently in *The Christian Century:* ". . . in the prophets you have the very best of Judaism. They're . . . well, in a very lofty way, they were sort of like radical journalists in their time, rushing around exposing evils, interrupting people and getting in dutch" (p. 1314). Of all the prophets, Stone prefers Isaiah, about whom he says:

> But Isaiah represents the activism that, to me, is particularly attractive in the Jewish tradition. It seems to me Judaism is a religion that isn't so much concerned with an afterlife as with a man's duty in this one, and with concern for others and a better social order. I think Judaism is an activist religion, concerned with building a better life *here*" (p. 1315).

It was in Hasidism that the Jewish activism described by Stone as the prophet's tradition and the mysticism of those Jews who loved God more than they loved the moral obligations of His Law, given when the Covenant was made with His people at Mt. Sinai, came together. Linking Sabbatianism, a popular Jewish messianic movement of the seventeenth century, and Hasidism, Gershom Scholem says:

> There is a . . . very important point in which Sabbatianism and Hasidism join in departing from the rabbinical scale of values, namely their conception of the ideal type of man to which they ascribe the function of leadership. For rabinnical Jewry . . . the spiritual leader of the community is . . . the student of the Torah. . . . Of him no inner revival is demanded; what he needs is deeper knowledge of the sources of the Holy Law, in order that he may be able to show the right path to the community. . . . In the place of these teachers of the Law, the new movement gave birth to a new type of leader, the illuminate, the man

whose heart has been touched and changed by God, in a word, the prophet (pp. 333–334).

Highly secularized and "anti-Jewish" in a way defined earlier in this paper, Mailer's activism, nevertheless, seen against the prophetic tradition and Hasidic impulses must be regarded seriously as uniquely Jewish—a curiosity perhaps, an American Jewish curiosity that Norman Mailer, who has made Hemingway his personal hero, who has idealized the hipster lifestyle of the urban black, who wishes to keep himself existentially open, without established function or role, and who declares himself, in *Armies of the Night*, the member of no sect, should retain an obvious place in the history of Jewish life and letters through his "authentic" self.

In the last chapter of *The New Novel in America*, I developed the argument that the spiritual activist mode of the hero in the novels discussed was embodied in the narrative of a quest for being, which was in fact the description of a process of becoming, and that this process in novels by American Jews was different from the same process in novels by American Gentiles. I do not wish to repeat that argument in detail: I will only say here briefly that the spiritual activist mode of Mailer's heroes, especially Sergius, Marion, and Rojack (as well as of Bellow's Augie March, Roth's Gabe Wallach, Malamud's S. Levin), reveals the Jewish messianic sense of the going toward a transcendent self, not toward—as is the case in the mode of novelistic heroes of some Christian writers—a self-transcendence. The Christian theology of a fallen, congenitally sinful nature of man makes it inevitable that the process of spiritual becomingness in the Christian imagination include a denial of the body and its possibilities while going toward a promised "grace" for the soul. The Jew, who has no theology of original sin, who sees himself created in God's image and fallen only in the sense of being expelled from the garden of unearned natural pleasures, whose soul does not have to be saved because it is safe in the Covenant (whether or not he fully accepts it), who relies on himself to go toward a better self since it is the way he has to participate in the world which will one day be redeemed by the promised messiah, believes he is able to achieve a fulfilled, completely authentic yet transcendent self-hood. That the heroes in the novels do not realize this transcendent self is irrelevant: that they will such a self and strive toward it is entirely relevant. Mailer's heroes demonstrate this striving, which I have called spiritual, in the novels; and later Mailer diverts the energy he has invested in creating them back into his own activist life, which is indeed still the writer's life—into his essays, journalism, play, films, as well as into political acts. Though in his most recent books of *reportage*, Mailer's emphasis is clearly on himself in the arena of the social, political, and ecological, it is especially here he retains within his consciousness those imperatives of self that shape his activist heroes of the novels according to the remnant spiritual motifs of a Jewish imagination: his life reverberates with the messianic urgency of Jewish wilfullness and this fact of his life is known and recognized in his work, his writing.

BIBLIOGRAPHY

BUBER, MARTIN. *Good and Evil.* New York: Charles Scribner's Sons, 1952.
_____. *Tales of the Hasidim: Early Masters.* New York: Schocken Books, 1961.
FIEDLER, LESLIE. *Waiting for the End.* New York: Stein and Day, 1964.
MAILER, NORMAN. *Advertisements for Myself.* New York: G. P. Putnam's Sons, 1959.
_____. *An American Dream.* New York: Dial Press, 1965.
_____. *Armies of the Night: History as a Novel, the Novel as History.* New York: New American Library, 1968.
_____. *Barbary Shore.* New York: Rinehart and Company, 1951.
_____. *Cannibals and Christians.* New York: Dial Press, 1966.

———. *The Deer Park*. New York: G. P. Putnam's Sons, 1955.

———. *Miami and the Siege of Chicago*. New York: Signet Books, 1968.

———. *The Naked and the Dead*. New York: Rinehart and Company, 1948.

———. *Of a Fire on the Moon*. Boston: Little, Brown and Company, 1971.

———. *The Presidential Papers*. New York: G. P. Putnam's Sons, 1963.

———. "Up the Family Tree," *Partisan Review*, XXXV (Spring, 1968), 234–252.

———. *Why Are We in Vietnam?* New York: G. P. Putnam's Sons, 1967.

Scholem, Gershom. *Major Trends in Jewish Mysticism*. New York: Schocken Books, 1961.

Stone, I. F. "With Atheists Like Him Who Needs Believers?" (interview with I. F. Stone), *The Christian Century* (November 4, 1970), 1313–1317.

Weinberg, Helen. *The New Novel in America: The Kafkan Mode in Contemporary Fiction*. Ithaca and London: Cornell University Press, 1970.

Sitting *Shiva*: Notes on Recent American–Jewish Autobiography

SANFORD PINSKER

There was a time when literary periods in America seemed to have definable beginnings, middles, and, best of all, ends. Critics talked about the twenties or the thirties or even the forties as if our society and its literature had been neatly arranged by decades. And for good reasons. After all, *everyone* knew when the twenties were over: the Stock Market had crashed (conveniently enough) in 1929 and suddenly the "jazz age" no longer seemed an appropriate metaphor of the country's mood. Ten years later the Stalin-Hitler pact and the outbreak of World War II had a similarly foreclosing effect on the 1930's.

But history has a way of happening independently, without the advice or consent of literary scholars. Weighty events occur willy-nilly, as often in the middle of decades as at either end. All of this tends to create unfortunate side-effects, particularly where the old classifications are concerned. To be sure, the "decade" may have always been a decidedly limited yardstick. However, it has become increasingly clear that literary movements not only refuse to die on schedule, but very often they refuse to die at all!

Jewish-American writing is probably the most striking example of this phenomenon. For some time now critics have hovered over the would-be corpse while visions of obituary danced in their heads—only to discover the patient lingering endlessly between one bowl of watered-down chicken soup and the next. Like Faulkner's Dilsy, they "endure"—or, to use a more appropriate word, *survive.* Professor Irving Howe has suggested that the matter may be one of literary overcompensation. As he puts it:

> The great battles for Joyce and Eliot and Proust had been fought in the 20's and mostly won; and now, while clashes with entrenched philistinism might still take place, they were mostly skirmishes or mopping-up operations (as in the polemics against the transfigured Van Wyck Brooks). The New York writers came at the end of the modernist experience, just as they came at what may yet have to be judged the end of the radical experience, and as they certainly came at the end of the Jewish experience. One shorthand way of describing their situation, a cause of both their feverish brilliance and their recurrent instability, is to say *they came late.*[1]

Of course, what Howe describes as the peculiar condition of New York Intellectuals in the 1930's is (with only slight modifications) very likely to be the circumstance of any writer at virtually any time. The best always appears to have been thought, said, and, worst of all, *published.* Surely the New York Intellectuals were not the first ones to discover that the Biblical expression "There were giants in those days!" could have sobering connotations. Still, Howe's description is a useful one, not only as a way of charting the peculiar rise-and-fall of Jewish-American writing, but as a way of understanding what happened to American literature at large. It might be argued, for example, that nearly *everyone* "came late" —at least where the twentieth century classics are concerned.

And, yet, it was the Jewish-American writer who felt most cheated by the nightmare of history, especially when it became clear that much of the best modern literature was *of* him and possibly even *for* him, but hardly ever *by* him. The prototype of Jewish-American fiction in the 1920's was Abraham Cahan's *The Rise of David Levinsky* (1917), a novel which provided the bolt out of which innumerable up-from-the-ghetto sagas would be cut. However, at the very moment when Jewish versions of Horatio Alger were working hardest to establish their credentials, to become "American," the great expatriations to Paris were in full swing. The ironies that resulted were savagely Sophoclean, particularly when all the missed directions and crossed purposes took literary shape. For example, a figure like the "wandering Jew" evoked radically different responses depending on "when" and "to where" you crossed the Atlantic. For the disillusioned expatriate, it was an apt metaphor of the modern condition. And whether the treatment was by Joyce (Bloom as modern literature's penultimate wanderer) or Hemingway (Cohn as ALIEN among the "alienated"), Gentile writers explored the Jewish psyche and its fascinating "difference" at a time when most Jewish-American writing was seeking a kind of salvation in sameness. Besides, expatriation had no appeal for a people who had been expatriated both physically and psychologically since 70 C.E. Like Huck Finn, they had been there—and, in the 20's, they were happy enough to stay at "home."[2]

However, for their *sons*, "starting out in the thirties" (to borrow the title of Alfred Kazin's recent autobiography) was fraught with negatives, full of experiences not really felt and places not really seen. *They* had never lived in the ghettos of Eastern Europe nor had *they* walked the banks of the Seine. Of course, there was Brownsville for those who wanted ghetto life and the East River for those who wanted rivers, but they added up to cruel reminders and little more. That the country at large was in a severe depression only made things grimmer. What these writers needed was not so much *experience* as a way of giving a cohesive form to that experience, a mode of expression which would complement literary modernism (already in the process of decay) and, at the same time, speak of their ambiguous status as urban Jews in search of new gods. They may have inherited a socialism of sorts, but they virtually *discovered* the essay. And into it was poured nearly equal doses of energy, ideology, polemic, social emphasis, and, of course, brillance. Howe relates their particular chronicle with the affection of one who first learned to admire such dazzling, well-wrought writing and then to do it himself.[3] But there is no need to retrace more than the general outline of Howe's chronicle here. A thumbnail sketch should be sufficient to make my point: *Beginning*—a somewhat ill-defined and largely unacknowledged common law marriage in which common histories and common ambitions served as the double rings in a ceremony no one remembered; *Middle*—a prolonged history of marital spats and even occasional separations, but always with visitation rights built in and the possibility of reconciliation always held out; *End* (?)—official recognition, approval, and power (the marriage declared to have been, like Tom Jones, legitimate all along!), a fate generally agreed upon as worse than divorce and certainly crueler than death.

For Howe, the thirties and early forties were a matter of paying dues and establishing credentials—what my sketch above calls the "Beginning" and "Middle." However,

> By the end of the Second World War, the New York writers had reached a point of severe intellectual crisis, though as frequently happens at such moments, they themselves often felt they were entering a phase of enlarged influence and power. Perhaps indeed there was a relation between inner crisis and external influence. Everything that had kept them going—the idea of socialism, the advocacy of literary modernism, the assault on mass culture, a special brand of literary criticism—was judged to be irrelevant to the postwar years. But as a group, just at the time their internal disintegration had seriously begun, the New York writers could be readily identified. The leading

critics were Rahv, Phillips, Trilling, Rosenberg, Abel, and Kazin. The main political theorist was Hook. Writers of poetry and
fiction related to the New York milieu were Delmore Schwartz,
Saul Bellow, Paul Goodman, and Isaac Rosenfeld. And the
recognized scholar, as also the inspiring moral force, was Meyer
Schapiro.[4]

To be sure, the Second World War affected more than the outlines of a small band of Jewish-American writers. The reaction to
World War I was largely one of disillusion and/or liberated hedonism. However, the Nazi holocausts of World War II produced,
first, shock and then a kind of moral reappraisal. Suddenly the
urban Jew (who had seemed limited by the parochial boundaries
of the Hudson River and the *Partisan Review*) was a matter of
national attention and literary concern. But *this* time the Jewish-
American writer was ready—or, at least, that was the way it
seemed in the fifties. American culture became both sensitized to
and saturated by Judaization. And, yet, for all its apparent successes, the renaissance of Jewish-American literature failed to
produce—with the possible exception of Saul Bellow—even a
likely candidate to run against the likes of Faulkner or Hemingway or Fitzgerald—to say nothing about Joyce or Mann or Proust.
Leslie Fiedler has suggested that

> . . . the moment of triumph for the Jewish writer in the United
> States has come just when his awareness of himself as a Jew is
> reaching a vanishing point, when the gesture of rejection seems
> his last possible connection with his historical past; and the
> popular acceptance of his alienation as a satisfactory symbol for
> the human condition threatens to turn it into an affectation.[5]

It was hardly a surprise when Fiedler's predictions turned out to
be true, all too true. The whole affair began to smell of meta-
phorical fish—as if a literary plot had been hatched in some
Manhattan delicatessen by the editors of *Commentary*. Jewish char-

acters were everywhere, always trailing clouds of allegorical suffering and looking as if they had just arrived from a four thousand year trek across the desert.

However, for all of Bernard Malamud's insistence that (1) Jews "suffer for the Law" (usually always ill-defined and self-constructed) and that (2) "All men are Jews," the gulf between memories of a Jewish Tradition and the individual Jewish-American talent grew steadily wider. The protagonist of Bruce Jay Friedman's novel *Stern* (1962) puts the matter this way:

> As a boy, Stern had been taken to holiday services, where he stood in ignorance among bowing, groaning men who wore brilliantly embroidered shawls. Stern would do some bows and occasionally let fly a complicated imitative groan, but when he sounded out he was certain one of the old genuine groaners had spotted him and he was issuing a phony. Stern thought it was marvelous that the old men knew exactly when to bow and knew the groans and chants and melodies by heart. He wondered if he would ever get to be one of their number. He went to Hebrew School, but there seemed to be no time at all devoted to the theatrical bows and groans, and even with three years of Hebrew School under his belt Stern felt a loner among the chanting sufferers at synagogues. After a while he began to think you could never get to be one of the groaners through mere attendance at Hebrew School. You probably had to pick it all up in Europe.

And this is how Jewish-American fiction ends (or, rather, *fails* to end)—not with a bang or a whimper, but a kind of prolonged *kvetch*. As Jewish material grew ever thinner, the death rattles of self-parody became louder and more insistent. *Portnoy's Complaint* (1969) may have killed the golden chicken, but, as Philip Roth had discovered, most of its eggs were tarnished anyhow.

To be sure, there were no real obituaries for Jewish-American fiction, no actual funeral to attend. Still, Jewish-American writers visited the graveyards of the heart, mumbled a half-remembered *kaddish* and prepared to sit *shiva* in the ghettos they had left some forty years before. Perhaps the Willie Stark of Robert Penn Warren's *All the King's Men* is right when he claims that

> A man goes away from his home and it is in him to do it. He lies in strange beds in the dark, and the wind is different in the trees. He walks in the street and there are the faces in front of his eyes, but there are no names for the faces. The voices he hears are not the voices he carried away in his ears a long time back when he went away. The voices he hears are loud. They are so loud he does not hear for a long time at a stretch those voices he carried away in his ears. But there comes a minute when it is quiet and he can hear those voices he carried away in his ears a long time back. He can make out what they say, and they say: Come back, boy. So he comes back.[6]

For Willie Stark, the return takes him back to a farm in the red-neck country; for Alfred Kazin, it is the Brownsville section of New York City:

> Every time I go back to Brownsville it is as if I had never been away. From the moment I step off the train at Rockaway Avenue and smell the leak out of the men's room, then the pickles from the stand just below the subway steps, an instant rage comes over me, mixed with dread and some unexpected tenderness. It is over ten years since I left to live in "the city"—everything just out of Brownsville was always "the city." Actually I did not go very far; it was enough that I could leave Brownsville. Yet as I walk those familiarly choked streets at dusk and see the old women sitting in front of the tenements, past and present become each other's faces; I am back where I began.
>
> It is always the old women in their shapeless flowered housedresses and ritual wigs I see first; they give Brownsville back to me. In their soft dumpy bodies and the unbudging way they occupy the tenement stoops, their hands blankly folded in each other as if they had been sitting on these stoops from the beginning of time, I sense again the old foreboding that all my

life would be like this. *Urime Yidn. Alfred, what do you want of us poor Jews?*[7]

And, yet, when a Moses Herzog is overcome by the ". . . need to explain, to have it out, to justify, to put into perspective, to clarify, to make amends," the result is very different from the sort of lyrical nostalgia Kazin serves up so generously in *A Walker in the City.* The timelessness he insists upon—old women on primordial stoops—merely falsifies what the actual experience of growing up in Brownsville was like and, more importantly, why it was crucial for Kazin to come to terms with it.

Starting Out in the Thirties (1962) is a sequel to *A Walker in the City,* but there are enough differences in perspective and subject matter for it to be more than the same yard goods rerolled. In fact, the sequel is a more satisfying book. Rather than the lyrical affection which tended to grow tiresome in his first book, *Starting Out in the Thirties* is a fairly straightforward account of the literary and sociopolitical climate between 1934 and 1940. To be sure, Aunt Sophie is still around (and still unmarried), but so are Malcolm Cowley and a host of other figures from the thirties. Kazin's recollections of the "scene" cannot help but become a valuable bit of literary lore, however much one might want to quarrel with the outlines of a particular portrait. And, when *literary* matters are at stake, Kazin writes with a passion and control that is undeniable:

> What young writers of the Thirties wanted was to prove the literary value of our experience, to recognize the possibility in our own lives, to feel that we had moved the streets, the stockyards, the hiring halls into literature—to show that our radical strength could carry on the experimental impulse of modern literature.[8]

But one cannot help but suspect that he protests a bit *too* much when claims like the following are made: "Although I was a

'Socialist,' like everyone else I knew, I thought of socialism as orthodox Christians might think of the Second Coming—a wholly supernatural event which one might await with perfect faith, but which had no immediate relevance to my life."[9]

However, it is the final lines of the book which bring Kazin's autobiography full circle. Suddenly we understand—in an image of terrifying clarity—just why a book like *A Walker in the City* came to be written:

> One day in the spring of 1945, when the war against Hitler was almost won, I sat in a newsreel theatre in Piccadilly looking at the first films of newly liberated Belsen. On the screen, sticks in black-and-white prison garb leaned on a wire, staring dreamily at the camera; other sticks shuffled about, or sat vaguely on the ground, next to an enormous pile of bodies, piled up like cordwood, from which protruded legs, arms, heads. A few guards were collected sullenly in a corner, and for a moment a British Army bulldozer was shown digging an enormous hole in the ground. Then the sticks would come back on the screen, hanging on the wire, looking at us.
>
> It was unbearable. People coughed in embarrassment, and in embarrassment many laughed.[10]

Of course, distinguishing between declared "fiction" and declared "autobiography" is never an easy matter. The differences are likely to be ones of degree rather than of kind. Wallace Stevens once claimed that "poetry is the supreme fiction"; in this sense, autobiography may well be the "ultimate fiction," the story we tell about ourselves by creating *character* from the myriad and often contradictory experiences which make up an actual life. Howe puts his finger on more than just the problems in Kazin's work when he suggests that

> The youthful experiences described by Alfred Kazin in his autobiography are, apart from his distinctive outcroppings of temperament, more or less typical of many New York intellec-

tuals—except, at one or two points, for the handful that involved itself deeply in the radical movement. It is my impression, however, that Kazin's affectionate stress on the Jewish sources of his experiences is mainly a feeling of retrospect, mainly a recognition in the 50's and 60's that no matter how you might try to shake off your past, it would still cling to your speech, gestures, skin and nose, it would still shape, with a thousand subtle movements, the way you did your work and raised your children. In the 30's, however, it was precisely the idea of discarding the past, breaking away from families, traditions, and memories which excited intellectuals.[11]

Kazin's autobiographies came at a time when the sub-genre of up-from-the-ghetto literature had all but exhausted itself. As Leslie Fiedler pointed out: "The autobiography of the urban Jew whose adolescence coincided with the Depression, and who walked the banks of some contaminated city river with tags of Lenin ringing in his head, who went forth (or managed not to) to a World War in which he could not quite believe, has come to seem part of the mystical life history of the nation."[12] And so he has—although to see the matter as one of myth is to deny the immediacy which makes for Art. Perhaps that is the difference between recollections made after too much tranquility and the fine brush strokes with which a writer like Isaac Bashevis Singer re-creates the world of *In My Father's Court.*

And, yet, the trip was worth the taking, if only to show the limitations of nostalgia. For the Jewish-American writer, poking among the ashes of his past would continue, but in other forms and from more oblique angles. One thing, at least, was clear: he did not intend to sit at the *shiva* for Jewish-American writing without a story of his own to tell.

In the introduction to *Making It* Norman Podhoretz gives a decidedly new wrinkle to the normal expectations of an up-from-the-ghetto autobiography:

To be sure, the story I tell here resembles the traditional success story in tracing the progressive rise of a young man from poverty and obscure origins. In contrast to the traditional success story, however, its purpose is not to celebrate that rise, but rather to describe certain fine-print conditions that are attached.[13]

. . . .

For taking my career as seriously as I do in this book, I will no doubt be accused of self-inflation and therefore of tasteless-ness. So be it. There was a time when to talk candidly about sex was similarly regarded as tasteless—a betrayal of what D. H. Lawrence once called "the dirty little secret." For many of us, of course, this is no longer the case. But judging by the embar-rassment that a frank discussion of one's feeling about one's own success, or the lack of it, invariably causes in polite com-pany today, ambition (itself a species of lustful hunger) seems to be replacing erotic lust as the prime dirty little secret of the well-educated American soul.[14]

Making It takes a hard look at avatars of Sammy Glick—al-though this time without the need to disguise or justify the ambi-tions which make them publish rather than run. For Budd Schulberg's character, the mecca was Hollywood and the stuff that dreams are made of. For Podhoretz, success was close enough to be a subway token and yet far enough to seem virtually impossible:

> One of the longest journeys in the world is the journey from certain neighborhoods in Brooklyn to certain parts of Manhat-tan. I have made that journey, but it is not from the experience of having made it that I know how very great the distance is, for I started on the road many years before I realized what I was doing, and by the time I did realize it I was for all practical purposes already there.[15]

The sensitive, young boy who began in Brooklyn—dressed in a "tee shirt, tightly pegged pants, and a red satin jacket with the legend 'Cherokees, S.A.C.' (social-athletic club) stitched across the back"—arrived, some twenty years later, as the Editor of *Commentary*, full of the sound-and-fury that signifies *everything* in Manhattan. As his high-school teacher fondly observed (through heavy layers of WASP-ish condescension), Norman was destined for better things than the "filthy slum children" who surrounded him. So far it all sounds like *Winesburg, Ohio*, with George Willard transferred to the city *a priori* and somehow circumcised along the way. We have grown fond of such stories. Perhaps that is why Podhoretz's confession that his heroes at Columbia were *critics* (rather than creative writers) smacks of betrayal:

> Then what do you want to be now when you grow up, little boy? *A literary critic*. An unlikely answer today, perhaps, for anyone so ambitious as I was at nineteen, but in the late 1940's, the opening of what Randall Jarrell was later to call "The Age of Criticism," nothing could have been more natural. . . . In my circle at Columbia, for example, we awaited the arrival of the quarterlies in which criticism flourished—magazines like *Partisan Review* and *Kenyon Review*—with the avidity of addicts, and we read the essays of such "New Critics" as Cleanth Brooks, R. P. Blackmur, and Allen Tate with an excitement that equaled, if indeed it did not surpass, the passion we brought to the poems and novels they were writing about. If we could all quote at length from the poetry of T. S. Eliot, we could also quote at length—and with, in truth, a greater feeling of assurance—from his critical essays.[16]

Podhoretz has a genuine talent for making the purely personal sound like the publicly important. He had learned early (with, say, the publication of "My Negro Problem—and Ours") that *certain* confessions can lead to controversy—which is to say attention. And, for Podhoretz, the notion that *attention must be paid* takes on the force of aesthetic credo, more important than all the shoes of all the Sammy Glicks. Of course, the sort of "attention"

Podhoretz has in mind is not only parochial, but somewhat ludicrous:

> Every morning a stock-market report on reputations comes out in New York. It is invisible, but those who have eyes to see can read it. Did so-and-so have dinner at Jacqueline Kennedy's apartment last night? Up five points. Was so-and-so *not* invited by the Lowells to meet the latest visiting Russian poet? Down one-eighth. Did so-and-so's book get nominated for the National Book Award? Up two and five eighths. Did *Partisan Review* neglect to ask so-and-so to participate in a symposium? . . . In the months that followed the publication of *Doings and Undoings* , I hardly dared look at the listings for fear of finding myself wiped out. . . .[17]

However, D. H. Lawrence has warned us all to "Trust the tale, not the author!" and the advice is doubly true for autobiography. Podhoretz's stated intention may be to make a "frank Mailer-like bid for literary distinction, fame and money all in one package,"[18] but *Making It* has more to do with SUCCESS than the small print costs of earning it. When Irving Howe suggests that success is always "heavy with moral risks and disappointment . . . debts, overwork, varicose veins, alimony, drinking, quarrels, hemorrhoids, depletion, the recognition that one might not prove to be another T. S. Eliot. . . ,"[19] we have an inkling about the sort of book a Podhoretz might have written, but, evidently, could not.

Vladimir Nabokov's *Speak Memory* (1951) is worth extended citation if only for what he has to say about the special art of autobiography. However, the following anecdote is particularly valuable where a work like Leslie Fiedler's *Being Busted* (1969) is concerned:

> One afternoon at the beginning of the same year (i.e. 1904), in our St. Petersburg house, I was led down from the nursery into my father's study to say how-do-you-do to a friend of the family,

General Kuropatkin. To amuse me, he spread out a handful of matches on the divan where he was sitting, placed ten of them end to end to make a horizontal line and said, "This is the sea in calm weather." Then he tipped up each pair so as to turn the straight line into a zigzag—and that was "a stormy sea."

. . . This incident had a special sequel fifteen years later, when at certain point of my father's flight from Bolshevik-held St. Petersburg to southern Russia, he was accosted, while crossing a bridge, by an old man who looked like a grey-bearded peasant in his sheepskin coat. He asked my father for a light. The next moment each recognized the other. Whether or not old Kuropatkin, in his rustic disguise, managed to evade Soviet imprisonment, is immaterial. What pleases me is the evolution of the match theme; those magic ones he had shown me had been trifled with and mislaid. . . . The following of such thematic designs through one's life should be, I think, the true purpose of autobiography.

For Leslie Fiedler, *Being Busted* is more history than autobiography and more "parable" than anything else. It deals with two events—one in the Newark of 1933, the other in the Buffalo of 1967—which take on the dimension of an insidious thematic design. Fiedler puts it this way:

Essentially then, this is, despite its autobiographical form, a book not about me, or indeed individuals at all, so much as one about cultural and social change between 1933, when I just missed being arrested, and 1967, when I made it at last. Its true subject is the endless war, sometimes cold, sometimes hot, between the dissenter and his imperfect society.[20]

Critics have a way of taking on the postures usually reserved for their literary heroes. Fiedler's has always been Huck Finn, the *puer eternis* continually on the lam. But, for Fiedler, the territories the artist lights out for are always within, at a spot where dream and myth coincide and Indians are really black men in red face (or is it the other way around?) and everyone, at bottom, is a Jew.

All of these critical pyrotechnics have singled Fiedler out for that special contempt reserved for those who have the ability to publish scholarly articles in *PMLA*, but who prefer the pages of *Fuck You: A Journal of the Arts* instead.

However, this time Fiedler's war is with the cops and those who send them rather than the critics. After all, it is one thing to deal with the absurdities in, say, Kafka's *The Trial* and quite another to be on trial yourself. It is even more painful when one has the uncomfortable feeling that he is in the wrong play and, furthermore, always has been:

> A pattern had set itself though I would not know it for a long time. The events that followed, back in 1933, should have convinced me that my encounters with the law were destined to seem comic in retrospect forever after, no matter how painful at the moment they occurred. I myself learned to look a little better than I had on Bergen Street (at least to myself); but, alas, the police never cooperated. And how can a man—at sixteen or twenty or forty or fifty or whatever—come on like Thoreau or Dreyfus, Joe Hill or Sacco and Vanzetti or Tom Mooney, when the cops fate has chosen him for him are always straight out of some Keystone Comedy or nineteenth-century farce? I do not mean that I have not suffered on my account since, and suffered the more when those around me have become targets of comic malice for my sake, but I have continued to feel that I am doomed to be robbed always of the final solace of finding my suffering noble, since what falls on my shoulders is likely to be a rubber truncheon, what hits me in the face a custard pie.[21]

But, for all the seeming good cheer, this time Fiedler was had. Being busted in Buffalo made him a public figure—with all the hoopla and misunderstanding that comes with the territory:

> . . . young people are likely to assume that because I have been busted, I am not merely *Kosher*, but a real Head in professor's clothing; just as their parents, on the basis of the same evidence, may assume that I am not merely a member of the

marijuana lobby but some sort of unreconstructed, if aging
swinger . . . they tend to conclude that I must have something
to teach them more real and true and dear than how to read
Dante or Dickens or Mark Twain; though, in fact, to me there
is nothing more real and true and dear than this—or if there is,
I have it still to learn from *them*. And this leads to all sorts of
absurd misunderstandings, which I should, I suppose, resent,
but which in truth I relish and even consume with all the writer's insatiable appetite for material, all the comedian's hunger
for the play of cross purposes.[22]

But the scenario has had some comic twists even a Fiedler could
not have predicted, much less control. As the legal situation
worsened, Fiedler found himself flying into Buffalo for hurried
meetings with his accountants and lawyers, looking more like a
Maffioso gangster than a university professor. And on Thursday,
April 9, 1970, the ironies that had been building all along outdid
themselves: Professor Fiedler was found guilty of "maintaining
a premise" where marijuana had allegedly been smoked—after a
trial in which the prosecution had read long sections of *Being
Busted* as proof, from the horse's mouth, that he was an unsavory
character.

Not surprisingly, the dreams which gave birth to *Love and Death
in the American Novel* go on, although now we tend to see them on
the evening news or in the pages of *Playboy*. Very often they
amount to little more than a curious sort of *mea culpa* chanted
over the thick books of modernism, as if Fiedler were ashamed
that he had been taken in by Joyce for so long. The issue is clear:
modernism is dead. Long live post-modernism.

But if Leslie Fiedler seems happy enough to drink at Fin-
negan's wake and eat hard-boiled eggs at the *shiva* for Jewish-
American writing, people like Irving Howe are not convinced. To
be sure, sons replace fathers and the new triumphs over the old,
and yet, for Howe, there is still a hope that he might be able to
rally the old crowd around the typewriters once more:

What, after all, would be risked in saying that we have entered a period of overwhelming cultural sleaziness? . . . precisely at this moment of dispersion, might not some of the New York writers achieve renewed strength if they were to struggle once again for whatever has been salvaged from these last few decades? For the values of liberalism, for the politics of a democratic radicalism, for the norms of rationality and intelligence, for the standards of literary seriousness, for the life of the mind as a humane dedication—for all this it should again be worth finding themselves in a minority, even a beleaguered minority, and not with fantasies of martyrdom, but with a quiet recognition that for the intellectual this is likely to be his usual condition.[23]

We have not heard the end of such appeals—or their rebuttals. The *experience* may be over and the days when Jewish-American literature swam in the mainstream past, but autobiography is a special way of remembering how it was and why it mattered. This is one *shiva* that is likely to go on and on. And who knows, if I. B. Singer is right, they may even be visited by a lively *dybbuk* or two.

N OT E S

1. Irving Howe, "The New York Intellectuals: A Chronicle & A Critique," *Commentary*, XLVI (October, 1968), 32. To be sure, Professor Howe's definition of the New York intellectuals includes more than Jewish-American writers—although he claims that, "by birth or osmosis," all of them are Jews. In any event, Howe's term is a convenient shorthand, one that puts the special dilemma of Jewish-American writers into sharp focus. For the purposes of my argument, then, the terms become nearly synonymous.

2. But if the bulk of Jewish-American writers in the twenties seemed decidedly parochial, not *all* of them were. It was Gertrude Stein, after all, who labeled Hemingway and his crowd "the lost generation."

3. I have long suspected that Irving Howe is a conglomerate, rather than an actual person. Imagining five or six professors who all write

under the pseudonym "Irving Howe" not only gives solace to those of us who are less productive, but it is a neat way of explaining how he is able to edit *Dissent*, review dozens of books, teach classes at Hunter College, and still find time to write articles like "The New York Intellectuals."

4. Howe, p. 36.

5. Leslie Fiedler, *Waiting for the End* (New York, Stein and Day, 1964), p. 66.

6. Robert Penn Warren, *All the King's Men* (New York, Harcourt Brace), chapter one.

7. Alfred Kazin, *A Walker in the City* (New York, Harcourt Brace, 1951), pp. 5–6.

8. Alfred Kazin, *Starting Out in the Thirties* (New York, Harcourt Brace, 1962), p. 15.

9. Ibid., p. 4.

10. Ibid., p. 166.

11. Ibid., p. 31.

12. Fiedler, *Waiting for the End*, p. 65.

13. Norman Podhoretz, *Making It* (New York, Random House, 1967), p. xii.

14. Ibid., pp. xvi-xvii.

15. Ibid., p. 3.

16. Ibid., pp. 40–41.

17. Ibid., pp. 350–351.

18. Ibid., p. 356.

19. Ibid., p. 41.

20. Leslie Fiedler, *Being Busted* (New York, Stein and Day, 1969), p. 7.

21. Ibid., p. 18.

22. Ibid., p. 232.

23. Howe, p. 51.

Mr. Bellow's Perigee, Or, The Lowered Horizon of *Mr. Sammler's Planet*

MAX F. SCHULZ

His nephew Elya Gruner's dying and his daughter Shula's purloining of a scientific treatise on colonization of the moon provide the immediate context for several days in the life of Mr. Sammler. As for the greater public rhythm after which at a distance his private life pulsates, Mr. Sammler watches his nephew act out the perigee of death ("death to dust . . .") as the rest of the nation follows the drama of astronauts Armstrong and Aldrin's impending moonwalk. And between this oldest and newest of human acts, Mr. Sammler the geonaut picks his way through the excrement-fouled walks of New York City on his routine earthbound orbit, "once around Stuyvesant Park, an ellipse within a square."[1] Surely the irony implied in the juxtaposition of these events is not accidental: the nation proudly awaiting man's first walk on the moon, with the great attendant unknown about man's adaptability to life in space; while Mr. Sammler's world revolves around the petty details of urban survival, fixing breakfast in his bedroom from foods kept on the windowsill, running a daily gauntlet on the street among pickpockets, muggers, dogs, and drunks. Here is no rash appetite for life, nor hunger for selfhood, such as kept Augie March, Henderson, and Herzog turning on the spit. A knell of stridency and despair is sounded instead that was unheard in their *sehnsucht*. Bellow's ambivalent faith in the human capacity to realize itself virtuously in relation to others, a vision of man never affirmed easily nor other than in an uneasy balance between assertion and submergence of ego, has darkened in *Mr. Sammler's Planet*, with Bellow reversing his previous vote of confidence in man. The relentless claim of the individual for "a name, a dignity of person" (p. 235), which so gripped the imaginations of Augie, Henderson, and Herzog, now prompts Mr. Sammler to scoff at what he considers to be a "limitless demand" (p. 34) translated "barbarously and recklessly into personal gesture" (p. 235). Furthermore, the regulating role of society, to which Augie, Henderson, and Herzog lovingly submitted a portion of their individuality, appears to Mr. Sammler to be bent on "personal humbling" (p. 7). Urban existence, the achievement of civilization, is realizing its own forms of barbarism, of "historical ruin": "Most outdoor telephones were smashed, crippled. They were urinals, also. New York was getting worse than Naples or Salonika. It was like an Asian, or African town, from this standpoint" (p. 7). Rather than the product of an ennobling tension between "the single Self and the multitude,"[2] Mr. Sammler bleakly considers the possibility that "the real purpose of civilization is to permit us all to live like primitive people and lead a neolithic life in an automated society" (p. 227).

In 1963 Bellow remarked in his essay "Some Notes on Recent American Fiction": "Undeniably the human being is not what he commonly thought a century ago. The question nevertheless remains. He is something. What is he?"[3] One can read Bellow's novels as successive attempts at an answer to this question. For all their foibles and selfishness, Augie, Henderson, and Herzog are men of generous heart, ultimately capable of self discipline and restraint. Keith Opdahl is right, however, to note that Mr. Sammler is instead a man of analytical mind, still able to feel pity and outrage.[4] This shift in emphasis unveils a very different philosophy of man. Like Herzog, Mr. Sammler continues fitfully to perform the civilized office of keeping alive in us the agony of consciousness. Yet his relentless rationality sees primarily the "extremism and fanaticism of human nature" (p. 219), its insatiable demand for more than "the sum of human facts could . . . yield" (p. 83). To his mind, modern man's "liberation into individuality" has "brought misery and despair" (p. 235):

> Hearts that get no real wage, souls that find no nourishment. Falsehoods, unlimited. Desire, unlimited. Possibility, unlimited. Impossible demands upon complex realities, unlimited. Revival in childish and vulgar form of ancient religious ideas, mysteries, utterly unconscious of course—astonishing. Orphism, Mithraism, Manichaeanism, Gnosticism. (p. 229)

Modern man's fever for originality of soul has put "too great demand upon human consciousness and human capacities" (pp. 229, 232). Ironically his grasp for uniqueness is now additionally compromised by his equal success in satisfying his material desires. The result is a blurring of the hard-fought distinction between individuality and materiality. The "gay new ornament" of the Self, the modern personality, is all too recognizable as a product of our mass-produced, consumer-oriented culture, a product "from the Woolworth store, cheap tin or plastic from the five-and-dime of souls" (p. 234).

A propos of Bellow's work, Earl Rovit could write in 1967 that the total reach of his "six novels, several plays, a handful of short stories and essays—constitutes his attempt to define habitable limits for contemporary man, within which he can rest secure and still seize hold of the day with a partial power and the responsibility for his employment of that power."[5] In his latest novel, "habit-

able limits for contemporary man" are so drastically shrunken as
to be virtually nonexistent. Elegantly written with all the eloquence Bellow can muster when he wishes, *Mr. Sammler's Planet*
reflects a Bellow in retreat, turned off by the spectacle of a great
city in disintegration and in recoil from a people bewildered by
"new leisure and liberty" (p. 228). The extravagant achievement
of America putting a man on the moon becomes an occasion for
assessing the impulses of man. And the assessment takes the form
of a debate between civilization and barbarism in Mr. Sammler's
mind, in which the new order of things is seen to be a resurgence
of the old savagery:

> The labor of Puritanism now was ending. The dark satanic mills
> changing into light satanic mills. The reprobates converted into
> children of joy, the sexual ways of the seraglio and of the Congo
> bush adopted by the emancipated masses of New York, Amster-
> dam, London. Old Sammler with his screwy visions! He saw the
> increasing triumph of Enlightenment—Liberty, Fraternity,
> Equality, Adultery! Enlightenment, universal education, uni-
> versal suffrage, the rights of the majority acknowledged by all
> governments, the rights of women, the rights of children, the
> rights of criminals, the unity of the different races affirmed,
> Social Security, public health, the dignity of the person, the
> right to justice—the struggles of three revolutionary centuries
> being won while the feudal bonds of Church and Family weak-
> ened and the privileges of aristocracy (without any duties)
> spread wide, democratized, especially the libidinous privileges,
> the right to be uninhibited, spontaneous, urinating, defecating,
> belching, coupling in all positions, tripling, quadrupling, poly-
> morphous, noble in being natural, primitive, combining the
> leisure and luxurious inventiveness of Versailles with the hibis-
> cus-covered erotic ease of Samoa. Dark romanticism now took
> hold. As old at least as the strange Orientalism of the Knights
> Templar, and since then filled up with Lady Stanhopes, Baude-
> laires, de Nervals, Stevensons, and Gauguins—those South-
> loving barbarians. Oh yes, the Templars. They had adored the
> Muslims. One hair from the head of a Saracen was more pre-

cious than the whole body of a Christian. Such crazy fervor! And now all the racism, all the strange erotic persuasions, the tourism and local color, the exotics of it had broken up but the mental masses, inheriting everything in a debased state, had formed an idea of the corrupting disease of being white and of the healing power of black. The dreams of nineteenth-century poets polluted the psychic atmosphere of the great boroughs and suburbs of New York. Add to this the dangerous lunging staggering crazy violence of fanatics, and the trouble was very deep. Like many people who had seen the world collapse once, Mr. Sammler entertained the possibility it might collapse twice. He did not agree with refugee friends that this doom was inevitable, but liberal beliefs did not seem capable of self-defense, and you could smell decay. You could see the suicidal impulses of civilization pushing strongly. You wondered whether this Western culture could survive universal dissemination—whether only its science and technology or administrative practices would travel, be adopted by other societies. Or whether the worst enemies of civilization might not prove to be its petted intellectuals who attacked it at its weakest moments—attacked it in the name of proletarian revolution, in the name of reason, and in the name of irrationality, in the name of visceral depth, in the name of sex, in the name of perfect instantaneous freedom. For what it amounted to was limitless demand—instatiability, refusal of the doomed creature (death being sure and final) to go away from this earth unsatisfied. A full bill of demand and complaint was therefore presented by each individual. Nonnegotiable. Recognizing no scarcity of supply in any human department. Enlightenment? Marvelous! But out of hand, wasn't it? (pp. 32–33)

The rhetoric of this passage is remarkable for its utterance of the liberal's felt frustration over what seems to be wholesale deterioration of those values which have historically elevated man above the animal—and justifies, I hope, such extended quotation. Mr. Sammler finds evidences of the new barbarism wherever he looks. He is a collector of dour prognostications of the imminent collapse of civilization, that is, of social decorum. Public telephones no longer function. Dogs foul the sidewalks. Soot covers everything. Winos and drunkards litter the parks and streets. Fashionably dressed pickpockets tyrannize bus passengers. Blacks assert their sexual power. Holiday acquaintances commit group intercourse, strangers fellatio. Mr. Sammler's world—and Bellow's—is reduced to "this death-burdened, rotting, spoiled, sullied, exasperating, sinful earth" (p. 278).

A student of anthropology, Bellow has always regarded man as having evolutionary kinship with the animal world; and he has not hesitated in the past either to "invest animals with 'human' characteristics" or to show that "brute animality resides deeply and subtly in [his protagonists'] basic natures." But, as Earl Rovit is quick to insist, "The difference between the human animal and brute," for Bellow, remains "a matter of essential kind rather than degree."[6] Man has the saving grace (and the eternal curse) of selfconsciousness. In *Mr. Sammler's Planet*, however, Bellow seems to be having difficulty in keeping this distinction in mind. As if to underscore his darkening view of the Adam in man, Bellow repeatedly resorts to bestial imagery that transforms man into animal without the old alleviating reservation. The black pickpocket, who perpetrates his thefts with unselfconscious effrontery in a fashionable camel's hair coat (and why black if not an expression of Bellow's conservative Jewish outrage at the state of the nation?) is equated with a puma, his penis with both a snake and "the fleshly mobility of an elephant's trunk" (p. 49). Indeed, in possibly the most memorable episode in the novel, the pickpocket's display of himself appears to both Mr. Sammler's and our eyes as an instance of total brute power. The novel abounds with such portraits of man. After his lecture on Orwell at Columbia University is interrupted by a foul-mouthed radical student, Mr. Sammler characterizes the protests of contemporary youth as "confused sex-excrement-militancy, explosiveness, abusiveness, tooth-showing, Barbary ape howling. Or like the spider monkeys in the trees . . . defecating into their hands, and shrieking, pelting the explorers below" (p. 43). "Arrested in the stage of toilet training," youth have "made shit a sacrament" (p. 45). Here is no alleviating recognition that today's youth are also one of the most idealistic of generations. Instead man is seen from below. Like Mr. Sammler's relative Walter Bruch, man no longer converses: he gobbles, quacks, grunts, swallows syllables (p. 57). It is difficult to understand, given the almost Swiftian revulsion felt for people on occasion by Mr. Sammler, how Irving Howe can still claim that "Bellow now writes from a conviction that even today men can establish a self-ordering discipline which rests on a tentative-sardonic faith in the value of a life without faith."[7]

Mr. Sammler is a man who was killed by the Nazis, but who Lazarus-like clawed his way out of the ditch in which he had been left for dead back into the life of this world. For the thirty years since that freak occurrence, life has been for him distinctly apocalyptic. It qualifies his view of mankind, for whom "the sole visible future" seems to be death (p. 75). The Six-Day Arab-Israeli War draws him irresistibly, not as a witness of what John Braine trumpets to be an instance "for once" of Jack killing the giant, of "A race which had been led like sheep to the slaughter for two thousand years" slaughtering the butchers,[8] but as a witness of the blood bath, of the smell of rotting flesh and the sight of mangled bodies. For Mr. Sammler new beginnings are occasions for "finalities . . . summaries" (p. 278). The "hop to the moon" (p. 149) affects him less with wonder and pride than with the sense of impending doom, the sense of a conclusion to "our earth business" (p. 148), of "the end of things-as-known" (p. 278). The "utopian projects, experiments," of both the U.S.A. and U.S.S.R. appear ironically to Mr. Sammler, the *Ostjude,* as a "wading naked into the waters of paradise, et cetera. Bur always a certain despair underlining pleasure, death seated inside the health-capsule, steering it, and darkness winking at you from the golden utopian sun" (p. 158). And this sense of the imminence of apocalypse has its frame of reference not only in the ironic juxtaposition of man's conquest of space with his failure to maintain law and order in his cities ["New York makes one think about the collapse of civilization, about Sodom and Gomorrah, the end of the world," (p. 304)], but also in the hospital room of the dying Elya Gruner.

Nowhere is Bellow's change in attitude more pronounced than in his conception of the novel's characters and in his treatment of Elya's death. In none of his previous novels has he handled his fictional creations with quite the same unalleviated disrespect. The three most fully developed women in *Herzog*, for example— Madeleine, Ramona, and Sono—are not shown as faultless creatures; yet we are allowed, like Herzog, to admire them for their integrity of personality, for their fidelity to self. In each blooms a vitality, a *joie de vivre*, that is attractive, and that provides a counterweight to the excesses of their humanity: Madeline's intellectual arrogance, Ramona's shopworn sexuality, and Sono's fatalistic hedonism. These deficiencies are excusable, actually the obverse side of the strengths in each to which we respond.

No such explanation immediately offers itself for their counterparts in *Mr. Sammler's Planet*, who are given to us abstractedly almost as puzzling products of a society that has lost its sense of history and of humility. With the exceptions of Mr. Sammler, his nephew Elya, and the Indian scientist Dr. Lal, practically everyone is depicted as incompetent, crazy, and/or dishonest—as reductive mutations of a malfunctioning culture. And the language used to portray them is implacable in its disapproval. Mr. Sammler's daughter Shula is a scavenger, a nut, a thief, "with loony, clever, large eyes," a "rucked-up skirt," "shopping bag with salvage, loot, coupons, and throwaway literature," and cheap wig of "mixed yak and baboon hair" (pp. 23, 34). Her husband Eisen, like Mr. Sammler a survivor of the Holocaust, is "equally crazy," with homicidal tendencies to boot. His steady efforts at self improvement—"deposited starved to the bones on Israel's sands; lice, lunacy, and fever his assets; taken from internment in Cyprus; taught a language and a trade"; and now "gone on to become an artist"—arouse only derision in Mr. Sammler's heart. To the ex-Bloomsbury Anglophile, Eisen's aspirations to make "something important, beautiful," to do "something like a human being" (p. 171), are offensive, are one more instance of contemporary man's excessive desires. A pity "you could not tell recovery where to stop," he bitterly remarks. Wallace Gruner also "fell into the Shula category" (p. 88). A sophisticated version of Tommy Wilhelm in *Seize the Day* (whose father also was a hard-headed businessman-doctor), he is a persistent disappointment to his family, "a creep" to his sister (p. 297), a man who has the ability to be almost anything he wishes but who lacks whatever is necessary to be more than "nearly . . . a physicist . . . nearly . . . a mathematician, nearly a lawyer . . . nearly an engineer, nearly a Ph.D. in behavioral science. . . . Nearly an alcoholic, nearly a homosexual" (p. 88). Unlike Wilhelm, whose loving nature is developed with sufficient sympathy to discount his obvious personal deficiences, who accepts his "peculiar burden" of being human, of feeling "shame and impotence" and tasting tears (ch. 4) for both his and a stranger's mortality, Wallace is portrayed as a man without a shred of sentiment, self-centered, worried only that his father may die without disclosing where he has hidden money earned from performing abortions for New York underworld figures. Flying a Cessna in a harebrained money-making scheme, a few hours before his father dies, he is dismissed by Mr. Sammler who watches him buzz a house: "Unto himself a roaring center. To us, a sultry beetle, a gnat propelling itself through blue acres" (p. 267). Like Madeleine in *Herzog* (who is "a mixed mine of pure diamond and Woolworth glass," p. 299), Angela Gruner is a compound of "low comic and high serious. Goddess and majorette" (p. 164). Unlike Madeleine, who conveys intellectual vitality and a forceful commanding personality, Angela communicates only the powerful odor of sex, "smearing all with her female fluids" (p. 278), a voluptuous woman with "a big mouth, a large tongue," (p. 70), an elegant façade masking a coarse "woman who has done it in too many ways with too many men" (p. 178), and who is bitterly dismissed by her father as "a dirty cunt" (p. 177). Feffer is "an ingenious operator, less student than promoter" (p. 38), charming but untrustworthy, a man on the make and not overly scrupulous about his means. Walter Bruch is a sixty-year-old masturbater who falls in love with women's arms. And even Margotte, "boundlessly, achingly, hopelessly on the right side," is maladroit, her cups and tableware greasy, her tablecloth splattered, her toilet unflushed. Worse, she is a high-minded bore. "She talked junk, she gathered waste and junk in the flat, she bred junk" (pp. 20–21).

Elya Gruner's death similarly is less an occasion for "the consummation of [the] heart's ultimate need" in an affirmation of man, of "another human creature," as is the funeral scene concluding *Seize the Day*, than a "droll mortality" play (p. 294) on the sins and vices of contemporary life, with Elya cast as the American Everyman, Mr. Sammler as Good Deeds, Wallace as Kindred, and Angela as Beauty in micro-mini skirt. Associated with loonies and thieves, a morbid "collector" (as his name implies) of the dissociations of the age, Mr. Sammler is also a spokesman for old-fashioned virtues, for the stoic ethic of Middle America. His eulogy of Elya is a compendium of the Horatio Alger attributes that make up one form of the American Dream:

> Husband, medical man—he was a good doctor—family man, success, American, wealthy retirement with a Rolls Royce. We have our assignments. Feeling, out-goingness, expressiveness, kindness, heart—all these fine human things which by a peculiar turn of opinion strike people now as shady activities. Openness and candor about vices seem far easier. Anyway, there is Elya's assignment. That's what's in his good face. That's why he has such a human look. He's made something of himself. He hasn't done badly. He didn't like surgery. You know that. He dreaded those three- and four-hour operations. But he performed them. He did what he

disliked. He had an unsure loyalty to certain pure states. He knew there had been good men before him, that there were good men to come, and he wanted to be one of them. I think he did all right. (p. 303).

Here is a consecration of life in diminuendo as compared to Tommy Wilhelm's tears, Henderson's drunken rage, and Herzog's neurotic ardors.

It has been suggested that Mr. Sammler is Herzog twenty-five years older and wiser, "a Herzog gone exquisitely sane, and playing Prospero to his former role as mad King Lear."[9] The implications of the Prospero-Lear analogy are sound enough. Herzog experiences some of Lear's fatal involvement with people, and Mr. Sammler much of Prospero's disdainful detachment. But the fact is that Bellow does not repeat himself in his delineation of characters. In his capacity for drawing endlessly different types he displays one of the marks of a major novelist. More pertinent to the discussion though is that Herzog and Mr. Sammler reflect divergent responses of Bellow to the contemporary scene. Herzog is a half-mad yea-sayer, a man of feeling, who like all men has had his "schooling in grief" but who nevertheless will not preach the fashionable "doctrine or theology of suffering" (p. 317), will not tout the void (p. 93). He rejects both the brutal solutions of Himmelstein and the despairing absurdist importations of Shapiro and Mermelstein, choosing instead to praise man's will to survival. In contrast, Mr. Sammler may be eminently sane, but his sanity partakes of that cold pessimism which delights in observations of the bestial antics of *homo sapiens.* An advocate of "law and order," he likens himself to a "curate of wild men and progenitor of a wild woman; registrar of madness" (p. 118). He is an old man, a European intellectual, who deplores social change. He opts for regularity and habit. "All mapmakers should place the Mississippi in the same location, and avoid originality," he declaims.

It may be boring, but one has to know where he is. We cannot
have the Mississippi flowing toward the Rockies for a change.
Now, as everyone knows, it has only been in the last two centuries that the majority of people in civilized countries have
claimed the privilege of being individuals. Formerly they were
slave, peasant, laborer, even artisan, but not person. It is clear
that this revolution, a triumph for justice in many ways—slaves
should be free, killing toil should end, the soul should have
liberty—has also introduced new kinds of grief and misery, and
so far, on the broadest scale, it has not been altogether a success. . . . We have fallen into much ugliness. (p. 228)

The tone of the 1960's conservative is heard in his litanies of the
failure of modern soical engineering. It is Dr. Lal, not Mr.
Sammler, who asserts the credo, the *O altitudo* of man, and of
Augie, Henderson, and Herzog. In defense of the moon launching, he exclaims:

Still, there is a universe into which we can overflow. Obviously
we cannot manage with one single planet. Nor refuse the challenge of a new type of experience. We must recognize the
extremism and fanaticism of human nature. Not to accept the
opportunity would make this earth seem more and more a
prison. If we could soar out and did not, we would condemn
ourselves. We would be more than ever irritated with life.
(p. 219)

In Mr. Sammler's eyes not the urge for growth, progress, full
realization of the human potential, but the desire to live with
order and restraint (if not constraint) is "the fundamental biolog-
ical governing principle" (p. 216).

Keith Opdahl has noted that in *Augie March* "the secondary
characters provided the theories, and they were amusing and
eccentric," whereas in *Mr. Sammler's Planet* "the protagonist supplies them and they are in deadly earnest."[10] The unfortunate
consequence is a loss of dramatic interest. The excitement of the

novel resides almost entirely in Mr. Sammler's ruminations. His ideas have the makings of good essays but not of good fiction. Bellow in writing *Mr. Sammler's Planet* must have temporarily forgotten the words he gave to Gooley MacDowell in his "Address . . . to the Hasbeens Club of Chicago." Gooley decries the "dome of thought" suffocating us. People are "dying of good ideas," he remarks, "deafened, hampered, obstructed, impeded, impaired and bowel-glutted with wise counsel and good precept, and the more plentiful our ideas the worse our headaches. So we ask, will some good creature pull out the plug and ease our disgusted hearts a little?"[11] To the world's load of "wise counsel" Mr. Sammler adds another hefty bit of "good precept"—in marked contrast to the previous Bellow protagonists like Augie and Herzog who are on the run from the "reality instructors."

An authentic part of Bellow's literary contribution has been his willingness in novel after novel to cleanse the soot-filled eyes of twentieth century vision, to confront the "issue of the single Self and the multitude."[12] And in *Mr. Sammler's Planet* the theme is encountered again; but the tension, the dynamic equipoise one finds in the earlier novels between private life and public consciousness is absent. The explanation lies partly in the nature of Mr. Sammler, whom Bellow has conceived of as a man no longer striving as had his fictional antecedents simultaneously to be true to himself and to the collective will. The explanation also lies in the direction of Bellow's gaze. He is too absorbed in the reportorial job of decrying the dirt and disintegration of urban America and too bent on the philosophical job of formulating a Hobbesian view of man,[13] in short, too concentrated on touting the void to attend to the hard intellectual discipline of holding alternatives in equilibrium. Otherwise why the shocking "improbable possibility" of the episode in which the elegantly dressed black pickpocket exposes himself to Mr. Sammler in a demonstration of silent threatening animal power? And why the early biographical facts of Mr. Sammler, his survival of the Holo-

caust—of concentration camp, partisan warfare, and blood lust—
facts known by Bellow with the mind, not, as by Elie Wiesel and
Jerzy Kosinski, on the pulse? And why the exposition of Mr.
Sammler's journalistic tour of the Arab-Israeli War of 1967, with
its concentration of blood, sand, and corpses? The gratuity of the
latter episode, in its encrustation on the narrative, is reminiscent
of the merchant marine sequence in *Augie March*. That each has
been treated fictionally by Bellow is not independent of his having served as a merchant seaman in World War II and as a
correspondent during the Six-Day War. Bellow is an economical
writer, making use of every scrap of his experience. One has no
quarrel with this proceduce, of course, unless as in these two
instances the author has extra literary designs on the reader and
tacks the material onto his narrative structure without scrupulous
attention to the fictional carpentry. Bellow's ability to formulate
a narrative that carries the theme has never been one of his
strong points as a novelist; and in *Mr. Sammler's Planet* his propen-
sity to intellectualize, to compose essays on the state of society,
gains the upper hand. The tension generated derives less from
narrative conflict than from Bellow's visceral response to contemporary America.

   In his previous novels Bellow identifies life with the maintenance of socially useful individuality; in *Mr. Sammler's Planet* the
private self has deteriorated into eccentrics and crazies like Wallace and Shula. Mr. Sammler has all but dispensed with the responsibility of the private person. Whereas in the earlier heroes
excess dominates, in Mr. Sammler a sense of limits, of the normative, prevails. He leads a claustrophobic existence, always in
somebody else's room, the dimensions of his world shrunken by
his desire for safety and uneventuality. His memories of the old
country are no match for Elya's hunger [like Herzog's obsession
with "ancestor worship and totemism," (*Herzog*, p. 78)] to know
about obscure members of the family. His daughter, his nephews
and nieces, are kept at a dignified distance. Like the other Bellow

protagonists, Mr. Sammler prefigures his death; but he does not triumph over it psychically, redeemed in the knowledge of himself as a loving man committed to accommodation with the "ordinary middling human considerations" of society. No bone-breaking burden of individuality overwhelms him as it does Tommy Wilhelm and Herzog; only complacency informs Mr. Sammler's notion of himself. Personally uninvolved, the observer, with a running commentary on all and sundry, he lives by accepting the generosity of others: the Pole Cieslakiewicy who fed him in hiding in a cemetery, his nephew Elya who supported him for decades in America, and the Jesuit Father Newell who shepherded him around the Syrian front. The intense emotional compassion of Augie, the personal involvement of Herzog, are not Mr. Sammler's *modus operandi*. He survives by opting out of history, by "keeping his own counsel for . . . seven decades of internal consultation" (p. 144). Even his fondness for his dying nephew is qualified by his tasteless analogies of Elya's aneurysm, for example, to Wallace's flooding of the attic (p. 259). In the fictional conceptions of Bellow's middle years, the primal " 'law of the heart' in Western traditions" (thus Herzog formulates the principle, p. 119) provides a counterbalance to the modern code of the dehumanized *Lumpenproletariat*, "shaggy . . . malodorous, peculiarly rancid, sulphurous" (thus Mr. Sammler describes man, p. 40). With Mr. Sammler, the moderate contemplations of intellect not the mad exaltations of blood become the *desiderata*, calculated perseverence not reckless striving the ideal, careful collecting not generous expending the key to survival.

The impoverished view of man Bellow gives us in *Mr. Sammler's Planet* is dramatically appropriate to the cynical-wise "cultivated Old School European"[14] that is Mr. Sammler. One of the questions the novel raises, however, ultimately concerns the validity of this perspective that Bellow trains on his contemporaries. Is Mr. Sammler's dismissal of mankind the valetudinarian withdrawal of the septuagenarian from the "salmon-falls" and the "mackerel-crowded seas"? Or is it a Swiftian recoil from the "modern expectations" of boundlessness and of senseless engagement "to capacity" (p. 202) of the limited sexual being that is poor bare-forked man? In choosing an elderly person for his spokesman, Bellow begs the question. Whether *Mr. Sammler's Planet* reflects a real shifting of philosophical ground and of idea of man or a momentary, fictionally undigested reaction to the frustrations of mid-twentieth century existence only subsequent writing will confirm.

NOTES

1. Saul Bellow, *Mr. Sammler's Planet* (New York: The Viking Press, 1970), ch. 3. The other Bellow novels quoted from are *Seize the Day* (New York: The Viking Press, 1956) and *Herzog* (New York: The Viking Press, 1964).

2. Saul Bellow, "Some Notes on Recent American Fiction," *Encounter,* XXI (November, 1963), 24.

3. Ibid., p. 29.

4. Review of *Mr. Sammler's Planet* in *Commonweal,* XCI (February 13, 1970), 535–536.

5. Earl Rovit, *Saul Bellow* (University of Minnesota Press, 1967), p. 8.

6. Ibid., p. 13.

7. "Fiction: Bellow, O'Hara, Litwak," *Harper's Magazine,* CCXL (February, 1970), 106.

8. "Bellow's Planet," *National Review,* XXII (March 10, 1970), 266.

9. Christopher Lehmann-Haupt, "The Monotonous Music of the Spheres," *New York Times* (January 26, 1970), p. 45.

10. *Commonweal,* XCI (February 13, 1970), 536.

11. *Hudson Review,* IV (1951), 225-226.

12. Saul Bellow, "Some Notes on Recent American Fiction," *Encounter,* XXI (November, 1963), 24.

13. It is not insignificant that Bellow has most recently eschewed fiction to attack New York City in a straightforward journalistic piece, "World-Famous Impossibility," *New York Times* (December 6, 1970), pp. 1A and 12A. The resort to editorial, however, does not improve Bellow's

control over his material. *Mr. Sammler's Planet* is eminently more quotable than the essay, its language encompassing a greater range of experience. Bellow's imagination is evidently released more by a fictional than an expository framework. Even so, one must acknowledge that Bellow's imaginative vision has been realized less fully in *Mr. Sammler's Planet* than in *Seize the Day* and *Herzog*.

14. Anatole Broyard, "What a Complicated Machine an Old School European Is," *New York Times Book Review* (February 1, 1970), Sect. 7, p. 1.

Dissent and Dissent: A Look at Fiedler and Trilling

L. S. DEMBO

I

"What is a rebel?" asks Camus. "A man who says no, but whose refusal does not imply a renunciation." Leslie Fiedler began crying No! (*in thunder*) at the age of sixteen, as he tells it, from a soapbox on a ghetto street corner in Newark and, in a way, his rebellion was no less metaphysical, if considerably more oratorical, than Camus' universal *homme revolté*. Expanding upon Melville's description of Hawthorne ("He says No! in thunder; but the Devil himself cannot make him say *yes*. For all men who say *yes*, lie. . . ."), Fiedler was to define nay-saying as one of the hallmarks of "serious" literature:

> It pays to be clear about the nature of the "No! in thunder," which is quite different from certain lesser *no's* in which a thriving trade is always done: the *no* in newsprint, for instance, and the *no* on manifestoes and petitions. . . . [which] carry with them a certain air of presumptive self-satisfaction, an assurance of being justified by the future. They are Easy No's, merely disguised *yes's,* in varying degrees sentimental and righteous. . . . The "No! in thunder" remains a *no* forever; like the *no*

implicit in the whole work of the Marquis de Sade, or the deeper *no* of Huckleberry Finn. . . .

There is some evidence that the Hard No is being spoken when the writer seems a traitor to those whom he loves and who have conditioned his very way of responding to the world. When the writer says of precisely the cause that is dearest to him what is always and everywhere the truth about all causes —that is has been imperfectly conceived and inadequately represented, and that it is bound to be betrayed, consciously or unconsciously, by its leading spokesman—we know that he is approaching an art of real seriousness if not of actual greatness.[1]

To be a rebel, in at least one crucial respect, is not to be a revolutionary, for the latter's devotion to a cause is precisely what the former denies himself in loyalty to "truth" itself. And what is more important is that the rebel acquires his identity through words (negative) not allegiances or destructive acts.

Is it an accident at all that Fiedler, to his mock astonishment, had to wait until he was fifty before being "busted," and then on allegedly trumped-up charges? Really committed only to the act of saying "no," he found himself to be the Ambiguous Man, as early as his undergraduate years at NYU, where, as a member of a Trotskyite group, he participated in mass meetings and demonstrations but "saw them all as a kind of tourism" and "always ended by going home." On the other hand, though a diligent student, he could not identify himself with the university: "[I] never considered for a moment the possibility of dropping *out*," he wrote, "because I never could believe that I was yet quite in." And he goes on to say,

> With the B.A., M.A., Ph.D., I told myself, I would have a louder voice, more access to the centers of power, a better fulcrum, and greater leverage with which to heave over the whole rotten mess out of which I had been trying in vain to crawl. (*BB*, 21)

Perhaps the "louder voice" is the thing, but the "I told myself"
suggests that the older Fiedler had no idea why the younger
Fiedler stayed in school—if he had any reason at all.

The urge to say "No" for its own sake did not abandon Fiedler
after he had attained his degrees. In Italy on a Fulbright in 1951,
he found himself, "for whatever reasons," joining a procession
of his neo-Fascist students: "They were howling in unison as they
marched for Trieste, '*Italianissima Trieste,*' an odd slogan for
someone with my beginnings to echo, but I howled along with the
rest of them" (*BB*, 26). Although the police closed in and began
cracking skulls, Fiedler (as usual, he laments) escaped unscathed.
The whole episode is, of course, quite symbolic.

I should mention at this point that Fiedler warns that his autobiography is more parable than history. But if the Fiedler it
describes is in any way a Platonic projection of himself, the case
for his literal "ambiguity" seems all the stronger. In *Being Busted,*
the author, perhaps, becomes one of his own characters, but
evasive though he may be, arguing that the narrative "I" is the
name of us all, Fiedler is clearly drawing on actual personal
experience, and the mask, if there is a mask at all, looks like Leslie
Fiedler. Or rather it looks like what Leslie Fiedler would look like
to Leslie Fiedler.

The autobiography is throughout, then, the story of the "ambiguous" rebel: the naval intelligence officer trained in Japanese
who was not a Naval Intelligence Officer, the "controversial"
professor at Montana State ("JEW COMMIE, GO HOME"), who reluc-
tantly, and led on by circumstances, was the prime mover in a
successful effort to unseat the chancellor; finally, the "controversial professor" at SUNY, Buffalo, unapologetic possessor of a large
house, in a desirable neighborhood, and a Buick ("I long for the
sleek and shiny comforts produced by the miserable world");
and, though forswearing drugs himself, suspect enough to be
made the victim of a phony charge of "maintaining premises
where narcotics are used."

Whatever he is not, the rebel has a keen sensitivity to people who play what they are not. Baro Finkelstone, the hero (antihero) of *Back to China*, is driven to conclude that no one "seemed content anymore merely to live out the ethnic role to which he was born." The whole passage is worth quoting:

> Just as Susannah [a Gentile] had longed apparently to become a good Jewish wife, Shizu [a Japanese] had tried desperately to pass as a midwestern co-ed; and the young, whatever their origins . . . , yearned to be black. Meanwhile, of course . . . , the Negroes must be pretending to be white as fast as emancipation permitted.
>
> Yet such passing from stereotype to stereotype was . . . a less ignoble strategy than acting out—with even more abysmal lack of conviction—one's inherited role: being a professional Jew like Shapiro, a professional Indian like Irwin Grayfox, a professional Japanese like Hiroshige; or worst of all, somehow, a professional WASP like Harry D. Ransome.
>
> In the end, caught between two equally distasteful possibilities, he has been left absolutely nowhere—the loser in a game of ethnic musical chairs that had become America's favorite sport, indoor and out. (pp. 212–213)

The real problem lies with the meaning of "ethnic role," for Fiedler knows, as Finkelstone must learn, that a positive cultural identity outside the ghetto or reservation is a very elusive ideal indeed. Does the Last Jew in America exist as an "authentic" or a professional Jew? The "vestigial" Jews, who pass as WASP academics and send their children to church, or those who become "part" of the business community and take Gentile wives, are obvious targets of satire. Jacob Moskowitz, the old man, who desperately organizes a *minyan* for a Yom Kippur service to be presided over by his dying friend, Louie Himmelfarb, in a Catholic hospital room, is obviously sympathetic. The service, to the old man's surprise, is well attended (theme of the secret compulsion or sense of obligation that binds Jew to Jew whatever his professed attitudes?) but the proceedings turn out to be farcical. *The Last Jew in America* can only, in the final analysis, be an ambiguous tale because Fiedler cannot and will not define the proper "ethnic role" for the American Jew. He came closest to such a definition in his essay on the Yiddish novelist I. L. Peretz, but he spoke in generalities: "We have become aware that we must achieve, if we are unwilling to become shadows of shadows, a double assimilation, back to a stable past as well as forward to a speculative future" (*NIT,* 96). A double assimilation. But is there such a thing and can it be willed or even learned? And are we not confronted with that most impossible of all impossible questions, What is a Jew? More credible perhaps than the notion of double assimilation is its obverse, double unassimilation, the rebel's ultimate belief that he must say "No" in his own house (if he has one to begin with) as well as outside the enemy walls.

What is true about ethnic identity is even more evident in professional identity. An academic for most of his life, Fiedler, at least in his written work, has refused "assimilation" into the "WASP community of scholars," an assimilation, he notes in *Waiting for the End,* that has claimed a myriad of urban Jewish intellectuals. This refusal means denying some of the fundamental values associated with academic methods. "I tell myself," Fiedler wrote of Frederick Hoffman's *The Twenties,* "that it is orderly, well-documented, immune to the more ridiculous prejudices about the period with which it deals; a combination of the most admirable attributes of old-fashioned scholarship and newfangled criticism. . . . It is, in short, good-tempered, well-informed, inclusive, balanced—and thoroughly unreadable." Hoffman's chief sin is an excess of objectivity and Fiedler admits to a "low tolerance for detached chronicling and cool analysis" (*NIT,* 153-4). Clearly this attack, for all its shock-value, comes from the depths; it is a battle in Fiedler's long war against "genteel" (formalist) criticism and scholarship, approaches that allegedly exist in a cultural vacuum and, though they shed the light, lack the heat necessary for life. Decorous antipolemics cannot be the way of the rebel.

Again, this attitude has a persuasive rationale behind it and should not be mistaken for arrogant posturing.

> What irks our age and drives us to the more shameful excesses of "scholarship" . . . is that we feel ourselves trapped among the clichés of anti-cliché that we have inherited from the stereotype mongers of the twenties. We should be ashamed to be as nakedly square as Fitzgerald, as unawarely sentimental as Hemingway or Faulkner, as prone to maudlin self-pity as Ezra Pound, as ignorant or as absurdly self-educated as any of these. Yet our irony, sensibility, objectivity and culture have not made us capable of seeing around the literary platitudes of the twenties. (*NIT,* 155).

Fiedler's major criticism is devoted precisely to discovering the archetypes and stereotypes—of women, Jews, Indians, Negroes —that inhere in American life. He calls it literary anthropology but the word No, sometimes in thunder, sometimes in a whisper, sometimes merely in a gesture, echoes throughout.

As Fiedler is quick to admit he does not readily take to theorizing, and the fact is significant. His formal attack on the New Criticism and his attempt to define the relationship between the poet and the poem in "Archetype and Signature" (*NIT*) eventually degenerates into Jungian jargon and oversimplification. On the other hand, he is quite right that the formalist critic—if by that we mean the critic who is interested chiefly in the structure and language of the text and believes that an art-work is autonomous—is forced to explain away or ignore, say, stereotypes of the Jew produced by Hemingway, Fitzgerald, Eliot, and Pound, among others. Clark Emery, I believe, in his detailed exegesis of the *Cantos,* has an extended list of the possibilities and motivations of Pound's antisemitism, a list that becomes more evasive and embarrassing the longer it gets. And what expounders of the intricacies of *The Sun Also Rises* and *The Great Gatsby* have not had to parry "naive" undergraduate questions, perhaps by explaining the description of Robert Cohn as a projection of Jake's jealousy and anxiety and the group's paranoia, and attributing that of Meyer Wolfsheim to Carraway's midwestern "innocence"—thus leaving Hemingway and Fitzgerald free and clear? A critic like Fiedler, attuned to what David Daiches has called the "maximum context" of a literary work or works, will rarely find himself in this situation. He'd be much more concerned with pointing out, as Fiedler does in *Waiting for the End,* that not until the emergence of the Jewish novelists of the fifties and sixties were the literary stereotypes of the Jew created by the twenties and preceding generations of writers dispelled.

Still, sociological or myth criticism has grave limitations of its own, even when practiced with sensitivity. *Love and Death in the American Novel,* Fiedler's tour-de-force, suffers from the same major problem as that all-encompassing work to which it is meth-odologically related, Northrop Frye's *Anatomy of Criticism:* litera-ture is used as evidence to support a sociological or cultural thesis and major and minor works are given importance in the perspective of this thesis, rather than in terms of their inher-ent literary quality. Indeed, Fiedler seems to have little con-cern for the integrity of an art-work, even though he does add in an appendix (consolidated with the text in a later edition) long analyses of single novels. "Inherent literary quality" and "integrity of an art-work" are, I realize, formalist terms, but they are scarcely shibboleths and one scorns them at his peril. Moreover, contempt for close reading courts the inaccuracy that makes the brilliant generalization an emperor without clothes.

Here, as a random example, is Fiedler on *Tender Is the Night:*

Early in *Tender Is the Night*, Dick Diver comes upon Nicole in Europe, and, dazzled by her "cream-colored dress . . . her very blonde hair . . . her face lighting up like an angel's," thinks of her as "a scarcely saved waif of disaster bringing him the essence of a continent. . . ." He reads into her, that is to say, the conventional meanings of the Good American Girl. But before his marriage with her has finally unmanned him, he comes to see her as an "evil-eyed" destroyer, and longs "to grind her grinning mask into jelly." (p. 314)

Do not be misled by the appearance of details here; they are the only ones Fiedler refers to and they are intended to prove a sociological and psychological point:

Nicole, the goddess who failed, is postulated in the novel as a schizophrenic, in an attempt to explain her double role as Fair Lady and Dark, her two faces, angelic and diabolic, the melting and the grinning mask. But the schizophrenia is really in Diver, which is to say, in Fitzgerald, which is finally to say, in the American mind itself.

Not unconvincing, appealing, in fact, when Fiedler adds that there are not two orders of women (Fair and Dark) but two orders of male expectations in "a land of artists who insist on treating them as goddesses or bitches," both of which roles deny women's humanity. In their confusion women "switch from playing out one to acting out the other" to the outrage and despair of artists like Fitzgerald. (Whether women are merely the victims of male expectations is not the issue here.)

But Fiedler has not taken into account a crucial fact about Dick Diver, one that plays havoc with his evaluation of Fitzgerald ("sentimental and whining") and makes his ultimate thesis an oversimplification. That Diver is dazzled by Nicole is quite true but he is no *naif* falling for the Great American Beauty; he is a psychiatrist bedazzled by a patient and he knows full well the consequences of an involvement:

"I'm half in love with her—the question of marrying her has passed through my mind."

"Tch! Tch!" uttered Franz.

"Wait." Dohmler warned him. Franz refused to wait: "What, and devote half your life to being a doctor and nurse and all—never! I know what these cases are. One time in twenty its finished in the first push—better never see her again!"

"What do you think?" Dohmler asked Dick.

"Of course Franz is right."[2]

Franz *is* right and Diver knows it. He is wholly aware that he "is possessed by a vast irrationality" and that to marry Nicole is to marry Ophelia. That he cannot help himself is his tragedy. Nicole, therefore, is not "the goddess who failed," for, since Diver never believed he was entering the "sentimental paradise of married love" (as Fiedler says of him), he could never really be disillusioned. His greatest hope, to effect a cure, was held in the knowledge that even success here might end in failure of the marriage, as it subsequently did.

Diver's decline, then, is not ascribable to shock over the Golden Lady's becoming a Royal Bitch. It was caused by nothing in particular and everything in general—"emotional bankruptcy," if we take Fitzgerald's word for it, or just the fated progress of the romantic sensibility. We do Fitzgerald a profound injustice if we believe him to be simply a creature of "outrage and self-pity." He knows all that Diver knows and, whatever his limitations, achieved more in his art than Diver in his psychiatry. *Tender Is the Night* demands "close reading" if any novel ever did.

Fiedler's Fitzgerald is a tile cut to fit a mosaic of two centuries of American writing, along with its European prototypes. That mosaic portrays the fortunes of "The Sentimental Love Religion," which emerged in fiction with Richardson and, conditioned by social and psychological forces, took many avatars down to the present. "So deeply," writes Fiedler, "had the formulae of degraded Richardsonianism impressed themselves on the American imagination, that in the United States, well up into the twentieth century, no novelists, however committed and talented, could treat the relations of the sexes without falling prey to their influence. Only by bypassing normal heterosexual love as a subject could such writers preserve themselves from sentimentality and falsehood." (*LD*, 104) Richardson's *Clarissa*, we are told, is a "tragedy of seduction," Clarissa being "the Persecuted Maiden, a projection of male guilt before the female treated as a sexual object," a "Protestant Virgin" who "offers salvation" and upon whose purity "depends not only her own eternal bliss but that of the male who attempts to destroy it," a "bouregeois Maiden, whose virginity is an emblem of the ethical purity of her class" (p. 67).

To his credit, Fiedler recognizes that *Clarissa* achieves its archetypal quality without sacrificing verisimilitude, by remaining a "scrupulous portrayal of contemporary manners and modes of consciousness." He also notes that Clarissa has (unspecified) weaknesses. The trouble is that the more one is captured by the verisimilitude, the less relevant the archetypal classifications seem to become. If we read the novel, for instance, as the story of a sensitive young girl, in rebellion against a society and a family that have no regard for her feelings, and a singleminded seducer who is even less compassionate—a girl whose pride is both her undoing and her salvation, a man whose aristocratic charm and intelligence make him a powerful, but not powerful enough, adversary—does it really increase our understanding to reach for the anagogical level? Whatever Clarissa means in terms of neoclassical society, both bourgeois and aristocratic, her eight volumes of letters add up to a much fuller character than Protestant Virgin and Persecuted Maiden.

Because Fiedler is intent upon discovering archetypes or exposing psyches, he is often indifferent to an author's conscious or half-conscious symbolism, an element that, unlike archetypes and stereotypes, requires careful attention to internal organization. The discussion of Hart Crane in *The Return of the Vanishing American* (a book that applies the methodology of *Love and Death* to a consideration of white visions of the American Indian) illustrates the problem in one of its acutest forms. Now, Crane's flirtation with mythopoeia exposes him to the kind of skeptical abuse he has received from those critics who pay more attention to what Crane said he was doing than to what he actually did do. For his part, Fiedler is concerned with Crane's use of a stereotype that had established itself in American literature long before his time; namely, that of Pocahontas, the Indian Princess. Fiedler seizes upon Crane's remarks to Otto Kahn concerning "The Dance" ("I . . . become identified with the Indian and his world, before it is over") and proceeds to "psych out" the poet:

> "*His* world," Crane says, and the "his" is a giveaway, a reve-
> lation that the poet has not been telling quite his own truth in
> his adaptation of the myth of Pocahontas—that what he yearns
> to celebrate is not the legendary Indian Princess at all . . . but
> the dusky Indian Prince whom he imagines his as well as her
> true lover . . . and it is to him, not to Pocahontas, that the poet
> chants the phallic song in which his verse—elsewhere flaccid
> and unconvincing—comes to life. . . . (p. 88)

Crane exposed as the homosexual we all knew him to be! But clearly Crane has throughout *The Bridge* been at pains to make Pocahontas a personification of the continent, an object of the nature-worship of the Indians that the white man must recapture if he is to escape his technological hell and at least partially redeem his crimes. Furthermore, the speaker's identification with the Indian in a sacrificial dance is Crane's vision of that hope realized by the questing poet; indeed, the earlier stanzas of "The Dance" trace the poet's gradual initiation into mysteries of the Earth known to the Indian ("I learned to catch the trout's moon whisper") and his preparatory purification ("A distant cloud, a thunder-bud—it grew/ . . . I heard it; 'til its rhythm drew,/— Siphoned the black pool from the heart's hot root!"). All these things make Fiedler's comments beside the point. Certainly there are ambiguities in the relation of Crane to Maquokeeta and Pocahontas, and there may indeed be a homosexual "leopard ranging always in the brow" as Crane writes, but the real issue is that the poet is caught up in a mystical vision whose implications of death and rebirth transcend the sexual.[3]

Fiedler has said that he felt himself to be more "the poet" than the scholar. And in many ways the feeling is justified—not simply by dint of the fact that he has written as much fiction as criticism or even, less charitably, that his criticism is often a form of fiction. Rather, it is justified by his view of the serious writer as a dissenter. I wrote earlier that Fiedler pointed out that it took the Jewish novelists of the fifties and sixties to break the stereotype of the Jew created by antisemitic or ignorant writers. But his argument continues:

> The very notion of a Jewish-American literature represents a dream of assimilation, and the process it envisages is bound to move toward a triumph (in terms of personal success) which is also a defeat (in terms of a meaningful Jewish survival.) If today Jewish-American writers seem engaged in writing not the high tragedy of Jewish persistence in the midst of persecution, but the comedy of Jewish dissolution in the midst of prosperity this is because they tell the truth about a world which neither they nor their forerunners can consider themselves guiltless of desiring. (*WFE*, 70)

Fiedler himself does not desire such a world and his work cries out against it. If he has endured harassment by bigots, cops, jittery administrators, and formalist critics, is his identity not all the more confirmed?

I I

Urbane where Fiedler is flamboyant, reflective where Fiedler is melodramatic, and virtually unconcerned with subcultures, Jewish or otherwise, Lionel Trilling is the very image of the American Scholar. His is an entirely different world from Fiedler's and there is little transition between the two. If Fiedler's "Jewish-Wasp academics" in *The Last Jew in America* are in any way a reflection on the achievement of Trilling (and many others), then Trilling's achievement makes Fiedler's characters mere caricatures and stereotypes.

Whatever the case, Trilling's novel, *The Middle of the Journey*, is the story of an intellectual among intellectuals and depicts a world without Jews (although one character with a walk-on role is so designated). Rather it is interested in the psychological and philosophic relations among fellow-travelling liberals, their response to the defection of a Party member who had heretofore held sway over them, and their interaction with the people of a New England town. Essentially an interplay of ideas, the work, almost plotless, is so verbose that one cannot be sure whether the characters are meant to be sympathetic or ironic. Beneath all the talk, however, is the failure of John Laskell, the central figure, to establish any real bonds with the persons around him, whatever the trappings of friendship, influence, and camaraderie he may enjoy. The object of his most intense feeling, experienced during a siege of scarlet fever, is a rose, and even after he has recovered, the feeling retains its significance for him. His brief sexual encounter with the wife of a handyman does not relieve the reader's suspicion that he is epicene. Perhaps Laskell's condition is symbolic and Gifford Maxim, the highpowered disaffecting Party member whom everyone insists has gone insane, is right when he tells him, and the group in general, "Like any bourgeois intellectual, you want to make the best of every possible world and every possible view. Anything to avoid a commitment, anything not to have to take a risk."[4]

But *The Middle of the Journey* is also a novel of ambiguities and opposites, of the self existing for its own sake and the self requiring a public identity, of man in love with a rose and man in a community, of life to be lived in an eternal present and life to be dedicated to the future. And Trilling's quarrel with liberalism lies precisely in its paradoxical denial of the claims of individual feeling. Thus the preface to *The Liberal Imagination:*

> . . . in the very interests of its great primal act of imagination by which it establishes its essence and existence—in the interests, that is, of its vision of a general enlargement and freedom and rational direction of human life—it drifts toward a denial of the emotions and imagination. And in the very interest of affirming its confidence in the power of the mind, it inclines to make mechanical its conception of the nature of the mind.[5]

Trilling is concerned here about what he calls the organizational impulse of liberalism, which values ideas "that can be passed on to agencies and bureaus and technicians," a liberalism that must be recalled to the "lively sense of contingency and possibility" that is essential to the spirit. Both organization and contingency, political action and the romance of the rose, are a part of life.

Predisposed to liberal values himself, Trilling is, after his own fashion, a dissenter to his own cause:

> We cannot very well [he writes] set about to contrive opponents who will do us the service of forcing us to become more intelligent, who will require us to keep our ideas from becoming stale, habitual, inert. This we will have to do for ourselves. . . . a criticism which has at heart the interests of liberalism might find its most useful work not in confirming liberalism in its sense of general rightness but rather in putting under some

degree of pressure the liberal ideas and assumptions of the
present time. (p.6)

And this argument has its counterpart in Trilling's interpretation
of Freud. The whole burden of *Freud and the Crisis of Our Culture*
is to establish the value of an "opposing self" and, correspond-
ingly, call into question the (liberal) idea of the absolute nature
of culture as a criterion for judging the individual. Freud's bio-
logical determinism, the belief in a given human nature that is
immutable,

> proposes to us that culture is not all-powerful. It suggests that
> there is a residue of human quality beyond the reach of cultural
> control, and that this residue of human quality, elemental as it
> may be, serves to bring culture itself under criticism and keeps
> it from being absolute.[6]

Trilling argues that every great writer for the last two centuries
has been on the side of the self against culture. (The essays in
such appropriately entitled collections as *The Opposing Self* and
Beyond Culture attempt to document this view.)

Freud and the Crisis of Our Culture appeared in 1955 after having
been delivered before the New York Psychoanalytic Institute and
Society but its preoccupations go back at least as far as 1944, the
date of "Of This Time, of That Place," Trilling's best known
piece of fiction.[7] Fielder, among others, has made much of the
fact that Allen Ginsberg was the model for the "mad" student,
Ferdinand Tertan (although Trilling has denied it). The instructor, Joseph Howe, Fiedler tells us, must finally prefer Tertan's
madness, even though he must inevitably betray it, to the sanity
of his well-adjusted classmate, "bound for success in the same
world in which the instructor seeks to be recognized, though the
latter will publish poetry, while the fomer sells insurance" (*NIT*,
151-152). Fiedler concludes that the Tertan-Ginsbergs will not
tell of their college experiences; it is their teachers, "loved for

having, with whatever doubts, protected the right of others to 'flip' but despised for not having dared cross that frontier themselves, for having preferred academic security to insanity, who must write the record as best they can" (p. 152).

But "Of This Time, of That Place" is not just a record of Tertan or Ginsberg; it is as much the story of Joseph Howe, the "liberal," academic poet who encounters contingency in the form of a student. Howe is comfortable in the whole academic milieu, but he remains something of an outsider. Indeed, although he suspects the motives of his reviewer, he has been attacked in print for writing obscure and socially irrelevant poetry. His true crisis comes, however, when he is forced to commit himself to the system he respects (civilization, culture) or to obey his impulse to recognize and preserve the unknowable (the "unconditioned" spirit, the opposing self):

> He must not release Tertan to authority. Not that he anticipated from the Dean anything but the greatest kindness for Tertan. The Dean would have the experience and skill which he himself could not have. One way or another the Dean could answer the question, "What is Tertan?" Yet this was precisely what he feared. He alone could keep alive . . . the question, "What is Tertan?" He alone could keep it still a question. Some sure instinct told him he must not surrender the question to a clean official desk in a clear official light to be dealt with, settled and closed.

But he does surrender the question to the Dean. Now it should be kept in mind that Tertan is not an aggressive rebel, out to undermine or overthrow Howe's authority. Quite the contrary, he sends a letter to the Dean that when revealed to Howe leaves him with the impression that "this was love . . . he could not destroy the effect upon him of his student's stern affectionate regard." Howe really had a choice and he chose, as he fully realizes, to betray Tertan.

Fiedler says that Howe preferred Tertan's insanity to the sanity of his well-adjusted classmate destined to be an insurance executive. But Trilling's irony is sharper yet, for the classmate, Blackburn, turns out to be, in his own obsession with success, no more balanced than Tertan. Having failed an examination, Blackburn has wheedled Howe into allowing him to take another; the second exam turns out to be as bad as the first, but Howe gives it a C-minus. No less outraged at this grade, Blackburn taunts and threatens Howe, who answers him by reducing the grade to an F. Blackburn crumbles and, pleading to have the grade restored, is about to fall to his knees:

> Howe . . . thought, "The boy is mad," and began to speculate fantastically whether something in himself attracted or developed aberration. He could see himself standing before the Dean and saying, "I've found another." This time it's the vice-president of the Council, the manager of the debating team and secretary of Quill and Scroll.

Howe does not go to the Dean, however, and eventually passes Blackburn in the course—just to get rid of him, as he later tells the boy himself.

"Of This Time, of That Place" is, in a sense, a tragedy of labels. Howe betrays Tertan as soon as he classifies him as being "mad." And what possibly stops Howe from going to the Dean a second time is that Blackburn is "vice-president," "manager," and "secretary,"—mad, perhaps, but scarcely unknowable. Howe has indeed made his choice, and his righteous (and rightful) indignation at the slippery Blackburn on graduation day is no doubt directed as much against himself.

This is not to say, however, that, politically, the decision was an easy one; the same choice—in favor of society over the opposing self—could have been made by the group of Marxist sympathizers described in *The Middle of the Journey*, or, as it was in fact made, by Matthew Arnold. In his sympathetic intellectual biography of Arnold (a product, we do well to note, of the thirties), Trilling explained his subject's theory of social determinism:

> In Arnold's . . . organic conception of society, the individual is scarcely a member of an aggregate [as he is in Mill's atomistic view], but, as it were, a particular aspect of an integral whole. His individual does not join society, but springs from it, is endowed by it; therefore it is difficult, if not impossible, to conceive of his rights as against or apart from the rights of society as a whole.[8]

Although Trilling did not wholly embrace this view, he found it more valid than Mill's view of society as an aggregate of individuals.

But the real issue is psychological, not political. In *The Middle of the Journey*, for instance, much is made of the inability of Nancy Crooms, a staunch liberal, to utter the word *death*. The significance of this phenomenon is made clear in Trilling's book on E. M. Forster. In his "positive and passionate naturalism," Forster, we are told,

> accepts the many things the liberal imagination likes to put out of sight. He can accept, for example, not only the reality but the power of death . . . and the fine scene in *The Longest Journey* in which Rickie forces Agnes to "mind" the death of Gerald is a criticism not only of the British fear of emotion but also of liberalism's incompetence before tragedy.[9]

Afraid of the word *death*, the liberal is perhaps all too partial to the word *mad* to describe things beyond his ken: a defecting Party member in fear for his life, a student who speaks and writes in a "torrential rhetoric" that never quite makes good sense.

And his response to Tertan is certainly the measure of Howe's qualities as a teacher, especially of modern literature. Some seventeen years after the appearance of the short story, Trilling gave an account of his own pedagogical problems ("On the Teaching of Modern Literature"). The chief difficulty lay in the nature of the subject: "Nothing is more characteristic of modern literature," wrote Trilling, "than its discovery and canalization of the primal, non-ethical energies." The trouble was that to avoid self-confession, the teacher had to present the material formalistically, as a structure of words from which he and the students were detached. This approach exacerbated the natural tendency of the students "to socialize the antisocial, acculturate the anticultural, and to legitimize the subversive":

> I asked them to look into the Abyss, and, both dutifully and gladly, they have looked into the Abyss, and the Abyss has greeted them with the grave courtesy of all objects of serious study, saying: "Interesting, am I not?"[10]

What is wrong with exam questions is not that they are ridiculous but that they make "such good sense that the young person who answers them can never again know the force and terror of what has been communicated to him by the works he is being examined on." Trilling finally decides to give the course "without strategies" or any attempt to conceal his "relation to the literature," his "commitment to it," his "fear of it," his "ambivalence toward it." This attitude is, I think, relevant to our judgment of Howe, who teaches literature by discussion, the very method, Trilling tells us in the essay, that is necessary to formalistic analysis. In any case, we do not really know what Howe feels about what he is teaching and ironically it is at the very moment that Tertan puts his finger on a crucial point in an Ibsen tragedy that he betrays what Howe takes to be brilliant madness. But whatever his approach, Howe's response to Tertan shows him to be guilty

of the same pigeonholing and categorization that marks the classroom domestication of modern literature.

Trilling's views on the teaching of modern literature are, as I
have implied, part of an overall conception of culture and the
opposing elements within and beyond it. Where Fiedler says
"No!" in thunder, Trilling says it with gentility, if no less persistently. But in his whole style Trilling reveals an undeniable commitment to culture. It is difficult to imagine him as the spokesman
for the irrational, and impossible to imagine him conjuring up
terror in the classrooms of 116th Street.

But aside from this, Trilling's formulation of the teaching
problem is based on an affective theory of literature—a belief that
modern works are "not static and commemorative but mobile
and aggressive." These are compelling words but do they indicate the whole picture? Camus' *The Plague,* for example, is as
much the study of a group of heroic men who refuse to play the
role of heroes as it is a vision of the Abyss. Sartre's *Nausea,*
another vision of the abyss behind familiarity, has behind it an
entire philosophy, a grasp of whose principles is essential to a full
appreciation of the work. That Absurd Man, Beckett's Molloy, is
so complex a bundle of contradictions that the reader is forced
to stand back and observe him in detachment before his impact
can be felt.

No, the contemporary poem or novel, like its antecedents,
contains much that requires cool thought as well as emotion,
objective analysis as well as pity and terror. That is really the only
excuse for bringing it into the classroom, for few teachers can
successfully play the role of *guru,* and, if they could, they would
no longer be teachers as the word is understood in the university.
"I asked them to look into the Abyss"—what kind of response did
Trilling expect from his students when his whole position was
that of official guide?

Trilling, like Fiedler, says that formalistic analysis (which he tried out in class) goes against his grain. The feeling is probably common to all social critics. But in both Fiedler and Trilling antiformalism is, again, part of a larger pattern of dissent, a pattern that in its turn is part of a total view of literature and society. Fiedler is the well-read *enfant terrible* and Trilling the erudite gentleman, and they each represent different kinds of dissent. Furthermore, where Fiedler is frankly given to extra-literary generalizations and is a self-styled "literary anthropologist," Trilling is much more sensitive to literary tradition and his insights are therefore more convincing. Yet both men can be the victims of their methodologies and a priori conceptions. It seems to be one of the truths of life that if the formalist is prone to myopia, the social critic is prone to hyperopia. Only a blind man can afford to prefer one to the exclusion of the other, and neither Fiedler nor Trilling is blind.

NOTES

1. *No! in Thunder, Essays in Myth and Literature* (Beacon Press, Boston, 1960), p. 7. Hereafter cited as *NIT*. Other works cited include *Love and Death in the American Novel*, rev. ed. (Delta, New York, 1966) (LD), *Waiting for the End* (Stein and Day, New York, 1964) (WFE), *The Return of the Vanishing American* (Stein and Day, New York, 1968), and *Being Busted* (Stein and Day, New York, 1969) (*BB*). Fiction cited includes *Back to China* (Stein and Day, New York, 1965) and *The Last Jew in America* (Stein and Day, New York, 1966).

2. *Tender Is the Night* (Scribners, New York, n.d. paperback ed.), pp. 140-41.

3. The *Indiana* section may be another story. I have myself asserted elsewhere that Crane, probably because of homosexual impulses, reversed the male-female symbols by assigning to "Larry" the role of the "prodigal" normally associated with the evanescent goddess. Since I was trying to explain a distortion in the pattern, rather than expose the

aberrations of the poet, I remain unabashed. The reader interested in pursuing this problem in methodology can find my discussion in *Hart Crane's Sanskrit Charge, A Study of* THE BRIDGE (Cornell, Ithaca, 1960).

4. *The Middle of the Journey* (Viking, New York, 1947), p. 301.

5. *The Liberal Imagination, Essays on Literature and Society* (Doubleday, Garden City, N.Y.: 1953, paperback ed.), p. 9.

6. *Freud and the Crisis of Our Culture* (Beacon, Boston, 1955), p. 48.

7. Originally published in *The Partisan Review*, the story has been widely anthologized. My own source has been *Fifty Best American Short Stories, 1915–1965*, ed. Martha Foley (Houghton Mifflin, Boston, 1965).

8. *Matthew Arnold*, (Meridian, New York, 1955, paperback ed.), pp. 237–38. (The book was originally published by Norton in 1939.) Trilling was obliged to defend Arnold against charges that he was a reactionary.

9. *E. M. Forster*, (New Directions, New York, 1964, paperback ed.), p. 23.

10. In *Beyond Culture, Essays on Literature and Learning* (Viking, New York, 1965), p. 27.

Jewish Mothers and Sons:
The Expense of *Chutzpah*

MELVIN J. FRIEDMAN

"The dean said, 'Jane Austen and a solid Jewish mother would agree on many things—particularly marriages.' "—Renata Adler, "Downers and Séances" (*The New Yorker*, February 13, 1971)

"I do once in a while, like this portrait of you I'm working on now, but I always go back to 'Mother and Son.' "—Bernard Malamud, *Pictures of Fidelman*

Memories of a Non-Jewish Childhood is the title of a recent novel by Robert Byrne. (Non-Jewish seems to suggest something which Christian does not!) We have reached the point of believing that the experience of the Jewish—especially involving the relationship between mother and son—is so special that everything must be measured in terms of it. Even in that Judeo-Irish family, Salinger's Glass clan—with an Irish mother née Bessie Gallagher—the Jewish clearly wins out. It is the "Jewish mother" who asserts herself in "Zooey": "Her [Bessie's] entrances into rooms were usually verbal as well as physical."[1] Her overpowering concern, as she first enters the bathroom and finds her son Zooey in the tub, is characteristically with "post-bath drafts." J. D. Salinger is himself half-Jewish as was Marcel Proust before him. It was Proust, we should remember, who probably introduced into modern literature that obsessive attachment between mother and son; it is difficult to forget those frustrating moments in *Swann's Way* when the narrator Marcel waits for his mother's goodnight kiss.

All the to-do about this relationship between mother and son, Jewish-fashion, seems to be very much with us at the moment. The subject has found its ideal chronicler in Philip Roth, but other talented writers like Herbert Gold, Bruce Jay Friedman, and Wallace Markfield have continued to make us aware of its splendid comic possibilities. It has almost reached the point where Jewish writers must apologize for either depicting a serious mother-son relationship or else ignoring the subject entirely. Mrs. Portnoy and her near-relatives in Bruce Jay Friedman, Herbert Gold, and Wallace Markfield have displaced the type of the resigned, retiring, and gentle mother.

Before the current vogue in assertive, overpowering Jewish mothers, which has found its way into advertising, television, and the popular press, as well as into fiction, there was a less colorful, less aggressive figure who displayed uncommon good sense in an unspectacular way. This earlier Jewish mother, part of the ghetto world of eastern Europe or the newly arrived immigrant group in urban America, was distinguished by her muted suffering, her calm devotion to family (especially to her husband and sons), her fine sense of balance and stability. Isaac Bashevis Singer, in his autobiographical book *In My Father's Court,* speaks of his own mother as being agreeably heterodox, as offering a buffer to the talmudic excesses of his rabbinical father. She was the ideal Rebbetzin for an unworldly husband who was more devoted to sacred texts than to the raising of a family. Her logic splendidly offset his mysticism.

The most appealing of this type of Jewish mother is doubtless

Mrs. Schearl in Henry Roth's *Call It Sleep*. She is the self-effacing immigrant mother and wife who reacts with extreme courage to poverty and displacement. She is a true figure of the diaspora, with a built-in sense of suffering and survival. Her devotion to her son David is one of the most compelling relationships expressed anywhere in the history of the novel, as Leslie Fiedler, Alfred Kazin, Walter Allen, and others have continued to remind us. Jewish mother and son turn Yiddish into poetry as they speak a special language of exclusions—which shuts out their poverty-ridden surroundings and the tyrannical threats of the pater-familias, Albert Schearl. Roth's mother and son are concerned with being and have discarded all notions of becoming. They are a long way from the Portnoys, mother and son, with their affluent society and their assured urban sophistication. *Call It Sleep* is a product of the Depression years—those years devastatingly chronicled in such books as Tom Kromer's *Waiting for Nothing*— and it nods toward the underprivileged, the deprived. The Jew, arriving in New York, just off the boat from eastern Europe in 1907 (in this case the Schearl family) has the same sense of urban desperation as those unfortunate victims of the years of priva-tion, the 1930's.

Isaac Singer's mother and Roth's Mrs. Schearl are products of a condition which seems almost a contradiction in terms, Jews without money (an expression, incidentally, which was used as the title of a 1930 book by Michael Gold). *Newsweek* reminded us recently, in the issue of March 1, 1971, devoted to "The Ameri-can Jew Today," how well off Jews are as they continue to make their presences felt in the more lucrative professions. It is difficult to reconcile this view of prosperity with the Jewish childhoods described in such books as Alfred Kazin's *A Walker in the City* and Norman Podhoretz's *Making It*. Kazin and Podhoretz depict their mothers with the kind of respectful sympathy which we associate with Henry Roth's treatment of Mrs. Schearl. Here is Kazin at his most lyrical: "Poor as we were, it was not poverty that drove my mother so hard; it was loneliness—some endless bitter brooding over all those left behind, dead or dying or soon to die; a loneliness locked up in her kitchen that dwelt every day on the hazardousness of life and the nearness of death, but still kept struggling in the lock, trying to get us through by endless labor."[2]

Jewish fiction writers since World War II seem to have abandoned this tortured, deprived, Depression-ridden view in favor of something more luxuriant. The Jewish mother of Henry Roth's novel and of Singer's, Kazin's, and Podhoretz's autobiographical writings is replaced gradually by the exaggerated comic figure who dedicates her unlimited leisure to extracting guilt from her son. Her anguish is of a very different sort from that of her predecessor; what matters most is insistently reminding her son of his ingratitude and filial irresponsibility—it becomes a full-time profession, with its own peculiar rewards.

Before turning to this latter type, it might be well to define an intermediary between Mrs. Portnoy and Mrs. Schearl. We find her most imaginatively realized in Romain Gary's autobiographical book, *Promise at Dawn*. Gary's mother, more the subject of these memoirs than himself, achieves success vicariously through her son. There is something picaresque about her, both in the way she moves about from place to place (an odyssey starting in Vilna and ending up in France) and in the way she engages in mild roguery—always for the sake of her son. Her ambitions for her son, much like those of Mrs. Portnoy and Bruce Jay Friedman's mothers, are boundless. But unlike them she is willing to sacrifice endlessly (not in words only). She emerges as a creature of rare and admirable heroism who reaches her grandest heights when concealing her own death from her son: "During the last few days before her death, she had written nearly two hundred and fifty letters and sent them to her friend in Switzerland. I was not to know that she was no longer there to support me—the undated letters were to be forwarded to me at regular intervals —this was, no doubt, what she was scheming with so much love when I had caught that naïve and cunning expression in her eyes, when we parted for the last time at the Saint-Antoine clinic."[3] She has a cunning and sophistication unknown to the ghetto mother and a genuineness unfamiliar to the guilt-extracting mother.

Romain Gary fittingly ends his autobiography by printing the last letter from his mother. One sentence in it is quite uncharacteristic of the later strain of Jewish mother: "Just as you never saddened me but gave me only joy." The mothers of Philip Roth, Bruce Jay Friedman, and Wallace Markfield would never admit— even in a death-bed farewell—that their sons gave them anything but *tzuris*. They hold on tenaciously to the precept that the Jewish mother is constitutionally a sufferer for her son's ingratitude.

Henry Roth's Mrs. Schearl and the mothers of Kazin's, Podhoretz's, and Gary's memoirs are acutely aware of the problems of survival and the horrors of poverty. When the Jewish mother begins to taste the move agreeable fruits of affluence, she then has the leisure to concentrate on her legitimate avocation (at least according to Philip Roth), the matter of extracting guilt from her son. American-Jewish sons came home in large numbers from the Second World War only to find this unexpected adversary ready to stuff their mouths with unbelievable quantities of food, ready to arrange marriages with "nice Jewish girls" for them, ready to run all aspects of their lives.

And this is where we presently stand in the coming of age of the Jewish mother. She is at the nerve center of the Jewish novel of the sixties. She has forced the father into a protesting but submissive background role and has isolated herself in direct confrontation with her son. In a sense, this mother-son relationship—usually very little touched by Freud and Oedipus[4]—has replaced a long-standing connection between ogreish father and tempting daughter, which has made its presence felt in literature from *The Jew of Malta* and *The Merchant of Venice* through *Daniel Deronda*.[5] The Jewish mother, armed to the teeth with such contemporary weapons as her son's feelings of guilt and her own assurance of self-sacrifice, manages to fight her son to a standoff; a psychoanalyst is often available to lead the son off protestingly to a psychiatric couch for a secular exercise in confession. The possibilites of this subject are far more tempting than those involving a beautiful daughter outwitting her tyrannical Jewish father by making off with her Christian lover, and they certainly appeal more to the contemporary imagination.

As I have already suggested, this new image of the Jewish mother has not only captured the fancy of the fiction writer but has also invaded other more popular areas. David Susskind's television talk show, which has always served as a convincing barometer of eccentricity, has twice acknowledged its relevance: once with a gathering of Jewish mothers, the second time with a group of Jewish sons. There is no such thing as a "famous" or "successful" Jewish mother (she is usually too busy making her son "famous" and "successful" to have any time left for herself) so Susskind rounded up unknowns for his mothers. When turning to the sons, however, he managed to come up with celebrities—who owe it all to the efforts of their mothers. Susskind seems to have been accommodating this mythos that the Jewish mother basks in obscurity while her son goes on to win fame and fortune; he is, after all, a famous Jewish son himself! The mothers spoke the language we have grown accustomed to since the days of Bessie Glass; there was little special about them other than their rhetoric and their pride in the accomplishment of their sons. The Jewish sons, who appeared more than a year later, included Mel Brooks, George Segal, David Steinberg, and Dan Greenburg (who had already distinguished himself in this area with that classic text *How to Be a Jewish Mother*). Mel Brooks, with superb irony, proceeded to dominate much of the discussion although he willingly admitted selling-out by marrying a *shiksa*, the actress Anne Bancroft.

We should now give some attention to the individual literary occurrences of this type of mother. Herbert Gold's *Fathers*, subtitled "a novel in the form of a memoir," offers some brilliant confrontations between mother and son. Mrs. Gold, with her "waricose weins," does three of the things we associate with the species: she distorts her son's age at every turn to suit her convenience; she lives in perpetual fear that he will not marry "a nice Jewish girl"; and she runs down his achievements to his face and praises him out of all proportion behind his back. We see the first two at work in the following exchange:

> "You're only fourteen years old."
> "Fifteen, going on sixteen."
> "You're too young to marry a shiksa."
> "Who said I wanted to marry anyone? Just because I'm in love with Pattie doesn't mean I can marry her." Sadistically, ominously, oedipally I added: "Yet."
> "Oh! oh! aie!" sobbed my mother, struck at her core.
> "Fifteen years old," I pursued her angrily. "Why can't I be my own age?"⁶

We notice the Jewish mother's irresistible logic doing full-time duty in this passage. She extracts a final promise from Herbert before she allows him to play baseball with the other boys: "No shiksas. A nice Jewish girl from a good family, plays the piano, not flat-chested, educated." (p. 144)

Herbert comes off badly when his mother compares him—which she does all the time—to Aunt Sarah's son Bernie ("such a go-getter!"). Yet in a head-on phone conversation with Aunt Sarah (another vintage Jewish mother) we get this rather differ-

ent slant: " 'So how's your Bernie? My Herbert shouldn't be
better, he got a all-A report card and with a B plus in gymnistics
[*sic*; the Jewish son is traditionally less good in gym than in the
academic subjects—his strength is in his mind, not in his body],
he gained two pounds by the scale. . . .' " (p. 138)

Herbert Gold's book, as its title indicates, is more about the
father than the mother. All that matters in Bruce Jay Friedman's
A Mother's Kisses is the mother. Friedman actually introduces the
type with great success into his first novel, *Stern*, but there makes
only occasional use of her. Stern is a thirty-four-year-old husband
and father of a son. Yet his mother has clearly not given him up.
When he announces on one occasion that he has an ulcer, his
mother's response is predictable: " 'That's what I needed. . . . I
don't have enough. That's the perfect extra thing I need to
carry.' " And after some remarks are exchanged, she continues:
" 'I'm not going to worry about it . . . , I can't kill myself. I've had
disappointments in my life, too. Plenty of them. I could tell you
plenty.' "[7] "I could tell you plenty" threads its way through most
of her comments and acts as a leitmotiv. Another dimension,
noticeable before only in Romain Gary's mother, is that she believes herself to be irresistible to men, a femme fatale.

In a sense, Stern's mother is a dry run for that remarkably
aggressive and overbearing central figure in *A Mother's Kisses*.
Joseph's mother is a veritable dynamo who arranges not only to
get her son into a Kansas college after Bates and Columbia have
emphatically turned him down but then moves in with him to
oversee an embarrassingly long stretch of his freshman year. Just
as Stern's mother's leitmotiv was "I could tell you plenty," Joseph's mother's is "you're going through some period." She
knows all the answers and keeps offering this incontrovertible bit
of evidence as to her infallibility: "Your mother's always wrong.
That's why they made her your mother."[8] The sexual is a very
important part of her makeup, as she prides herself on her own

irresistibility to men and urges her son on to successes with women. David Steinberg commented on the David Susskind show that "in New York all the Gentiles are Jews"; Joseph's mother extends the remark: "Everybody's a Jew these days." She can smoke out Jews from the remotest corners of Kansas and usually ends up by embarrassing them into admitting their carefully concealed identities.

A Mother's Kisses suffers from excessive exposure of the Jewish mother. Her too constant presence on stage leads in the direction of caricature and slapstick comedy. She is removed too far from a family situation to be entirely convincing. A novelist is often more effective when he introduces the Jewish mother only sparingly into the narrative and thrusts her into domestic conflicts. The pre-wedding (a wedding which never takes place) scenes in Myron S. Kaufmann's *Thy Daughter's Nakedness* are such an example. Mrs. Hollander increases doubts in her son's mind about the approaching marriage; she manages to touch on all the sensitive points: " 'That girl's been taking advantage of you. You said she was beautiful, but I don't see it. I think she's a little odd-looking. Cross-eyed, if you ask me.' "[9] Every Jewish son has been through this night-before-the-wedding ordeal with his mother but usually survives it and goes on to get married the next day. Not Leslie Hollander. The combination of his own reservations and his mother's gentle nudges causes untold embarrassment to the bride's family as the wedding guests are sent home without benefit of a marriage ceremony. In a fine moment, worthy of the most presumptuous and aggressive Jewish mother, Mrs. Hollander is seen trying to load the car with a great number of boxes, shouting to all interested parties, "These were all from our side." (p. 665) She characteristically exits with the "spoils."

Wallace Markfield belongs in our discussion, if only because of a whimsical review of Irving Stone's *The Passions of the Mind, A Novel of Sigmund Freud* which he wrote for the March 14, 1971,

New York Times Book Review. The review takes the form of a letter from Aunt Syl to her nephew (read Jewish mother to Jewish son). The word plays and syntax are precisely right in a sentence like this one: "As far as his writing is concerned—well, maybe you have an old-fashioned aunt, but I'm very happy Mr. Stone is a refined author of elegant style and doesn't give me *tzuris* like Uris, who's getting lately altogether too experimental." (p. 7) Aunt Syl proceeds to quote cliché-ridden samples of Irving Stone's prose and dialogue, justifying them on Jewish-mother grounds: she speaks of "his swell and matchless ear," "his gift for gab," his "scenes that really tear your heart out." She ends by suggesting that the book would make a fine movie and that it is regrettable that Paul Muni (the beloved of every Jewish mother) is no longer alive to play "Sigi" (Sigmund Freud).

Wallace Markfield's first novel, *To an Early Grave* has the ambience of Jewish intellectual New York but, alas, without a Jewish mother on stage. Barnet Weiner, "poet, critic, contributor to the literary quarterlies," does have a more than passing attachment for his mother. He extols her homemade applesauce and chicken soup and urges his current girl friend to visit her. On the way back from his friend Braverman's funeral at the end of the novel, Weiner tries to reach his mother by phone and after several aborted attempts gets through; his relief is as noticeable as his guilt was earlier. Markfield unfortunately denies us the phone conversation as he does the physical presence and dialogue of the mother.

In his latest novel, *Teitlebaum's Window*, we get the Jewish mother very much in the flesh, she of the "dropped stomach," the gargantuan stutter, and the dislocated syntax. Simon's mother hovers in the background but comes forward when needed to pronounce the expected sentiments and words: "In this spirit I want to wish my son *very very very* good luck in his present under taking [*sic*] also in all his endeavors, and what I want for him is what *he* wants and what will give *him* happiness, my hopes are unselfish hopes, only that he should have a happy mother with him at his side for a hundred and 20 years and that she should only only be in the best of health and that with the help of the ALMIGHTY she should have much better then [*sic*] she had."[10] The syntax and vocabulary are unmistakably right. Only a Jewish mother could manage all this in a single sentence. *Teitlebaum's Window* is the Brighton Beach-Coney Island version of the *Bildungsroman*, the Jewish boy coming of age with gentle and helpful proddings from his mother.

Philip Roth writes in *Portnoy's Complaint:* "The novelist, what's his name, Markfield, has written in a story somewhere that until he was fourteen he believed 'aggravation' to be a Jewish word."[11] Philip Roth understands better than any of his contemporaries, even Wallace Markfield, what constitutes aggravation and, in turn, a Jewish mother. On second thought, perhaps no better than Dan Greenburg, the Stephen Potter of the world of Jewish mothers and author of *How to Be a Jewish Mother: A Very Lovely Training Manual.* Greenburg's contribution to the literature of Jewish mothers is a slim volume in bold print with many line drawings, most of which look like figures in a geometry textbook and resemble in their feigned complexity Rube Goldberg's labyrinthine efforts. Like Potter's *Lifemanship* and *Gamesmanship,* Dan Greenburg's *How to Be a Jewish Mother* is a guide to outwitting your opponent without his realizing that he's been outwitted; in this case the Jewish mother, by a variety of stratagems, brings to the surface all the guilt she can manage in her opponent the Jewish son—mainly by opening filial wounds which he never imagined existed. (Greenburg's own mother was doubtless delighted that her son's book was a best-seller in 1965, but probably less than happy that the paperback edition continues to sell for only one dollar. The Jewish mother casts a practiced eye on her son's royalty checks, which are the surest—and indeed the only

—measure of his success.) One sentence from the "Foreword by the Author's Mother" makes the point incisively: "You'd think that it wouldn't be such a hardship on a young man who writes so nicely to write an occasional letter to his mother who loves him, but it seems there are more important things to a young man these days than his mother." The syntax of this sentence, like others we have observed already, brilliantly avoids logical structures and twists and turns like a snake. The sigh of resignation following the comma is unmistakable. Dan Greenburg is obviously tuned in on the cadence of the Jewish mother's rhetoric and knows how to reproduce its complex rhythms.

We should not delay much longer discussing Roth's third novel, *Portnoy's Complaint,* which benefits so remarkably from the atmosphere which surrounds the Jewish mother mystique. Following its publication every son received from his Jewish mother (present writer included) a note with the following rhetorical question, "am I a Mrs. Portnoy?" Roth has faithfully labored in the vineyards since his early collection of stories, *Goodbye, Columbus.* In the title story he gives us a variant on the Jewish mother in the person of Aunt Gladys. In a telephone conversation between Neil Klugman and his Aunt Gladys we have this incisively Jewish mother-Jewish son encounter:

> "You've got clean underwear?"
> "I'm washing it at night. I'm okay, Aunt Gladys."
> "By hand you can't get it clean."
> "It's clean enough. Look, Aunt Gladys, I'm having a wonderful time."
> "*Shmutz* he lives in and I shouldn't worry."
> "How's Uncle Max?" I asked.
> "What should he be? Uncle Max is Uncle Max. You, I don't like the way your voice sounds."
> "Why? Do I sound like I've got on dirty underwear?"
> "Smart guy. Someday you'll learn."[12]

The exchange of Jewish repartee goes on for another half page; it is clear that Roth is very close to the pulse beat of this very special language and syntax. If there is such a thing as a Jewish language (I am not thinking of Yiddish—although it does figure in—or Hebrew now) Roth has always known how to write it.

Roth is at his best, it seems to me, when writing about Jews. Thus his finest accomplishments have been *Goodbye, Columbus* and *Portnoy's Complaint,* with their unmistakably Jewish ambience almost from beginning to end. His weakest book *When She Was Good,* with its midwestern Protestantism, is far removed from his accustomed moral and verbal setting. Theodore Solotaroff, one of the few critics who liked it, seemed especially charitable in speaking of its "language of scrupulous banality." *Letting Go* is a good novel in its Jewish moments; much less good when it tries strenuously to make its contribution to American literature, via the genre of the academic novel (which incidentally goes back as far as Hawthorne's *Fanshawe*).

Portnoy's Complaint comes out of the best pages of *Goodbye, Columbus* and *Letting Go.* One can even extract from it a glossary of Jewish-mother language, favoring expressions like "someday you'll be a parent and you'll know what it's like," "you know me, I'll try anything once," "God *forbid!*", "I'm only asking you to do it for your own good," "maybe I'm too good," which are repeated ad nauseam. Roth has settled here on all the things he knows how to do best, especially in his creation of the urban Jewish family with the mother at its moral center. Jews have proved more tolerant of the kind of in-group exposure which Roth offers in *Portnoy* than blacks have when confronted with any variety of the Sambo image. Of course, the pill is easier to swallow when pleasantly sugarcoated by a member of the tribe. The white man putting on black face, be he Stanley M. Elkins, William Styron, or Amos and Andy, leaves the bitter taste of the outsider intruding where he is not welcome. Roth, the insider, somehow seems always to be welcome.

Roth has given it his all in *Portnoy's Complaint*, apparently not fearing reprisals from the antisemitic community, the Anti-Defamation League, or the ubiquitous bluenoses. He has gambled on our infatuation with the Jewish mother. While he only got his feet wet in the stories of *Goodbye, Columbus* and the Jewish pages of *Letting Go*, he has ventured into deep water, occasionally over his head, in *Portnoy*. He has played a somewhat daring game also in making the novel a staccato confession, in heavily free associative prose, with a foreign-born psychiatrist on the receiving end—waiting to utter the final ironical words of the book in a broken German-Jewish: "Now vee may perhaps to begin. Yes?" Lillian Ross had already brilliantly handled the Jewish psychoanalyst with her Dr. Blauberman (blabbermouth?) in *Vertical and Horizontal.* Now Roth lets us listen in on the almost unbroken monologue of the patient, Alexander Portnoy, from his reclining vantage point—respecting the silence of the analyst until the final line.

Portnoy begins with a section entitled "The Most Unforgettable Character I've Met"—this schoolboyish title refers naturally to Alex's mother. She is the dominant member of a family (what else can a Jewish mother be?) which includes the "genius" son Alexander, the perpetually constipated and henpecked insurance-salesman father, the stout older sister with small breasts and even smaller sex appeal. The family including a mother, father, son, and daughter is clearly one of the *données* of American-Jewish fiction; Roth saw its possibilities earlier in his career but failed to realize its full potential until *Portnoy's Complaint.* Each member of the family has become almost a literary set piece in Roth's dexterous hands. Predictably, the mother is fiercely aggressive and domineering (a near-relative of Salinger's Bessie Glass and the mothers of Bruce Jay Friedman, Romain Gary, and Wallace Markfield); the father is unduly apologetic about his constipation and his modest means; the son is vengeful, sexually active (in fantasy and in practice), and enviably clever; the daughter is devoted to hearth and home and all the other pieties and banalities.

It is the son who does the confessing from the analyst's couch and it is he who feels most keenly "the bonds obtaining in the mother-child relationship." Alexander Portnoy requires psychiatric help, not his Jewish mother. That is always the way. Mrs. Sophie Portnoy exudes confidence and knows all the answers. When Alex emerges from the single family bathroom (which his constipated father covets) after an extended and joyful siege of masturbation, he conceals his sins and destroys the evidence by flushing the toilet. When confronted with a moment of truth he pleads diarrhea. Here is his mother's response, the same one that Dan Greenburg's Jewish mother would probably offer:

> "Oh, don't you shout at *me*, Alex. I'm not the one who gave you diarrhea, I assure you. If all you ate was what you were fed at home, you wouldn't be running to the bathroom fifty times a day. Hannah [Alex's sister] tells me what you're doing, so don't think I don't know." (p. 23)

Alex thinks for an uncomfortable moment that his mother has finally found him out. But the Jewish mother has too many infallibly ready and morally right answers to worry about the truth; she can be counted on to miss the point:

> "You go to Harold's Hot Dog and *Chazerai* Palace after school and you eat French fries with Melvin Weiner. Don't you? Don't lie to me either. Do you or do you not stuff yourself with French fries and ketchup on Hawthorne Avenue after school?" (p. 24)

Alex gets even with his mother by extending his masturbatory practices behind the locked door of the bathroom until he is ready to fulfill his needs with the opposite sex—and usually (crime of crimes!) with *shiksas*. He reaches a kind of sexual crescendo in his affair with The Monkey, a nymphomaniac *par excellence*, but has several other relationships with the midwestern Antioch girl, Kay Campbell (who seems almost out of *When She Was Good*), and with a sophisticated New England girl, Sarah Abbott Maulsby, just graduated from Vassar. Alex clearly has *shiksa*-on-the-mind; he even suspects that his father must be carrying on with a Gentile spinster at the office whom he brings home one evening "for a real Jewish meal."

Alex is very successful in uncovering chinks in his mother's armor, but always at the expense, so he discovers later on, of his own too active feelings of guilt. His mother, as he says in the first line of the novel, is "deeply imbedded in my consciousness." He can taunt her with *shiksas*, with abuse of Rabbi Warshaw ("a fat, pompous, impatient fraud, with an absolutely grotesque superiority complex, a character out of Dickens"), with denial of religion, God, and the Jewish holidays, but her Yiddish-tuned voice always has the final say as it dismisses the entire Christian world with its *"goyische* taste."

Portnoy's Complaint never stops being about the mother-son confrontation. There are indeed other concerns in the novel, but somehow they have a way of bringing Alexander Portnoy back to his mother, for everything "can be traced to the bonds obtaining in the mother-child relationship." The free associative movement of the confessional has a kind of circular rhythm which could easily have suggested a book starting in the middle of a sentence, like *Finnegans Wake*, if Roth were not by nature a more tradition-bound writer than Joyce. If Roth had chosen to start in the middle of a sentence he could have used Joyce's first three words, "riverrun, past Eve," but not his fourth and fifth, "and Adam's."

Portnoy has given a conclusive form and texture to the image of the Jewish mother, something Friedman, Markfield, Gold, Salinger, and others have failed to do in their fiction. Sophie Portnoy has finally put the Jewish mother on the defensive. An article in *The Milwaukee Journal* (April 20, 1969) carried the title "Jewish Mother Image Irks Jewish Mothers." Mothers of prominent Jews were interviewed following the publication of *Portnoy's Complaint* and the general opinion seemed to be that there was not much difference among mothers, whether Jewish or Gentile. Philip Roth's own mother went along with the consensus, but with an interesting twist: "I think all mothers are Jewish mothers."

The matter was taken up again in "The Liberation of the Yiddisha Mama" (*The Village Voice*, February 11, 1971). Rachael Goldman, in this article, begins by engaging in a certain amount of self-caricature: "*I* speak for her [the Jewish mother] for I am she and she is me and I too am a victim and I am trying to liberate myself. Will I ever be able to simply say 'the coffee's on the stove' and not worry about *not* getting up?" (p. 26) Then she asserts the positive side of the issue and offers a quite compelling defense.[13]

We have probably by now concluded that the Jewish mother is too much with us. Perhaps she will have less effect on the fiction of the seventies than she had on that of the sixties. In any case, she is certain to undergo some sort of change, if only to accommodate such latter-day movements as Women's Liberation. In "The American Jew Today" (*Newsweek*, March 1, 1971), a magazine editor was quoted as saying: "The Jewish mother here used to say of her son, 'I hope he doesn't marry a gentile.' Now she says, 'thank God, the boy married a white girl.' " That represents real progress.

NOTES

1. J. D. Salinger, *Franny and Zooey* (Boston and Toronto: Little, Brown, 1961), p. 72.

2. Alfred Kazin, *A Walker in the City* (New York: Harcourt, Brace & World, 1951), pp. 69-70.

3. Romain Gary, *Promise at Dawn*, trans. John Markham Beach (New York: Harper, 1961), p. 332. All subsequent references will be to this edition.

4. Romain Gary's remark is fairly accurate and typical: "I have never had incestuous leanings toward my mother." (p. 64)

5. See Hyam Maccoby, "The Delectable Daughter," *Midstream*, XVI (November, 1970), pp. 50-60.

6. Herbert Gold, *Fathers* (New York: Fawcett, 1968), p. 144. All subsequent references will be to this edition. Elsewhere in the novel Gold offers one of the really fine definitions of that untranslatable Yiddish word: ". . . 'Chutzpah' means 'hubris,' that mad pride which led so many Greeks into trouble by assuring them that twenty-twenty vision and pubic hair all of one color do not make the man . . ." (p. 93).

7. Bruce Jay Friedman, *Stern* (New York: Simon and Schuster, 1962), p. 106.

8. Bruce Jay Friedman, *A Mother's Kisses* (New York: Simon and Schuster, 1964), p. 216.

9. Myron S. Kaufmann, *Thy Daughter's Nakedness* (Philadelphia and New York: J.B. Lippincott, 1968), p. 645. All subsequent references will be to this edition.

10. Wallace Markfield, *Teitlebaum's Window* (New York: Knopf, 1970), p. 31.

11. Philip Roth, *Portnoy's Complaint* (New York: Bantam, 1970), p. 107. All subsequent references will be to this edition. See my review of *Portnoy* in *Tempest*, II (Winter, 1970), pp. 33-36.

12. Philip Roth, *Goodbye, Columbus* (New York: Bantam, 1970), p. 54.

13. Before the appearance of *Portnoy*, Zena Smith Blau wrote "In Defense of the Jewish Mother," in the February, 1967, *Midstream*, acknowledging such intriguing things as "The well-known ambivalence of the Jew toward his mother, then, is part and parcel of his ambivalence about remaining a Jew" (p. 44). Samuel Irving Bellman wrote a very

persuasive article, leaning heavily on the literary side, "The 'Jewish Mother' Syndrome" (*Congress Bi-Weekly*, December 27, 1965, pp. 3–5). Mr. Bellman's piece touches on some of the Jewish mothers I discuss here. One should also consult the recent study by Allen Guttmann, *The Jewish Writer in America: Assimilation and the Crisis of Identity* (New York: Oxford University Press, 1971).

Two articles of considerable interest appeared after the completion of the present essay. See Alan Warren Friedman, "The Jew's Complaint in Recent American Fiction: Beyond Exodus and Still in the Wilderness," *Southern Review*, VIII, New Series (January, 1972), pp. 41–59; Harold Fisch, "Fathers, Mothers, Sons and Lovers: Jewish and Gentile Patterns in Literature," *Midstream*, XVIII (March, 1972), pp. 37–45.

Bernard Malamud and the

Jewish Movement*

SHELDON NORMAN GREBSTEIN

Only those too perverse or fuzzy-headed to recognize cultural facts now refuse to acknowledge the existence of a Jewish Movement in contemporary American writing, and especially the writing of fiction. Saul Bellow, its brightest luminary, has been at work for more than thirty years. Bernard Malamud, a less spectacular but no less durable writer, began in the early 1950's. Even Philip Roth, just yesterday a child prodigy, has been around for better than ten years. In terms of simple longevity, then, the Jewish-American novel is more than a vogue. And with three such writers as Bellow, Malamud, and Roth, all versatile and consistently productive, it seems unlikely to fizzle out. As yet no signs appear of self-imitation, sure clue of a movement's degeneration. There is also an entire second string of writers of varying ages and abilities, Leslie Fiedler, Herbert Gold, Bruce Jay Friedman, to name but three. Not to speak of the Popular Front: e.g., Herman Wouk, Leon Uris, Jerome Weidman. Even those not aligned with the Movement, Norman Mailer and J.D. Salinger, contribute

*This study was supported by a Faculty Research Fellowship awarded by the Research Foundation of the State University of New York.

to it indirectly with an occasional half-Jewish hero and secularized Jewish *schmerz.*

Let's call this coincidence and coexistence of so many able Jewish writers just plain luck. After all, genius exists where you find it. But if luck were the only reason for this curious abundance of Jewish literati, and for the emergence of the Jew as a kind of culture hero, it wouldn't explain why so many of us read their books or why we are so fascinated by the Jew as literary character, or why, after twenty years, the Movement continues to thrive, or why these writers have had so much impact upon our consciousness. We have had Jewish writers before who wrote about Jews: Abraham Cahan, Ludwig Lewisohn, Ben Hecht, Henry Roth, Daniel Fuchs, Michael Gold; but whatever the reception of individual works—and it was sometimes enthusiastic, as in the case of Gold's *Jews Without Money*—there was nothing that could be described as a movement. Thus it seems a safe assumption that this particular time and place holds something unusually salubrious to Jewish genius. Whence this phenomenon, then, that we have been witnessing for the past generation?

In part, it was engendered by a void, born to occupy the space left by the decline or demise of other movements. The time was ripe, just after World War II, for the Great War Novel, but that novel was never written. As it turned out, instead of an entire body of writing we were given a few good books, including two by Jews which presented significant and appealing Jewish characters, Mailer's *The Naked and the Dead* and Shaw's *The Young Lions.* Hemingway and Faulkner, great as they were, surrendered their domination of the scene when it became evident that their best work had already been done. The Southern School proved to be puny. And the black writers never have put it all together, their rage and their talent, though their day could still be coming.

But more important, the Jewish Movement responded to an urgent cultural need. In short, and this is now a truism, the Jewish writer was made the beneficiary of Hitler's death camps. We

Americans, spared the war's worst horrors, had to know more about those piles of corpses, teeth, shoes, we saw in the newsreels. Whether out of guilt, morbid curiosity, or both, the Jew became important to us. In the Western imagination the Jew had always played a special role as wizard, magician, possessor of secret knowledge, but never before, until Auschwitz and Buchenwald, had such moral authority been conferred upon him. From hated, feared, or ridiculed figure, lurking on the fringes of the culture, he was transformed into the Man Who Suffered, Everyman. To Americans especially, ever respectful of eye-witness reports and ready to listen to the man who was there, the Jew compelled attention. If, as many believed, the annihilation of the Jews signified the end of the liberal ideal for human character, at least by hearkening to the Jew we might participate in the mourning, vicariously share some of the misery he had undergone, and perhaps gain a deeper understanding of what life was all about. Who could better instruct us than the Jews, those most expert and experienced sufferers? Others had taken a beating, yes, but what other group in human memory had been marked out for genocide?

Thus, the dominant and recurrent theme of the Jewish Movement, a theme which unifies its various members however different in method, is the theme of suffering. Furthermore, although such European-Jewish novels as André Schwartz-Bart's *The Last of the Just,* Elie Wiesel's *Night,* and Piotr Rawicz's *Blood from the Sky* treat the same theme with the unsurpassed authority of those who survived the annihilation, their work does not comprise a movement. We cannot bear their nihilistic suggestion that the suffering produced naught; or worse, that the European Jews collaborated in their own slaughter. Our writers, just far enough away from the holocaust to feel its heat but not be scorched, retain a little optimism, a little affirmation. With us, the suffering is meaningful. It can even be redemptive, stirring up a faint hope for the goodness of man after all. Jewish heroes may be *shlemiels* or *shlimazels* but unlike the major trend of much other contemporary fiction which depicts man as joke, cripple, or cipher, the Jewish-American writer continues to emphasize the fundamental worth of life and the possibility of humanity. Yet he does not retreat into the safe orthodoxy of formal religion. His affirmation is tough, qualified, secular. He is religious in that he portrays man as more than matter, but he is not pious.

I have been speaking about that abstraction "The Jewish Writer," but all along I have really been thinking about Bernard Malamud. Bellow may be flashier and more intellectually impressive, Roth may be subtler, shrewder, and funnier, but Malamud is to my taste the most solid, the most consistently fulfilled, and —I might as well get this chauvinism right out into the open— the most *Jewish*. What I mean is that Malamud best represents the phenomenon of the Jewish Movement; not only is he one of its founders and major practitioners, he is probably its best single exemplar. In Malamud's work we most clearly perceive just those characteristics which define the entire Movement.

First and foremost, there is the theme of meaningful suffering, which in Malamud also implies the quest for moral resolution and self-realization. But the theme of suffering cannot alone sustain either a movement or a writer's career. We can take just so much bad news. Malamud's writing, like that of the Movement at large, is also richly comic. Paradoxically, the comedy is at once a mode of expression of the suffering and a way of easing it. With the Jew humor is an escape valve for dangerous pressures, a manner of letting out things too painful to be kept in. (Could it be that one of the reasons we have able black writers like Ellison and Baldwin but not a Black Movement, is the prevailing solemnity of these writers?) Finally, the Jewish writer speaks in a distinctive literary voice. With Bellow and at about the same time, Malamud invented and perfected a fresh literary idiom, a "Jewish style." This style consists of much more than the importation of Yiddish words and phrases into English, or a mere broken Yiddish-English dialect, long the staple of popular works presenting lovably silly Jewish stereotypes *(Abie's Irish Rose)*. Rather, it is a significant development and expansion of the American colloquial style, established as a vital literary medium by Mark Twain. The Jewish style is for the first time in our literary history a voice that conveys ethnic characteristics, a special sort of sensibility, and the quality of a foreign language, yet remains familiar and eloquent to non-Jews. Although dialects and dialect styles tend to be reductive, rendering their speakers either funny or absurd, Malamud's style can evoke either tragic dignity or comic foolishness, or, miraculously, both at once.

These are the points I will stress in the pages to follow: suffering, comedy, style, as typical of Malamud and, by extension, of the Jewish Movement.

I

About suffering it is hard to say anything new because others have said so much. Virtually every critic who has written of Malamud—and there is already a sizable body of criticism—has examined this aspect of his work. In his lucid and intelligent first book on Malamud, *Bernard Malamud* (New York, 1966), Sidney Richman names this theme "redemptive suffering," which implies that the meaning of the suffering is to redeem both sufferer and, to some degree, those for whom he suffers (but not entirely, that's Christianity). Malamud thus follows in the ancient Jewish tradition of the prophets, Amos, Jeremiah, the Second Isaiah, who announce suffering to be the Jew's special destiny, evidence of his unique covenant with God, proof of God's concern in that only those who are loved are chastised, and the means of the Jew's peculiar awareness of his identity. Could Malamud have had this biblical passage in mind when he wrote *The Fixer*? The coincidence seems too close for sheer accident, embodying as it does the novel's fundamental situation and symbolism:

> I have given you . . . as a light to the nations,
>   to open the eyes that are blind,
> To bring out the prisoners from the dungeon,
>   from the prison those who sit in darkness.
>
> (ISAIAH, 42:7)

But this begins to make Malamud sound too holy, to suggest that his writing functions as biblical parable, which is not at all the case. He is a good Jew in his way, but he is not trying to rebuild the temple. As Malamud himself has said, "The purpose of the writer is to keep civilization from destroying itself. But without preachment. Artists cannot be ministers. As soon as they attempt it, they destroy their artistry." His heroes all suffer deeply, but they are also secular men whose suffering is not always voluntary, undertaken wholly for exalted reasons, or blessed by great rewards. Malamud's real concern is for the social and moral aspects of suffering as they impinge upon personality. If his characters expect some recompense for their misery, they would like it in the here and now. In sum, although we have no conclusive biographical evidence to assess Malamud's personal religious commitment, the testimony of his work suggests him to be an agnostic humanist. Some of his own remarks support that deduction: "My premise is that we will not destroy each other. My premise is that we will live on. We will seek a better life. We may not become better, but at least we will seek betterment."[1]

This is Malamud's real toughness, the factor that prevents his treatment of suffering from deteriorating into drippy melodrama or comfortable piety. He has a view of man which perceives the property of conscience, the seeking to be better, not as a divine mystery but as natural to humans as skin, hair, voice. Yet this basically optimistic concept of human nature is checked by an almost equally persistent view of man as greedy, treacherous, lustful, and often vicious. Cheerful idealist and hard-eyed realist peer out through the same bifocals.

Consequently, Malamud's depiction of suffering is ambivalent; in each of his major characters altruism and materialism combine as motives for self-sacrifice. In Malamud's first hero, Roy Hobbs of *The Natural*, materialism overpowers altruism. He has impulses for good but keeps making the wrong choices for the wrong reasons: baseball for glory rather than the joy of the game, a girl for sex not love, winning for prizes and payoffs. He never learns to live by the wise Iris' dictum, "Experience makes good people better. . . . Suffering is what brings us toward happiness. . . . It teaches us to want the right things."[2] Roy's venality is symbolized by two climactic episodes in the novel, in which he is twice stricken in the lower organs, suggestive of his errors in responding to the dictates of his appetites rather than his heart. When at the last minute his conscience does take command, he ruins the chance by giving in to other base instincts, anger and revenge. Again we ponder a coincidence: Malamud's only hero who submits neither to love nor to idealism, and whose sufferings are consequently futile, is his only hero not a Jew.

The Assistant, Malamud's masterpiece, achieves his most complex portrayal of suffering. Morris Bober seems a paragon, a holy man, in his honesty, his tolerance, his compassion. The dingy, starving store is illuminated by his goodness, so that when he instructs Frank Alpine in the meaning of Jewishness, "I suffer for you . . ., you suffer for me," his words have the force of his example.[3] Yet if the store is his earthly trial and his fate, it also serves as a retreat from the buffets of the world, a tomb and a prison. His daughter's final thought about him, at his grave, may be uncharitable but it contains truth: "He could, with a little more courage, have been more than he was."[4] This weakness in Morris, a flaw in his character, is symbolized throughout the novel by his vulnerability to natural forces, fire, gas, and at last the wind and the cold, which have been his enemies from the start.

Frank Alpine's motives are about equally divided between altruism and materialism. Conscience he has; it brings him back to the store to expiate his part in robbing Morris. He also aspires to a better life than that of drifter and hoodlum. And he has ambitions in love, for Helen. But there is a practical side to it. The store is warmer than the street or cellars. A job there offers food and a few bucks. Even the lowly status of poor shopkeeper or clerk is better than that of bum. And the girl is luscious: "Her body was young, soft, lovely, the breasts like small birds in flight, her ass like a flower."[5] When at the end Frank endures circumcision and becomes, in Malamud's cryptic phrase "a Jew," he has attained not only a moral apogee, the height implicit in his name, but has executed a deft romantic strategy as well. Helen can never again call him "uncircumcised dog."

The very title of *A New Life* repeats one of Malamud's basic ideas and the motive driving his heroes to their quests. Levin arrives in Cascadia on the run from his past as derelict drunk, his only conscious aim to make good out West. He wants only to please, to pick up experience, and then to win tenure as a college teacher. But all sorts of messes get dumped into his lap, literally in the opening episodes, figuratively thereafter. From private man he is transformed, willy-nilly, into a champion of the liberal arts, departmental reformer, and tender lover of another man's wife. To settle for merely making good means to collaborate in the fractured state of things, a dilemma symbolized by the cracked pane of glass in his office window looking out upon the campus. Should he sit there in comfort and security, mouth shut, and earn success, or should he try to right wrongs, thus breaking his chances for advancement? For a Malamudian hero it's a foregone conclusion. Thus, although he arrives empty-handed, he leaves with his hands full: the other man's wife, whom he has loved but no longer wants, her children, and a child of his own growing inside her. Why does he accept the responsibility? Out of some nutty Jewish compulsion for self-sacrifice, a mystery, wonderfully dramatized in a culminating scene between Levin and Gilley, the novel's bad guy, who has just offered to let him off the hook:

> "An older woman than yourself and not dependable, plus two adopted kids, no choice of yours, no job or promise of one, and other assorted headaches. Why take that load on yourself?"
> "Because I can, you son of a bitch."[6]

The same motivation must apply to Yakov Bok, hero of *The Fixer*. He endures the dreadful misery of his imprisonment not because of any lofty ideals but because he *must* do it. Even when he is made aware that his case has become a national concern and that his fate will affect the destiny of all Russian Jews, he refuses to surrender to his captors' threats or be seduced by their deals, not because he is a saintly martyr or idealist but because he is too stubborn to give in. Hate for his tormentors sustains him much more than love for mankind. Where idealism does enter into the novel, it appears only in glimmers. The most splendid example of it is Bibikov, the magistrate, whose attempt to get Yakov fair treatment under law results in his own death—although it should be noted that Bibikov acts perhaps less out of charity for Yakov than out of his own strict sense of duty and legality. Nevertheless, in standing by the law, Bibikov becomes, in Malamud's definition, a true Jew. Another case is the guard Kogin, who intercedes to save Yakov's life at the cost of his own. And then there is Yakov himself, who gives his name to his unfaithful and runaway wife's bastard child.

But despite these occasional miracles of character refined by suffering, the book more often than not stresses how suffering brutalizes, and man's brutishness in general. If *The Fixer* teaches a lesson, I read that lesson to be how the death camps were possible. By simple tabulation there are far more demented, stupid, ruthless, or sadistic people in *The Fixer* than decent men. Grubeshov, Father Anastasy, Berezhinsky, Marfa Golov—these seem to be the norm for human character. Ultimately only two affirmations rescue the book from bleakest despair: Yakov has been physically bent and weakened by his imprisonment but he has not been broken; and he will, finally, have his day in court. The persecuted and despised Jew will at last be heard.

Contrary to his name, Fidelman, the hero of Malamud's recent work *Pictures of Fidelman* is not so faithful. Innocent abroad in crafty, depraved Italy, he races around with his heart in his pants and his eye on Michelangelo's ceilings. Between his ambitions in art and his hot pants, he falls into much suffering. The sex complications are nothing new in Malamud, though never before rendered in such quantity or gusto; Malamud's men are always wanting women who are not good for them, having them, and then paying more than they can afford in emotional or moral currency. Throughout his work Malamud intimates that a Jew can't have sex just for fun, that it always gets complicated; and if we adduce the testimony of such other works as *Herzog* and *Portnoy's Complaint,* there seems to be a concurrence of Jewish opinion on the subject.

But sex and its problems is not the real subject of *Pictures of Fidelman;* it only shapes the plot. The novel's real subject is art, and the questions the book poses under its comic breath are about art: What is the relation of art to life? Which is more important in the making of good art, the artist's vision (i.e., character) or talent? Or, in terms of the subject of suffering: How is the artist's experience (suffering) transformed into art? If I interpret the book rightly, the answers it seems to give back are essentially anti-formalistic. To translate the concluding episode into a paradigm, a translation it demands, it says that before one can become a craftsman one must submit oneself in love to another, and be taught craft by him and the experience of love. Malamud makes the point with a startling sexual metaphor: that the love which leads to craft begins with the actual penetration by another. Fidelman finally abandons bad art and becomes a good craftsman, just as he becomes a good lover—instructed in both craft and love not by a woman but by a man. The novel's concluding sentence is at once absolutely clear as a culmination to Fidelman's saga and tantalizingly ambiguous as a general suggestion for conduct: "In America he worked as a craftsman in glass and loved men and women."[7]

The same emphasis on loving and its costs that we have seen in Malamud's novels is reiterated in his stories, from the first tale in *The Magic Barrel*, which ends with a man undergoing an unjust trial to prove a worthiness already proven, to the last story in *Idiots First*, wherein a man kills himself to share the fate of the wife he has abandoned, herself a martyr to their vows. But as suggested in this story, "The German Refugee," and in such others as "Take Pity" and "The Death of Me," suffering for love can cost almost too much. If there are gains for Malamud's characters, they can usually be measured only in moral inches. Not always is man's capacity to suffer for his loving enough to fend off the angel of death, as it does momentarily in the fable "Idiots First." Malamud's affirmation burns too much to be everyone's dish of tea. It is a sweeter brew than the *goyische* wormwood and gall served by the likes of Burroughs and Beckett, but it is hardly bland. As Malamud himself admitted, he writes not with horror but with sadness.

I I

Much of the sweetening, or more accurately bittersweetening, comes from the comedy, almost as typical of Malamud's work as its concern with suffering. Characteristic of Jewish humor, Malamud generally avoids such generally common sources of wit as pun, word-play, intellectual humor (although one finds some of

this in Bellow). Traditionally, Jewish humor is stark, edged, cynical. It communicates the double view of the man who is supposedly superior to the common run of humanity because he has
been chosen, but finds in actuality that he has really been singled
out for extra knocks on the head, dealt by those to whom he is
presumably superior. Consequently, Jewish humor mocks, sneers
at human foibles and pretensions, and delivers ironic observations about itself and its practitioners, the chosen people. Frequently it verges on self-hatred ("An anti-semite is a man who
hates Jews more than he should"), or conveys the desperation of
a wisdom about moral conduct which is impossible to practice.
While scholars of Jewish culture tend to minimize or overlook it,
there is also a coarse and bawdy strain of Yiddish humor, as I
know from the jokes I heard as I was growing up, a humor of
natural functions: eating, evacuation, sexuality. Perhaps this latter humor was adapted from the peasantry who surrounded the
Jewish enclaves in Eastern Europe, sustained and enlarged in
America by what it took from the urban streets. Finally, there is
that rich vein of Jewish humor which deals with the fantastic, the
incredible, the bizarre, treating them as though they were commonplace.

Although, as I will demonstrate, Malamud draws upon all these
varieties of humor, I find the mode of fantastic comedy particularly interesting and successful. In this mode Malamud implies
the immanence of a spiritual dimension or realm of human experience without committing himself to a specific faith, doctrine, or
theology. In short, the fantastic and the metaphysical enter into
Malamud's world as though they were fact, and he solidifies them
and ties them to earth by depicting them in the same voice and
with the same solidity of specification that he uses for grocery
stores and Czarist prisons. One might say that this is Malamud's
version of the quasi-religious folklore and superstition permea-
ting *shtetl* life, and as much a fact of that life as its food and drink.

Until recently this entire mode of writing and the cultural experience it connoted was limited to Yiddish readers familiar with the work of such writers as Mendele Mocher Sforim and Sholom Aleichem. But in the past decade Isaac Bashevis Singer's fiction has become widely known in translation, and Singer himself a distinguished member of the Jewish Movement. Malamud is thus the heir to rich Jewish traditions, and worthy heir that he is, he remakes them his way and reinvigorates them.

Fantastic comedy recurs throughout Malamud's writing, in various forms. It can be the central plot of a work, as in such stories as "The Jewbird" and "Angel Levine." In the first, a bird with a Yiddish accent flies through the window of a New York apartment, and availing himself of the Jewish custom of granting lodging to vagrants and strangers who ask it, takes up residence with the family. But the father, a Jewish antisemite, resents the bird's influence with wife and son, harasses the creature, and finally, we deduce, murders it. The bird, dying, identifies his assassins only as "Anti-Semeets." This story-joke is funny to the end, but not too funny. It sends up disquieting reverberations. In "Angel Levine," another story-joke, a black Jewish angel arrives to solace a poor man and his sick wife, but is repelled and deprived of his angelic power to heal by the man's skepticism. It takes searching and an act of faith before Angel Levine can be restored and do his job. In a little parable of race relations the Angel for a time descends to the kind of debauched behavior the skeptical Jew imagines as proper to Negroes. Again the goofiness turns into sobriety just as the tale ends. The humor in these fables derives from the credulous and matter-of-fact rendition of the absurd: a talking bird? a black Jewish angel? Why not? Too, Malamud's homey colloquial style (more of this later) strengthens the effect. Were the style more elaborate, the language itself fantastic, the whole thing would be only a gag. But the writer's manner of narration makes these events seem as ordinary as bread. In this way Malamud employs an archetypal principle of comic technique: incongruous juxtaposition. He also communicates the idea of Jewish transcendence, the indissoluble and simultaneous merger of the spiritual and the real.

The novels also contain a strong element of fantasy, which has a double function, especially in such primarily realistic works as *The Assistant* and *The Fixer*. The fantasy could be described as the leavening in Malamud's realistic bread, making it rise a little toward heaven; it can be thus interpreted as an extrapolation of that something in man which insists he is more than animal. It also functions to modulate, making the bread easier to get down by alleviating the dry taste of misery with some fun. And, of course, there is an aspect of Malamud's work which depends largely upon fantastic comedy for its substance.

Malamud's first novel *The Natural* is largely a work of fantastic comedy, and though a flawed book, there is such verve in it and such an abundance of talent, one might have predicted that this was to be Malamud's *métier*. In brief, Malamud transforms the national game of baseball, familiar to all and in which all are experts, into a contest among demigods and conducted as though it were a sacred ritual in a cosmic arena. This placing together of unlike pairs, baseball and the universe, already inspires a comic response. For the literary reader Malamud provides an extra dimension of incongruity by juxtaposing a sports story, rendered with the appropriate data and terminology, against a mythic context which draws upon the myths of the Quest Hero, the Fisher King, and, to some degree, the White Goddess.

All sorts of highjinks go on. The hero has superhuman powers as an athlete and rewrites the record book with his magical bat, Wonderboy, but, Malamudian man, is afflicted with an uncontrollable yen for the wrong woman. Though a wizard who, at one point in the narrative, inexplicably produces out of thin air a dead herring, a salami, a rabbit, and streams of silver dollars, he is no magician at coming through in the clutch. Roy's exploits at the plate sometimes invoke celestial responses: at his first hit for the New York Knights a little rain falls upon the parched wasteland of a field; when he has agreed to throw a crucial game, heaven sends down thunder, lightning, and darkness, and Wonderboy shatters in his hands. Too, there is an entire supporting cast of evil spirits: two dark and beautiful temptresses, a one-eyed gambler, a sinister judge who occupies a dark room at the top of a tower, and a malicious dwarf named Otto Zipp.

The pervasive dreariness of *The Assistant*, with its central locale of the dark store, is relieved and modulated by occasional but effective comic moments, notably one brief yet vivid episode of fantasy in which Morris Bober receives a visit from the devil and succumbs to his temptation. However, in keeping with the general method of the book, the agent of evil appears not in a spectacular scene but in a muted little encounter so close to credibility it can almost be taken as actual. I quote part of it here:

> At the counter stood a skinny man in an old hat and a dark overcoat down to his ankles. His nose was long, throat gaunt, and he wore a whisp of red beard on his bony chin.
> "A gut shabos," said the scarecrow.
> "A gut shabos," Morris answered, though shabos was a day away.
> "It smells here," said the skinny stranger, his small eyes shrewd, "like a open grave."
> "Business is bad."
> The man wet his lips and whispered, "Insurinks you got—fire insurinks?"
> Morris was frightened. "What is your business?". . . .
> "A smart man hears one word but he understand two. How much you got insurinks?"
> "Two thousand for the store."
> "Feh."
> "Five thousand for the house."
> "A shame. Should be ten."

"Who needs ten for this house?"
"Nobody knows."
"What do you want here?" Morris asked, irritated.
The man rubbed his skinny, red-haired hands. "What does a macher want?"
"What kind of a macher? What do you make?"
He shrugged slyly. "I make a living." The macher spoke soundlessly. "I make fires."[8]

In this scene we can discover how Malamud blends the fantastic with the realistic, for in such a novel as *The Assistant* the wholly bizarre and surrealistic would be an intrusion.

First, there is a basis of probability in the visit of a stranger whose profession it is to set fires, because among small businessmen facing bankruptcy, the fortuitous blaze—covered by insurance—is hardly an unknown phenomenon. Too, the macher's method, the strip of celluloid, is exactly that used by professionals. Furthermore, his argument, the guiltlessness of an act by a poor little man against the vast, rich, impersonal insurance company, consists of just the right logic for such a situation. Finally, a "macher" is, by definition, a man of affairs, an entrepreneur, one who knows what success is and how to get it. In this sense the macher appears as a familiar figure to all men.

But then Malamud cues us into the stranger's true nature with cunning, seriocomic hints. Harmless, even ludicrous, in appearance, he disarms by the way he looks. In his age he suggests the longevity of evil. The old hat and dark overcoat lend him the necessary cover of poverty and inconspicuousness, for machers who make fires should not call attention to themselves. The devil is all the more persuasive for looking ordinary. Yet we wonder about the costume. Does it also cover horns and a tail? The greeting of the good sabbath on the wrong day leads to the sure conclusion that the stranger is not a true Jew; or, to stretch the point a little, that the devil keeps his own holidays. The refer-

ences to the stranger's gauntness, close by the mention of open
graves, seem to portend man's mordant destiny—both the physical death and, if one participates in the exchange of "success" for
an evil deed, the soul's death as well. Then, the tiny red beard
and the red-haired hands suggest little tongues of flame. At last,
the scene is completed when Morris descends (note that) to set
the fire, only to be rescued by Frank. By this time, in Malamud's
magical way, the interlude is neither so fantastic nor so funny.
However, it has functioned both to underscore the novel's
themes and to lighten its mood. In the same way the slapstick
episode at Morris's funeral, when Frank falls into the grocer's
grave at precisely the moment when the bereaved are over-
whelmed by sorrow and burst into tears and lamentation, coun-
terpoints the scene's sentiment by turning it for an instant grimly
funny. Like the macher episode Frank's pratfall has moral significance, but in this case the downward movement signals an upward trend.

The fantastic component in *The Fixer*, to some degree anticipated by the characters' dreams and visions in *The Assistant*,
consists entirely of Yakov's dreams, fevers, and hallucinations
during his long and dreadful confinement. But these, however
farfetched, are often too painful to be comic, even when they
stage such improbable scenes as Yakov's imagined confrontations with the Czar. Indeed, the bitterness of Jewish humor is
nowhere better exemplified than in *The Fixer*. A prevailing source
of comedy comprises examples of the incredible misconceptions
and superstitions about the Jews held by the Russians, misconceptions for which the Jews, not the Russians, suffer. I doubt if
a more horrendous humor exists in any culture than this sort,
frequent in *The Fixer*:

> The days were passing and the Russian officials were waiting
> impatiently for his menstrual period to begin. Grubeshov and

the army general often consulted the calendar. If it didn't start soon they threatened to pump blood out of his penis with a machine they had for that purpose. The machine was a pump made of iron with a red indicator to show how much blood was being drained out. The danger of it was that it didn't always work right and sometimes sucked every drop of blood out of the body. It was used exclusively on Jews; only their penises fitted it.[9]

This is the double view of Jewish humor, with a vengeance, wherein the absurd stupidity of the Gentile—always good for a laugh—turns fearfully against the possessor of the superior intellect. Perhaps the only form of "comedy" more terrifying would be jokes about the gas ovens at Dachau, but we have yet to hear them. Another example of the inferior mentality of the Gentile, demonstrating that the persecutor is worse than those he despises, can be seen in a prison guard's recommendation of the New Testament to Yakov, all the more funny because of the grain of rough-and-ready logic in it. "The Old won't do you any good at all," Zhitnyak said. "It's long been used out and full of old graybeard Jews crawling around from one mess to another. Also there's a lot of fucking in the Old Testament, so how is that religious? If you want to read the true word of God, read the gospels."[10]

The comedy of *A New Life* and *Pictures of Fidelman* abandons fantasy almost entirely. Rather, these novels depend upon zany and often bawdy situations and employ the earthy humor, burlesque, and slapstick which derive from human lusts, mistakes, and misconduct.

Two typical and hilarious examples of burlesque in *A New Life*, really two variations on the same joke, involve the condition of undress. In the first Levin disrobes to crawl into the hay, literally, with a waitress, only to have his clothes stolen *in medias res* by a Syrian rival. Perhaps Malamud means to comment on the way things are between the Arabs and the Jews, with the Arabs spoiling not only the Jew's pleasure at just the moment he is to take it, but also his relations, so to speak, with the Gentile world. In the second episode Levin faces his freshman class at the opening of the semester and, enthralled by the class's close attention to his every murmur and what he assumes to be their rapt sympathy with his lofty pedagogical ambitions, builds himself up to an almost ecstatic fervor for his mission:

> In his heart he thanked them, sensing he had created their welcome of him. They represented the America he had so often heard of, the fabulous friendly West. So what if he spoke with flat a's and they with rocky r's? Or he was dark and nervously animated, they blond, tending to impassive? Or if he had come from a vast metropolis of many-countried immigrants, they from towns and small cities where anyone was much like everyone? In Levin's classroom they shared the ideals of seeking knowledge, one and indivisible. "This is the life for me," he admitted, and they broke into cheers, whistles, loud laughter.[11]

Only he discovers, a minute later, that what he had mistaken for empathy and intellectual comradeship was, in fact, his students' bemusement with the open front of his trousers. This is another instance of the prevailing motif in Malamud, sometimes painful, sometimes funny, most often both at once, that Jews without their pants on are particularly likely to get into trouble. Indeed, these episodes presage the novel's major action, Levin's maladroit love affair with Pauline Gilley, wife of his department chairman.

Quite aside from the burlesque sexuality of *A New Life*, a matter which Malamud treats with decreasing emphasis and increased seriousness as the novel proceeds—and sex becomes love, and love becomes commitment—*A New Life* demands comment as the only instance to date of Malamud as satirist. Although the satire finally collapses under the weight of too much academic detail and too much debate, for a time Malamud's fantastic gift exhilarates his depiction of Cascadia College and its English department. In this respect the novel's scene temporarily partakes in the great tradition of satire as fable: Gulliver's Lilliput, Martin Chuzzlewit's America, Sinclair Lewis's Zenith, all of them peopled not by *homo sapiens* but by goblins in human costume. The problem in *A New Life* is that the satire turns too grittily truthful, too near the quality of a *roman à clef*, and Levin, lovable and interesting as *shlemiel*-cum-lover, becomes something of a bore as academic crusader. Consequently, the novel is too playful to persuade entirely as realism and not playful enough to persuade as satire.

Pictures of Fidelman avoids that mistake. Although hardly Malamud's largest achievement, it is surely his most accomplished as a comic work. The humor arises from the antic misadventures in Italy of a would-be art student and painter. Perhaps the richest comedy is that of deliciously bawdy sexual farce, as when Fidelman can gain the favors of his landlady, for whom he has lusted in vain, only by masquerading as a priest. Surely this scene, which concludes an early episode, must be among the strangest absolutions depicted in a literary work:

> She grabbed his knees. "Help me, Father, for Christ's sake."
> Fidelman, after a short tormented time, said in a quavering voice, "I forgive you, my child."
> "The penance," she wailed, "first the penance."
> After reflecting, he replied, "Say one hundred times each, Our Father and Hail Mary."
> "More," Annamaria wept. "More, more. Much more."
> Gripping his knees so hard they shook, she burrowed her head into his black-buttoned lap. He felt the surprised beginnings of an erection. "In that case," Fidelman said, shuddering a little, "better undress."
> "Only," Annamaria said, "if you keep your vestments on."
> "Not the cassock, too clumsy."
> "At least the biretta."

He agreed to that.

Annamaria undressed in a swoop. Her body was extraordinarily lovely, the flesh glowing. In her bed they tightly embraced. She clasped his buttocks, he cupped hers. Pumping slowly he nailed her to her cross.[12]

But as hilarious as such scenes are, Malamud grounds them upon certain hard actualities which keep the book from dissipating into mere ribald spoofing. There is the authentic context of the Italian locale: of cold, poverty, venality, a people scrabbling for the next meal, including Fidelman himself. Simultaneously, there is the presence of great art, part of the air breathed in Italy, and the irresistible appeal to attempt it oneself. Thus Fidelman's wild sexual encounters are played off against his increasingly desperate and futile attempts to become an artist. The incongruous juxtaposition in *Pictures of Fidelman* is, then, that between the coarsely sexual and the sublimely aesthetic.

Too, the novel may be viewed as a kind of comic *bildungsroman*, intermixed with the International Theme and structured as a picaresque story cycle. Fidelman arrives in Italy respectably dressed and with the worthy ambition to become an art critic. Then, just as in the first episode he is robbed of his attaché case containing the initial chapter of his projected book, and swindled out of his extra suit of clothes, the layers of his superficial identity are stripped away episode by episode in a series of comic but also bitter encounters, until he is no longer definable as a middle-class American Jew. Instead, he gains a more basic identity: craftsman and lover. Furthermore, he has travelled there the hard way, through privation, failure, humiliation, abuse, crime, and fakery —an experience which brings him in the book's surrealistic penultimate episode face to face with the devil. In Fidelman Malamud has created his own version of an enduring Jewish comic prototype, the *luftmensch* with feet of clay. We have known worse people.

III

So far in this essay nothing has been said about Malamud's style, a subject the critics have largely avoided, as Leslie and Joyce Field point out in the introduction to their recent collection of Malamud criticism.[13] Yet, as indicated earlier, among Malamud's chief distinctions as an artist is his command of a particular literary idiom. This idiom not only bears Malamud's own signature, it has so permeated Jewish-American writing that the Movement itself is in some measure distinguished by it. Furthermore, the style is integral to those very themes and motifs we have been discussing. In a fundamental sense the suffering and the comedy are embedded in the language, and their peculiar simultaneity or proximity, the sweetly tragic and the bitterly comic, must to a significant degree be attributed to the style. In his own way Malamud captures in English what has been called an untranslatable quality of Yiddish, the admixture of the jocular and the solemn, "the fusion of the sacred and the profane."

But style cannot be studied in isolation from the writer's method at large. Before proceeding to a discussion of it, two important points must be made about Malamud's technique.

First, he avails himself of what is perhaps the most versatile and fluent of narrative modes, selective omniscience. In this mode the writer retains the objectivity, the freedom to move through time and space, and the power to know all, which are the great advantages of the traditional third-person outside narrator; yet by refraining from editorial intrusions and maintaining the focus on a single character or a few characters, the writer can shift into interior monologue or take a stance which allows him to perceive as through the character's eyes without any obvious break in the narrative seam or detection by the reader. This is, of course, a modern technique, and one at the service of many resourceful writers. It is the narrative perspective Malamud has employed in all his novels and, with rare exceptions, his stories as well. *Pictures of Fidelman,* though in part experimental, generally follows this narrative mode. Consider this passage, illustrative of selective omniscience, which recounts one of Fidelman's earlier, failed attempts at union with his landlady:

> She embraced him, her hairy armpits perfumed. He responded with postponed passion.
> "Enough of antipasto," Annamaria said. She reached for his member.
> Overwrought, Fidelman, though fighting himself not to, spent himself in her hand. Although he mightily willed resurrection, his wilted flower bit the dust.
> She furiously shoved him out of bed, into the studio, flinging his clothes after him.
> "Pig, beast, onanist!"
>
> At least she lets me love her. Daily Fidelman shopped, cooked, and cleaned for her. Every morning he took her shopping sack off the hook, went down to the street market and returned with the bag stuffed full of greens, pasta, eggs, meat, cheese, wine, bread. Annamaria insisted on three hearty meals a day although she had once told him she no longer enjoyed eating. Twice he had seen her throw up her supper. What she enjoyed he didn't know except it wasn't Fidelman.[14]

By writing this entirely as dramatic scene and in the objective mode, except for the one direct interior monologue statement "At least she lets me love her," Malamud achieves the immediacy and vividness of the I-narrative without paying the heavy price of limitation in time, place, and knowledge.

Another example, from *A New Life,* demonstrates how Malamud employs this particular narrative voice to inform us of the character's thoughts without seeming to tell us directly:

Levin was moved to discover he cherished what he had best cherished. For the first time since he had parted from Pauline the world seemed home, welcome. He had, as men must, given birth to it; he was himself reborn. Proof: leafy trees stippling green of earth on sky. Flowers casting bright color everywhere. Vast fires in cosmic space—all nature flowing in Levin's veins. He felt tender to the grass. "God's handkerchief," Whitman called it. He watched with pleasure a flat-footed bluejay hopping up and down branches in the blooming cherry tree. He was amiable even to Mrs. Beaty's cat, licking herself on the lawn at night, her whiteness, light. And Levin wanted, still, to be closer to men than he had been. The good you did for one you did for all; it wasn't a bad way to love.[15]

Here we begin outside Levin's head but move inside with a perception which can be either the narrator's or the character's ("Proof, leafy trees . . . space"); then, before the sentence is completed, we are back to the omniscient perspective with "all nature flowing in Levin's veins." Then, as the paragraph concludes, we move inside again: "The good you did for one you did for all; it wasn't a bad way to love." This is Levin's voice, not Malamud's, but the voices blend so well they cannot be distinguished one from the other.

Examples are legion in Malamud's work but the matter need not be further argued. Perhaps his most accomplished use of selective omniscience may be observed in *The Assistant*, wherein Malamud alternates between objective narration and the private minds of his three major characters, Morris, Frank, and Helen, though with swift incursions into the perceptions of even such minor figures as Julius Karp and Ward Minogue. In contrast, Malamud's most deliberately limited and intensive use of the selective omniscient is in *The Fixer*, in which the concentration entirely upon Yakov Bok and the total immersion in his perspective, undistracted and unmodulated by side glances into any other character, reinforces the claustrophobic atmosphere in the novel. This is the formal equivalent to the action, which consists largely of Yakov's experiences in solitary confinement. In a sense, by using this narrative mode, Malamud makes the reader undergo solitary confinement with Yakov.

A second vital point about Malamud's technique, preparatory to a discussion of his style but also intrinsically related to style, is the writer's symbolism. I have hinted that Malamud's best work is realistic, though it should be clear from the frequent and important presence of fantastic comedy that it breaks through strict categories. Indeed, although Malamud is a realist, as demonstrated in *The Assistant, The Fixer,* and the major part of *A New Life,* he is of the best sort: a symbolic realist. The Jewish sense of the Transcendent merged with the Actual expresses itself in Malamud's technique in a hard-rock verisimilitude, in which we smell garbage and know exactly how much money lies in the cash register or what a sadistic prison official does with his fingers when he searches a prisoner. At the same time, we are ever aware of the play of the human imagination upon experience and the inexhaustible intimations of the protean natural world. Symbols and emblems recur everywhere in Malamud's fiction, obtrusive only in the case of his first book, *The Natural,* and even there not inappropriate to a work with a frame of myth. Elsewhere they are wholly integrated.

So, for example, to develop some suggestions made earlier about *The Assistant,* the characters' movements in that work— quite normal in a building containing a cellar, a first-floor store, and living quarters above—assume symbolic purport. As already implied, these movements constitute a dramatic metaphor for the characters' moral conditions. Frank comes up from the cellar where he has been hiding to the store, and then to a room on the floor above. This parallels his climb from bummery to decency. Conversely, Morris goes upstairs to sleep and dream, his only escape from his prison—the store. In his one concession to evil, he goes downstairs to set fire to his business but is saved from this by Frank, who has already experienced what things are like in the cellar. In another important scene, Frank's descent into the grocer's grave signifies his inheritance of the grocer's miserable life, but it is also a kind of ascension. Furthermore, Malamud renders the symbolism ironic and thereby more profound (perhaps inspired by Hemingway's practice) by sometimes reversing the usual connotations and associations. Frank climbs up the airshaft to spy on Helen's naked body in the bathroom, just as he aspires to possess Helen, but morally his action is down. In rescuing Helen from Ward Minogue's assault, he lifts her up, but then, overcome by his own desires, he pushes her to earth to take her himself.

This sequence of movements, noted here only in part, comprises but one of several symbolic patterns in *The Assistant*. In that novel as elsewhere Malamud utilizes many others: heat and cold, light and dark, fragrance and stench, the indoors and the outdoors, to mention a few. Too, throughout his work he consistently uses weather, season, climate, as corollary and symbolic context for his characters' actions and moral conditions. He also skillfully employs emblems: mirrors, books, articles of clothing, for example. Thus whether the locale be a run-down grocery somewhere in Brooklyn or a glass works on the island of Murano, and whether the mood be realistic or comic, there is always much more to see in Malamud's stories than what will happen next.

With this cursory treatment of matters deserving separate and detailed study in themselves but necessarily reduced here to a mere preface, we come finally to Malamud's style. I speak of Malamud's style as though it were a single entity. More accurately, there are three styles, or a confluence of styles.

First there is a "straight" or standard belletristic style; that is, a style composed of the same linguistic materials used by other modern writers, with a syntax familiar to all speakers of American English, and a diction drawn from the common vocabulary of standard-informal usage. The passage cited below, from *The Fixer*, exemplifies Malamud's standard belletristic style. Lucid and vigorous, it contains nothing intrinsically alien or exotic and little identifying it as specifically Malamudian if it were taken out of context and seen in isolation.

> At five in the morning the day began and never ended. In the early evening dark he was already lying on his mattress trying to sleep. Sometimes he tried all night. During the day there were the regular checks through the spy hole, and three depressing searches of his body. There was cleaning out ashes, and making and lighting the stove. There was the sweeping of the cell to do, urinating in the can, walking back and forth until one began to count; or sitting at the table with nothing to do. There was the going for, and eating, of his meager meals. There was trying to remember and trying to forget. There was the counting of each day; there was reciting the psalm he had put together. He also watched the light and dark change. The morning dark was different from the night dark. The morning dark had a little freshness, a little anticipation in it, though what he anticipated he could not say. The night dark was heavy with thickened and compounded shadows.[16]

I have named this a standard belletristic style because the informal elements, e. g., "five in the morning," "the psalm he had put together," are balanced against an occasional sonorous and formal literary phrase never heard in the speech of ordinary men: "thickened and compounded shadows." And, of course, the passage has other literary elements, notably the series of sentences beginning with the identical phrase "There was," by whose proximity and similarity Malamud means to convey the repetitiousness and monotony of Yakov's routine, a linguistic replication of what is happening, i. e., imitative form. However, while this passage testifies to Malamud's sophistication and craft, it says nothing of his special function as a Jewish writer.

A second Malamud style, that most unlike the standard belletristic, is a dialect style which deliberately evokes the sound of Yiddish. It demonstrates Malamud's familiarity with the old mother tongue, the common language once spoken by seven million European Jews regardless of their country of habitation. It also demonstrates Malamud's skill at transliterating that tongue into a kind of English. However, Malamud can hardly be credited with inventing the dialect style or being the first to use Yiddish dialect as a literary medium. Dialect styles in America go back well into the nineteenth century, the rustic and Negro dialects especially, and were practiced by such men as Josh Billings, James Russell Lowell, Artemus Ward, Joel Chandler Harris, and, of course, Twain. In the twentieth century Yiddish dialect has been a staple of comedy and of comedians for decades, although very rare in serious writing. This is a sample of Malamud's dialect style, from the superb story "The Magic Barrel." The speaker is Salzman, a marriage broker extolling the virtues of one of his clients to a dubious prospective customer:

> Salzman pulled his clasped hands to his breast. Looking at the ceiling he devoutly exclaimed, "Yiddishe kinder, what can I say to somebody that he is not interested in high school teachers? So what then are you interested?"
> Leo flushed but controlled himself.
> "In what else will you be interested," Salzman went on, "if you not interested in this fine girl that she speaks four languages and has personally in the bank ten thousand dollars? Also her father guarantees further twelve thousand. Also she has a new car, wonderful clothes, talks on all subjects, and she will give you a first-class home and children. How near do we come in our life to paradise?"
> "If she's so wonderful, why wasn't she married ten years ago?"
> "Why?" said Salzman with a heavy laugh. "—Why? Because she is *partikiler*. This is why. She wants the *best.*"[17]

The dialect elements are obvious: the direct importation of stock phrases ("Yiddishe kinder"), the mangled grammar, the inverted syntax, the emphatic mispronounciation—a kind of Yiddish accent—of ordinary words. Furthermore, as in most dialect styles, the total effect here is reductive in that the passage presents not only an inferior language but also inferior values, presumably "Jewish" values (money, status), as though they were the ultimate goods in marriage. It is another case of self-mockery, although by the time the story ends all its characters attain to a stature impossible for stereotypes.

The third style, the most complex and resonant and that which Malamud has impressed with his own signature, is a mixed or fused style which combines both the belletristic and dialect styles yet is wholly neither. Malamud can be named the co-inventor of this style; he and Bellow began to use it at about the same time, in the early 1950's, though apparently without the conscious indebtedness of either one to the other. The fused style gathers additional force from the juxtaposition or combination of lyric, eloquent, soaring phrases (the belletristic) and homely idiom and vulgate (the dialect). The belletristic exalts the vulgate, infusing it with dignity and seriousness; the vulgate pulls down the belletristic from its literary eminence and makes it speak for ordinary men and coarse experience. The juxtaposition of the two also makes possible that remarkable bitter comedy we observe in Malamud, Bellow, and Roth. I cite an example of the fused style from *The Assistant,* a passage notable as well for its synthesis of omniscience and interior monologue:

> Tight-jawed, he opened his book. She returned to hers, hiding her thoughts behind the antics of a madman until memory overthrew him and she found herself ensnared in scenes of summer that she would gladly undo, although she loved the season; but how could you undo what you had done again in the fall, unwillingly willing? Virginity she thought she had parted with without sorrow, yet was surprised by torments of conscience, or was it disappointment at being valued under her expectations? Nat Pearl, handsome, cleft-chinned, gifted, ambitious, had wanted without too much trouble a lay and she, half

in love, had obliged and regretted. Not the loving, but that it had taken her so long to realize how little he wanted. Not her, Helen Bober.

Why should he?—magna cum laude, Columbia, now in his second year at law school, she only a high school graduate with a year's evening college credit mostly in lit; he with first-rate prospects, also rich friends he had never bothered to introduce her to; she as poor as her name sounded, with little promise of a better future. She had more than once asked herself if she had meant by her favors to work up a claim on him. Always she denied it. She had wanted, admittedly, satisfaction, but more than that—respect for the giver of what she had to give, had hoped that desire would become more than just that. She wanted, simply, a future in love. Enjoyment she had somehow had, felt very moving the freedom of fundamental intimacy with a man. Though she wished for more of the same, she wanted it without aftermath of conscience, or pride, or sense of waste. So she promised herself next time it would go the other way; first mutual love, then loving, harder maybe on the nerves, but easier in memory.[18]

In this passage literary and Yiddish-colloquial elements are so tightly joined as to be nearly inseparable. The Yiddish voice, here subdued because the character is a thoroughly assimilated second-generation young woman, can nevertheless be heard in the inverted syntax and the odd treatment of verbs: "Virginity she thought she had parted with"; "Nat Pearl . . . had wanted without too much trouble. . . ." Too, the dominant mood, a kind of reflexive neither wholly passive nor active, is typical of Yiddish but scarcely exists in English. Then there are the constant interruptions and interjections of modifying or qualifying phrases and clauses, imparting a faintly alien air of brooding introspection and of constant self-examination. This quality contrasts with the normative briskness and directness of American speech, which depicts actions swiftly completed and thoughts concluded with a minimum of interruption. Malamud further spices this linguistic mixture with colloquialisms, sometimes remotely Yiddish in flavor but also those appropriate to the big city: "lay," "lit," "harder maybe on the nerves." In the latter phrase the interposed "maybe" turns a stock expression a little Yiddish. The effect of all this is, of course, to render Helen immediate, human, and accessible to the reader.

Yet we must not overlook the belletristic components in the passage, entirely appropriate to a character who is as bookish as Helen (the book she holds in the scene just quoted is *Don Quixote*). As the colloquial style makes Helen folksily human, the formal and literary elements make her deep and complex. Such phrases as "memory overthrew him," "ensnared in scenes of summer," "torments of conscience," and "the freedom of fundamental intimacy with a man," elevated above common parlance and smacking of her intellectual ambitions and idealism, are not only right for her character, they help define it. Helen herself is constructed of the same mixture of elements as her language: part lusting flesh, pat lofty aspiration. Moreover, these elements blend into the larger structure of the paragraph, with its parallel and balanced sentences, thesis/antithesis, reflecting the tensions in Helen's mind as it plays over its experience. These deliberations are reinforced by the strategic repetitions of key words echoed and re-echoed, all congruent to the subject of sex, love, morality, and ambition: "undo," "loved," "conscience," "wanted," "love," "loving," "future." The whole thing becomes transformed by this miracle of Malamud's craft, a miracle most modestly performed, from narrative into incantation.

Malamud's artistry proves itself not only in the creation and practice of these styles but also in the diverse narrative functions to which he puts them. In *The Assistant*, to continue our concern with that novel a moment longer, each of the three styles appears in a variety of uses and combinations. The dialect style, for example, functions appropriately in the conversations of those characters for whom Yiddish was the language of their youth, between

Morris and Ida, or Morris and Breitbart. We also hear this style
in certain interior monologues. Perhaps its most consistent use
in the novel is to depict Ida, I suspect as a way to fix her into a
kind of narrowness or limitation of vision. Of all the important
characters, hers is the meanest worldview. Note this instance, Ida
at Morris's funeral:

> Ida, holding a wet handkerchief to her eyes, thought, So what
> if we had to eat? When you eat you don't want to worry whose
> money you are eating—yours or the wholesalers'. If he had
> money he had bills; and when he had more money he had more
> bills. A person doesn't always want to worry if she will be in the
> street tomorrow. She wants sometimes a minute's peace. But
> maybe it's my fault, because I didn't let him be a druggist.[19]

But what is so artistic about using a dialect style for a dialect
character? We have the answer to that in Malamud's treatment
of Morris, because, in contrast, Malamud shrewdly avoids the
dialect style and renders him, whether by omniscient narration or
interior monologue, either in the standard belletristic style or the
fused style. This "straight" treatment of Morris reiterates his
identity as an Everyman figure and comprises the stylistic equivalent to the novel's thesis that all men are, potentially, Jews. To
depict him in the dialect style would be to insist upon his ethnic
identity and thus to weaken the characterization. Morris's character gains depth, too, in that Malamud shows him as capable of
different levels of speech, depending on the situation. To Ida he
speaks strictly in Yiddish dialect, as to Karp and others; to Helen
and Frank his speech remains homely but closer to standard and
almost purged of its Yiddishisms; to Detective Minogue he speaks
in a stilted but "correct" manner which reflects the strain he feels
dealing with this man within a formal, official context.

On the other hand, Helen and Frank can be rendered in a style
which at times borders on dialect in its loose colloquialism, yet
without risk of stereotyping. As Helen's style is slightly more

literary because of her aspirations and her education, so Frank's tends to be slangy, appropriate to his background as drifter. However, we perceive a subtle but progressive heightening of Frank's speech and interior monologue, as well as of the omniscient narration describing him, on those occasions when he delves into serious subjects either with Morris or Helen, and as his moral ascension continues. He achieves, in his best moments, a striking combination of literary eloquence and lowdown bluntness. A few lines will illustrate: "His goddamned life had pushed him wherever it wanted; he had led it nowhere. He was blown around in any breath that blew, owned nothing, not even experience to show for the years he had lived. If you had experience you knew at least when to start and where to quit; all he knew was how to mangle himself more. The self he had secretly considered valuable was, for all he could make of it, a dead rat. He stank."[20]

The various styles I have remarked in *The Assistant* operate throughout Malamud's work, although, of course, with suitable modification to the needs of each novel. For example, *The Natural* totally lacks Yiddish flavor, rightly so, yet the style is breezy and slangy—accurate to a world of baseball players. At the same time the earthy colloquialism sets up an artistically desirable tension against the novel's heavy mythic and allegorical machinery, with two beneficial effects: it provides an illusion of actuality; it produces a keen humor. *A New Life* is written largely in the fused style, again seemly to the subject and to the novel's hero, an urban Eastern Jew with an M.A. However, just as Levin's Jewishness overtly plays only a small role in the novel, the "Jewish" elements in his thought and speech are suppressed. As is appropriate to the hero's profession as college English teacher, the selective omniscient voice tends to be formal and literary; but it can never be pompous or recondite because it must always remind us of Levin's origins in the urban streets and of the base urgings of his very mortal flesh. In this novel, too, the mixture of colloquial and belletristic materials generates a comic under-current.

The same comic potentiality, inherent in any style which em-ploys idiom, helps to enliven *The Fixer* and prevent it from un-bearable morbidity. There is nothing at all humorous in the situation of a man falsely accused of ritual murder, nor is there any single episode or passage in the novel that can be described as funny—apart from the galling satire upon Russian ignorance and barbarousness (recall the blood-draining apparatus). Thus, the novel's style must carry most of the task of relieving its gloom. And Malamud does accomplish it, with a doubly ingenious method.

First, he establishes a continual contrast between the language of all the official proceedings, innately formal and bombastic, and the spontaneous simplicity and pungency of Yakov's own speech. Accordingly, there is posed the repeated incongruity between what is uttered by the various magistrates and functionaries, and the pithy, unaffected quality of what Yakov is saying inside his own head. The incongruity becomes even more absurd in that when Yakov replies to his persecutors, he usually does so in the same stilted manner they use. The result is a kind of chorus of voices. Second, the contrast of voices, of what is said and what is thought, communicates an authentic difference of tongues. Yakov thinks and speaks to himself or to other Jews in his native language, Yiddish, whereas he must speak to everyone else in Russian. Although Yakov has learned Russian well, it is not his original language and cannot be used with the fluency and natu-ralness of Yiddish. Consequently, Yakov's stilted responses to the Russian officials' stilted declarations imitates the truth of the hero's circumstances. The crucial difference is that Yakov always speaks sincerely, while the inflated and artificial mode of the official rhetoric gives it the lie. At the same time Malamud's voice, employing the fused style of an omniscient narrator outside the hero but never very far away, merges with Yakov's. Narrator and hero often become one in that both express themselves in the same way: lucidly, candidly, sometimes earthily, sometimes in short lyric flights. In sum, what Malamud does, linguistically, is to pit the good Jews (Malamud and Yakov) against the bad Russians. You can usually tell the bad guys by their bombast, if they have rank, or if lower class by their nasty, vulgar mouths.

Pictures of Fidelman indicates a further expansion and experimentation in Malamud's technique. Although the narrative is largely rendered in the fused style, Malamud flies higher with the belletristic and dives lower with the vulgate than in any of his other work. He also takes greater chances with narrative perspective, shifting from objective to subjective naration more frequently and swiftly than ever before. He makes other rapid and varied shifts as well: from the conventional narrative past tense to the immediate present, from exposition to dialogue, from interior monologue or selective omniscience to direct impression. Technically the book is as wild and unpredictable as its hero's adventures. Indeed, chapter five is a technical *tour de force*, a packed and dazzling virtuoso demonstration of Malamud's range, a stylistic splurge. One can only describe it as a neo-Joycean, comitragic, surrealistic, stream-of-consciousness, visionary sequence, perhaps a burst of true madness in poor Fidelman but also containing a portion of almost coherent narrative which advances the story line. There is nothing remotely like it in Malamud's earlier writing. I quote a small portion:

12 12 12 12 12 12 12 12 12 12 12 12 12 12 12 12 12 12 12 12
369 369 369 369 369 369 369 369 369 369 369 369 369
veyizmirveyizmirveyizmirveyizmirveyizmirveyizmir
123691236912369123691236912369123691236912369
Fidelman painteth three canvases. The Crucifixion he painteth red on red. The Descent from the Cross he painteth white on white. For the Resurrection, on Easter morning, he leaveth the canvas blank.

P

t o tem

L

E

Suss

King

Je vous enmerde. Modigliani.

Oil on wood? Bottle fucking guitar? Bull impaled on pole?
One-eyed carp stuffed in staring green bottle? Clown spooning
dog dung out of sawdust? Staircase ascending a nude? Black-
stockinged whore reading pornographic book by lamplight?
Still life: three apple cores plus one long gray hair? Boy pissing
on old man's shoe? The blue disease? Balding woman dyeing
her hair? Buggers of Calais? Blood oozing from ceiling on
foggy night?

From such writing there seems only one safe conclusion: we
cannot tell where Malamud is going next.

Although for all its virtuosity and comic gusto *Pictures of Fidelman* is a much less estimable work than such solid accomplishments as *The Assistant* and *The Fixer,* this novel does make a
number of important affirmations. For one thing, it affirms that
despite Malamud's association with the Jewish Movement and his
importance to it, his material is not restricted to the themes and
prototypes characteristic to that Movement. It affirms that he
retains the capacity to surprise us, a capacity always beyond the
scope of a minor writer. It affirms, moreover, that Malamud
continues to be devoted to the subject he believes the writer
must treat as his mission: the richness of the development of
human personality. Finally, it affirms that whether his treatment be somber or comic, his possibilities as a craftsman are
far from exhausted. If it is perhaps too much to expect the
Movement to continue its present momentum indefinitely, although it seems far from played out, on the basis of the hard
evidence already provided by his talent we can surely look

forward to further development on Malamud's part. I, for one, can hardly wait to see what he will do.

The Tenants appeared after this essay had been written, and too late to be included in it. However, from my first reading of the book I would amend my conclusions here in only one important respect: it seems to indicate that Malamud is capable of unmitigated pessimism, gloomier even than that in *The Fixer*. Or, we could take a little comfort from the ending of *The Tenants* by interpreting it as warning and object lesson to both Jew and Black: learn to get along, *or else*. In any case the novel confirms my belief that Malamud is still growing.

NOTES

1. Malamud has been quoted in print rarely and there is little biographical information available about him. The two quotations are taken from one of the few sources, a newspaper interview by Joseph Wershba, "Not Horror But 'Sadness,' " New York *Post*, Sunday, September 14, 1958, p. M2.

2. *The Natural.* Random House (Modern Library Edition), New York, no date, pp. 135–136. The original edition was published in 1952 by Farrar, Straus, and Cudahy.

3. *The Assistant.* Farrar, Straus, and Giroux, New York, 1957, p. 125.

4. Ibid., p. 230.

5. Ibid., p. 75.

6. *A New Life.* Dell, New York, 1963, p. 330. The original edition was published in 1961 by Farrar, Straus, and Cudahy.

7. *Pictures of Fidelman.* Farrar, Straus, and Giroux, New York, 1969, p. 208.

8. *The Assistant*, p. 241.

9. *The Fixer.* Farrar, Straus, and Giroux, New York, 1966, p. 139.

10. Ibid., p. 231.

11. *A New Life*, pp. 85–86.

12. *Pictures of Fidelman*, pp. 67–68.

13. Leslie A. and Joyce W. Field, editors. *Bernard Malamud and the Critics.* New York University Press, 1970.

14. *Pictures of Fidelman,* p. 58.

15. *A New Life,* pp. 250–251.

16. *The Fixer,* p. 214.

17. *The Magic Barrel,* Farrar, Straus, and Cudahy, New York, 1958, pp. 201–202.

18. *The Assistant,* p. 14.

19. Ibid., p. 230.

20. Ibid., p. 175.

The Self in the Modern World: Karl Shapiro's Jewish Poems

KARL MALKOFF

"These poems are not for poets," Karl Shapiro begins his Introduction to *Poems of a Jew*.[1] But perhaps they are. Certainly, Jewishness for Shapiro is less a matter of cultural, religious, or historical tradition than a mode of apprehending reality. Shapiro's Jew, obviously a symbol of the human condition in general, may be specifically the archetypal poet. "Poetry is everywhere at its goal, a wise critic once said. And one might add in paraphrase: the Jew is everywhere at his goal." (ix)

Later in the brief essay, Jewishness is defined as "a certain state of consciousness which is inescapable. . . . Being a Jew is the consciousness of being a Jew. . . ." A metaphor begins to emerge in which Jew comes to represent a particular quality of mind, one that is intimately related to the creative process. We are dealing with that aspect of consciousness that is conscious of itself, that is, in fact, obsessed with itself; it is "the primitive ego of the human race," attempting to survive against a "background of Nothing." (x) We may begin to suspect that we are dealing with those powers of imagination by which the individual gives shape to his reality, with which he comes to terms with the emptiness that threatens to engulf him.

The discovery of order in apparent chaos, of form in flux, was, of course, a theme that preoccupied the generation preceding Shapiro's, that of Pound, Eliot, Stevens. But important distinctions must be drawn. The older poets were products of the First World War, which called into final question the standards and systems of the civilization that gave rise to it. With all in disarray, structure seemed absolutely crucial. The Second World War, however, was shattering in a different way. Order became the enemy, the concentration camp, the totalitarian state. The nothingness persisted, but now almost as an ally rather than an antagonist; meaninglessness had to serve as the source of meaning. The Jew, then, is appropriate for Shapiro's metaphor not simply because the poet is himself a Jew, but because the Jew has become the terrible symbol of the holocaust, of man brought face to face with annihilation. He is, in short, the symbol of a new way of coming to terms with chaos; no longer wishing to set the universe in order, he must learn to settle for absurd victories or no victory at all.

Poems of a Jew tests the capacity of the Self to survive the chaos it must embrace. If the Self seems to triumph, however uneasily, in this particular volume, we must recognize that the triumph is not necessarily permanent. *Poems of a Jew*, the culmination of a specific phase of Shapiro's career, must finally be understood not only in terms of its own poems, but in the context of the poet's subsequent work as well. This is Shapiro's last book as a relatively formal poet; and there may in fact be some connection between his original commitment to traditional verse and his early faith in the ability of the Self to exist, both of which beliefs are seriously questioned in his later poetry.

Poems of a Jew is divided into three sections: the first seems largely concerned with symbols of the Jewish experience, frequently with art and language; the second specifically places Judaism within the context of a Christian world, a theme that is never far from the surface throughout the entire book; and the final section deals with archetypal figures, most of them Jewish, all in some way relevant to a consideration of Jewishness.

"The Alphabet" begins the first section; emphasizing the power of the word, the poem supports the suggestion that for Shapiro the Jew is above all a creator of form, a namer of things, in short, a poet. But he is a poet of disaster. The letters of the Jewish alphabet are "as strict as flames/Or little terrible flowers . . . ," they "bristle like barbed wire. . . ." (3) There is appropriate irony in the fact that the letters themselves are cruel, at least intimating that the tradition from which they emerge contains an element of self-destructiveness. But the barbed, burning symbols look backward to biblical origins as well as to the contemporary nightmare. "Singing through solid stone," they are man's link with God; a "burning bush," they illuminate the human condition. Finally, combining the sinister movement of the flames with the cutting edges of the barbed wire, these letters "are dancing knives/ That carve the heart of darkness seven ways." Evidence of the "almost natural crime," genocide, the letters underline a universal guilt; they are signposts of atrocity.

However, the negative vision does not contract into a deepening gloom. The flickering pyre begins to symbolize the death that precedes resurrection; from "the still speaking embers of ghettos,/ There rise the tinder flowers of the Jews." There is logic to Shapiro's introduction of a Christian frame of reference, with its promise of rebirth. The Jewish alphabet lies "in chain-line over Christian pages." The image of the little terrible flowers itself suggests Saint Francis, recalling the configurations of Bernard Malamud's *The Assistant.* Not surprisingly, the total relationship between the two traditions must be finally expressed in paradox:

the letters' fire "Unsacrifices the bled son of man/ Yet plaits his crown of thorns."

"University" is not a better poem than "The Alphabet," which, even if its suggestion of resurrection is not fully earned, is a remarkably moving performance. But the earlier poem is far more typical of Shapiro's poetic powers in that phase of his career that is culminated by *Poems of a Jew*. He begins with the characteristic flat, prosaic statement: "To hurt the Negro and avoid the Jew/ Is the curriculum." (12) The rest of the poem is simply the development of this phrase. Its clarity—not its content—is almost shocking; it reminds us that in order to write satire, what is most required is a distinct point of view, a place of detachment from which to observe what is being satirized, and a coherent self to inhabit that place.

Not that there is a complete lack of complexity or density in the verse. The entering boys are "identified by hats." Presumably, they are entering freshman. But quite naturally, the Jews, singled out by their skullcaps, are brought to mind as well. The imperious columns of the college buildings explicitly become antebellum girls, contemptuous of the "outlanders," whose desire is a potent threat. This, however, seems largely visual dexterity; it lacks the ambiguity of perspective that transformed Hebrew letters into dancing knives.

In "University," the lines of irony are clearly drawn. In fact, it is only Shapiro's wit that prevents the irony from becoming heavy-handed. The university, and the establishment associated with it, condescend to or exclude everything alien to their own traditions; "Like manor houses," the colleges represent that which is aristocratic, high-minded, culturally sound. Intellectual and social acuteness become interdependent: "Within the precincts of this world/ Poise is a club." But in the hills, cut off by choice or accident from the movements of American civilization, live the real descendants of the tradition of which the university claims to be heir; there, in their inbred, obsolete world, "The past is absolute." The school "shows us, rotted and endowed,/ Its senile pleasure." (13)

The university embodies for Shapiro not all of American society, but a specific and especially powerful aspect of it; the "Curriculum" is the pattern of behavior that has long excluded Jews and Blacks from the "club," but pays lip service to selected egalitarian ideals. Hypocritical and corrupt, betraying its own past, it is a part of the establishment for which Shapiro has little sympathy. Here, the poem shows signs of being dated; the singling out of Wasp society as the enemy, the implicit wish to first violate and then occupy the old manor houses, seem nearly naive and subservient in the light of all that has happened since Shapiro wrote the poem. But certain touches survive. Recalling Pound's "old bitch gone in the teeth," that "botched civilization," Shapiro's suggestion that the vicious snobbery of the aristocrats is a kind of spiritual syphillis thoroughly deflates the nobility of mannered brick and magnolia.

"University" is a very different poem from "The Alphabet." But the poems share at least one significant characteristic. In each case, the Jew is important not only in his own right, but as a defining attribute of the world in which he exists, or from which he is excluded. In fact, if we move beyond the evident social implications of the poems, the Jew becomes a metaphysical touchstone, one that reveals both the limitations and possibilities of human experience. The Jew is, in short, something that mankind must sooner or later come up against. He is presented in precisely that light in "The Synagogue." The synagogue itself is "the adumbration of the Wall." (8) Literally, of course, Shapiro refers to *the* Wall in Jerusalem; but it is also symbolic of any enforcer of boundaries. The separateness of the Jew is also suggested by the Wall, and reinforced in the reference to the "calendar that marks a separate race." The poem makes an attempt to define what lies on the Jewish side of the Wall, using the synagogue as emblem in the mode of the seventeenth century meta-physical poets.

While cathedrals draw the soul upward, connecting man with the heavenly spheres, the synagogue is very much of this world: "No relic but a place. . . . Not holy ground but factual holiness. . . ." It is a special kind of worldliness, not to be confused with the antiseptic materialism of glossy American society; it is rather the sense that the things of this world are holy in their own right and not because of any transcendent relation to the spiritual.

> Our wine is wine, our bread is harvest bread
> That feeds the body and is not the body. (9)

Here as elsewhere, Shapiro's province seems located in the ter-rain between Jewish commitment to this world and the Kierke-gaardian Knight of Faith, whose ultimate commitment is para-doxically to the finite.

Of special interest in the first section of *Poems of a Jew* is "The Dirty Word." It is one of Shapiro's earliest attempts at the free verse (or prose poems) that later comprise *The Bourgeois Poet*. The word, represented in the poem by a frightening black bird, a vulture perhaps, is, within the context of the book, an offensive term for Jew. But as is usually the case, it does service as a more generalized symbol of fear, shame, and self-hatred, a malignancy forced upon the young boy by the society in which he lives, but finally nurtured and even, in a perverse way, loved by the boy.

Although it is probably far more accurate to say that the poem is written in prose than free verse, it has a definite formal struc-ture. Three paragraphs (the first, second, and fourth) of approxi-mately the same length, and a short, sentence-long third paragraph: "And the bird outlives the man, being freed at the man's death-funeral by a word from the rabbi." (5) In spite of this prophecy of longevity, Shapiro, or the *persona*, claims to have outlived the bird, to have murdered it. And here is what is most effective in the poem. The bird is clearly evil and filthy; yet it is taken in by the boy and cherished, its destruction is described as a murder. There is an ambiguity about the poet's attitude toward this aspect of his experience, a suggestion that he is touching upon complexities difficult to unravel. The word, the ostracism, that so terrifies the small child becomes a source of comfort, a protector, so that stepping out from behind the obscenity and asserting one's own self becomes an act of high courage. And while there is no way of convincingly establishing causal relationships, it seems more than coincidence that Shapiro abandons strict meter (present in the other poems even when rhyme is not) just at the moment the perceiving self experiences ambivalence, just at the moment the ego is forced to share its triumphs with forces from beneath the surface of consciousness.

The wall between Jew and non-Jew, or rather the notion of Jew as boundary of the human condition, is touched on in the first section of *Poems of a Jew*. But the contact between Jewish and Gentile worlds forms the explicit subject matter for most of section two, as the very titles of poems in that section indicate: "The Confirmation," "The Jew at Christmas Eve," "Christmas Eve: Australia," "The Ham-Bone of a Saint," "Teasing the Nuns," "The Crucifix in the Filing Cabinet." Some of the more interesting poems, however, do not explicitly announce this theme, although they do in fact explore it.

"The First Time" describes a seventeen-year-old boy's visit to a prostitute; in it, the suppressed sexual side of the Jewish question, latent in such poems as "University," becomes the focus of attention. Increasingly detached from the reality of his experience, which begins with clinical imagery "in shadowy quarantine" and ends with the boy transfixed "in space like some grotesque,/ Far, far from her where he is still alone. . . ," his otherness is brought into focus by the girl's question: *"Are you a*

Jew?'' (28, 29) Here the alienation of the Jew and the alienation of the adolescent converge. Sex becomes a pit of darkness threatening to swallow the boy's manhood, as the bed "Spreads its carnivorous flower-mouth for all." Insecurity, tinged with terror, culminate in an attack not only on the boy's masculinity but on his humanness as well: he becomes a Jew, an abstraction, a violation of his own personal identity.

What is most remarkable about the poem is its tone. Shapiro walks the thin line between comedy—the poem's subject is, after all, the butt of the conventional joke—and pathos. The boy is bumbling rather than inept; he is so thoroughly anesthetized he can, if not overcome, at least survive his fear and shame. The girl is ironically younger than he is. The cruel question is asked "almost gently." The image that summarizes the entire poem is that of "A candle swimming down to nothingness/ Put out by its own wetted gusts of flame. . . ." A clear reference to the boy's detumescence in the face of his anxieties, it is also the symbol for ultimate annihilation, which is none the less final for its gentleness.

Formally, the poem stands with Shapiro's early work, metrically regular (though with interesting variations), a fixed stanzaic pattern (abcabc), with enjambment and tough, flat, prosaic statement as antidote to ceremonious shape. Shapiro has learned much from Yeats, and is not totally unsuccessful in playing off rigid pattern against a rich, sometimes surreal body of imagery, although one senses it might have gone either way.

One of Shapiro's finest poems, and one of his earliest, is "The Leg." With no specific reference at all to Jewishness, a note at the book's end is helpful, if not essential, in understanding the poem's place in the book.

> Freud speaks (it may be all too often) of "violent defloration" and "the fear of being eaten by the Father." In Freud's view,

as in that of every other Jew, mutilation, circumcision, and "the
fear of being eaten" are all one. *The Leg* is a poem written
during war and its subject is the wholeness even of the muti-
lated. The poem *Mongolian Idiot* has the same theme. (70)

The poem and note together offer a fine opportunity to examine
concretely the uses to which Shapiro puts Jewishness in his poetry.

The amputation of the leg is not in itself a specifically Jewish
experience. But Shapiro's note makes clear what can actually be
deduced from the poem: the missing leg becomes the prototype
of all loss. And whether, as in the Freudian view, the anxiety of
mutilation is the source of all anxiety, or, in a more existential
reading, the anxiety of mutilation is the specific symbol of the
dread of nonbeing, the lost leg, and the Jew, are placed at the
very limits of human consciousness; they become the means of
defining those limits.

Some important questions are raised, not least the entire problem of relations between mind and body. The soldier slowly
becomes aware of what he has lost; his hands must explore the
stump. Is the loss real, is the body anything but an extension of
the mind? If the mind persists after the loss of the leg, is the body
anything more than a conventional, an artificial, limit to one's
existence? Or is the reverse true? Is the centrality of the mind an
illusion, does each part of the body have its own connection with
reality?

> For the leg is wondering where he is. . . .
> He is its injury, the leg is his orphan,
> He must cultivate the mind of the leg. . . . (32)

I would not suggest that there is in any definite sense an answer
to these questions in the poem, but if Shapiro leans in either
direction, it is toward the primacy of the body; he is not a tho-

roughgoing materialist, but he demonstrates that same commitment to the physical world as in "The Synagogue." The chief
interest of "The Leg" lies precisely in that—for Shapiro—characteristically Jewish commitment.

It is a poem about a soldier coming to terms with a terrible fact:
the mutilation of his body. The expected means of reconciliation
would, for most readers, involve a rejection of the primacy of the
body; but Shapiro frustrates this expectation by insisting all the
more upon the body's importance, and finding his consolation
therein. Again, the commitment to the finite transcends the infinite. The limitation is itself the means of transcending all limits:
Now he smiles to the wall:/ The amputation becomes an acquisition." These lines place Shapiro within the tradition that runs
from Donne, who beseeches God to ravish him that he may be
chaste, to Hopkins, whose God's descending darkness is His
mercy; it is that tradition which views man's relation to God as
being most closely approximated in paradox. ". . . If Thou take
me angrily in hand," Shapiro concludes, "And hurl me to the
shark, I shall not die." (33) What is especially interesting here is
Shapiro's locating of the Jew at the precise center of the paradox.
For just as circumcision makes the Jew the quintessential muti-
lated man, so the horrors of the Second World War make him the
living emblem of loss. It is all very well to suggest that without
the note cited above, and without "The Leg" 's inclusion in this
particular volume of poetry, there would be no necessity to connect the loss with Jewishness. The correct response to this is not
that the original subject of the poem was probably Jewish, but
that the very fact that the soldier has experienced a terrifying loss
and, having been thoroughly crushed by it, explores it and comes
to find salvation through it, makes him a Jew.

It is loss, it is the encounter with the "background of Nothing,"
that defines the Jew; it is these things that define the boundaries
of the human condition; and it is these things that help create the
special relation to reality held by the artist. Edmund Wilson's

metaphor of the Wound and the Bow is itself a kind of gloss on "The Leg." The wound, the artist's inability to function effectively in the world, leads to his estrangement. But it also is the source of his creative powers. Making the amputation an acquisition: Shapiro's own image of the creative imagination, revealing with equal clarity both the limitations and possibilities of that process.

Of the seven poems of "Adam and Eve," which forms a substantial part of the last section of *Poems of a Jew*, Shapiro wrote: "The viewpoint of the sequence, that man is for the world, not for the afterworld, is Jewish." (71) And the viewpoint, from Adam's initial longing, to the final expulsion from the garden, is also specifically sexual. The significant variation on the traditional story lies in Shapiro's unspoken suggestion that banishment from the garden is the cure for the disease rather than the onset of the disease; Shapiro's special contribution to this variation is the notion that sexual consummation is not the prize that must be paid for in banishment, but is itself simply a means of asserting man's rightful place in the scheme of things—that is, in the world, not in the garden. Further, this worldliness is not ultimately rebellion against God, although it may superficially and temporarily take that form, but a cornerstone of God's plan:

> "Needing us greatly, even in our disgrace,
> Guide us, for gladly do we leave this place
> For our own land and wished-for banishment." (69)

The paradox that tempts man to escape the garden is closely related to the paradoxes at the heart of love, and of art. Originally in tune with nature, operating exclusively by instinct, Adam, for no apparent reason except the very quality of his being, enters the world of thought and self-consciousness: "Thinking became a garden of its own." (62) Thought makes a creator of man himself, but the price of this power is the sense of aloneness and separateness from all of the rest of God's creation. Man longs to reestablish unity, and the longing is made concrete in sexual desire. The eating of the apple is transformed into sexual eating.

> So wide
> Their mouths, they drank each other from inside.
> A gland of honey burst within their throats. (65)

The note to "The Leg" comes immediately to mind: "In Freud's view, as in that of every Jew, mutilation, circumcision, and 'the fear of being eaten' are all one." But we would not need the note to be aware of the anxiety that accompanies sexual desire throughout the sequence. The sexual world is also the world of time and change, the world of death; but it is because rather than in spite of this that it is welcomed, even as it is feared, by Adam and Eve. "Death is the mother of beauty," Wallace Stevens wrote. And Shapiro echoes this as the angel calls out joyously to the banished pair, who turn to see "Eden ablaze with fires of red and gold,/ The garden dressed for dying in cold flame." (69) It is precisely in its consumption (in its being eaten up) by flames that the garden is revealed as most beautiful.

The sequence of poems begins with Adam instinctively praising the nature of things; it ends with Adam and Eve staring in "dark amazement" at the beauty of a dying world. The movement is from union with nature and harmony with the totality of being to consciousness of the self as separate from the rest of creation: in short, a forging of the human ego. The sequence is an appropriate conclusion to *Poems of a Jew*, affirming as it does the value of "autumn and the present world," (69) asserting the power of the self to remain whole in the face of chaos. From instinct, to consciousness, to guilt, to wonder—that is the growth of the individual, that is the development of the artist.

It is probably no accident, then, that "Adam and Eve" spans most of the range of Shapiro's mastery of traditional meter and pattern; the triumph of form is the triumph of the integrated self. The meter of each poem is iambic pentameter. The first poem consists of quatrains (abab), the second a favorite seven-line stanza (ababcbc), the third a sonnet, the fourth (xabcbac) and fifth (abbccca) variations on the seven-liner, the sixth six-line stanzas composed of rhymed couplets, and the seventh quatrains with a difference (abba). Off-rhymes, run-on lines, and rough, prosaic rhythms permit a significant degree of variation within the relatively rigid structure. But a powerful sense of regularity and agreement dominates. And the movement from quatrain to more intricate patterns, back to a slightly different quatrain, is surely meant to embody the emotional development of the poem: it is cyclical with crucial changes taking place within the cycle, it is the transformation of praise into wonder.

Many of the pieces in *The Bourgeois Poet* are, from the point of view of subject, parts of *Poems of a Jew* written too late to be included. Many others would seem to have at least as much right as, say, "The Leg," to be included in any oblique attempt to define the Jewish consciousness. But whether or not the original book could survive these additions without being burnt to cinders is certainly open to question. What has happened, chiefly, is that the poet has been dislocated from the center of his poems; and, ironically enough, it is by adopting a more personal poetic mode that Shapiro achieves this dislocation.

"Always the character who yells, I insist, I insist on being a Jew!" Shapiro begins poem 61, "(Can't you forget it? Isn't it obsolete? Isn't it faking the evidence?)"[2] Among many possible references, specific and general, the description of the character insisting on being a Jew could well apply to Shapiro himself, in *Poems of a Jew*. But somehow this insistence is now perceived as at best no longer applicable, at worst a fraud. Why? It is possible, of course, that Shapiro's lines are a commentary on the possibilities of being a Jew in the modern world; poets do, after all, occasionally mean what they say. But it seems much more likely that the difficulties of being a Jew are simply local manifestations of the more inclusive difficulty of possessing coherent being in any form whatsoever.

Poem 74 is probably the clearest statement of this in *The Bourgeois Poet:* "The prophets say to Know Thyself: I say it can't be done. . . . Man is mostly involuntary. Consciousness is only a tiny part of us. . . . Those poets who study their own consciousness are their own monsters. Each look in the mirror shows you a different self. . . . Creation renewing itself forever does not look back. . . . The lost ones return to the same old self and sit there in the corner, laughing or crying." (95, 96) Poetry, then, is the expression of a totality of which consciousness is only a tiny part: there can be no clear image of personality, only a series of shifting mirrors. By implication, there can be no single shaping intelligence, no clear-cut perspective from which one can accost reality.

Formal pattern is an immediate casualty: the agreement of rhyme, the regularity of meter, may well depend upon a strong faith in the existence of the self as a possible arbiter of experience. This is a problem that most contemporary poets have had to come to terms with: those of mystical bent define the poem as an expression of that universal self of which the individual self is but a specific manifestation; others have rooted the form and rhythm of the poem in the order and pulse of the human body, in bone and blood, flesh and breath; others still have grounded the particular self in the general myth. Very few other than Shapiro have been content to perceive the disintegration of the self and not attempt instantly to reestablish wholeness; he is again almost Kierkegaardian in his insistence on the finiteness of prose as opposed to the universals of pattern and meter.

The second casualty is the poet's ability to use the Jew as a definer of human boundaries, although the Jew still appears frequently throughout the book. The difference can be clearly seen in a comparison between the concluding words of "The First Time," "*Are you a Jew?*" and the opening line of Poem 87 of *The Bourgeois Poet*, "Cat called me a Jewish pig." (107) In the earlier poem, the question, although gently asked, draws all attention to the vulnerability, the nakedness of the young man, which may in itself be thought of as a kind of essential Jewishness. But the second phrase, although uttered in anger, has not a similar power to wound, nor to define. The relationship between the young man and the prostitute is sharply enough drawn to be a cliché; the relationship between the poet and Cat is mired in ambiguity. Who is victim, who the tormentor? What is the basis of their relationship, the nature of their love? Where in the surreal imagery of the poem does the description of Cat's overt action end and the evocation of her inner world begin? What marks the boundaries between suggestions of sexual intercourse and visions of the slaughterhouse? As was always the case in Shapiro's poetry, there is a great deal of irony involved. But whereas, before, the irony even if double-edged was perceived from a single vantage point, perspective may now shift from line to line. And in many passages throughout the book, tone is for all practical purposes impossible to determine.

Shapiro has not necessarily abandoned all formal poetry; nor is it reasonable to suppose that he utterly disbelieves in the possibility of the integrated self giving shape to experience. Subsequent poems have certainly marked an inevitable retreat from the extremes of *The Bourgeois Poet*. But even within that volume, Shapiro has not totally ceased to proclaim the humanistic values dependent upon the existence of a coherent self; he has continued to affirm even when affirmation is by definition absurd.

NOTES

1. New York, 1958, p. ix. Subsequent references to this book will be followed by page numbers in parentheses.

2. *The Bourgeois Poet*, New York, 1964, p. 74. Subsequent references to this book will be followed by page numbers in parentheses.

Further Notes on the Dereliction of Culture: Edward Lewis Wallant and Bruce Jay Friedman

MARCUS KLEIN

Bruce Jay Friedman and the late Edward Lewis Wallant are writers of that kind who are uniquely valuable in a moment of history, and even imperative, not for their range or their depth or wisdom or cunning, but for their astonishing likeliness. So such a poet as Matthew Prior, for instance, really tells us more about the early eighteenth century—its tonal options, the dialectic of its manners, its sense of cultural exigency—than does, say, Alexander Pope. And indeed it is helpful that Friedman and Wallant both suffer some relative lack of imaginative will to create imposing fictions. Rather, they cast clarity by creating the realization of what we should have expected all along. Their talent lies in the fact that they create the shapes of a unitary common knowledge.

In terms of temperament, style, ambition, and in all obvious ways, Friedman and Wallant are absolute opposites. They are therefore in a position to be complementary. Friedman takes the low road; Wallant took the high road. Friedman, dancing on the edge of a breakdown, is obsessively funny and vulgar. Wallant's novels are liturgical and melancholy, despite some efforts—notably in *The Tenants of Moonbloom*[1]—at sprightliness. For Friedman the major metaphor is impotence. The metaphor in its turn breeds many jokes which yearn toward *machismo*. For Wallant the primary realization was existential, a sense of God's imperturbability, which sense had as its consequence a yearning toward secular, social communions. And within their oppositeness Friedman and Wallant also, deviously, confirm each other, and therefore they confirm the availability of their perception of the cultural moment. Or, more precisely, they confirm their construction of a culture which in fact remains unavailable, for they have in common the habit of substituting tokens for conditions, of manipulating a limited number of plausibilities in order to signify cultural distress. They both have the habit of literalizing common metaphor, rather than the other way around, with the result that the fiction is at once extreme, abstract, and simulative. And the fiction is peculiarly authoritative just because it isolates and develops clichés.

So, in Wallant's first novel, *The Human Season*,[2] the hero is a plumber, with proletarian appropriateness named Joe Berman. The story proceeds toward a vision of universal humanity. Given that ambition, it should be the case that the hero of the story might be anything, and the less specific, the better, but the persuasiveness of the climactic vision rests in a very great part on the fact that Berman is a plumber and nothing else. He is ignorant but intelligent, reflective and taciturn, muscular, honest, fastidious (for he can be assumed to know much of sewage), a detached inhabitant of the underworld of common humanity, experienced, practical, inarticulate usually to the point of muteness but not without eloquence and slow passion, dependable, skeptical, and so forth. He is named by his job, from which in an ironic way he is not alienated. He has for modern mankind a significance equivalent to that of a golden-hearted prostitute or a bootblack in an earlier time. And at the end as at the beginning we know that plumbers are exemplary.

In Bruce Jay Friedman's novel *The Dick*,[3] the story is for the most part a function of the title. The hero is by profession a public-relations man in a police department, a "quasi-dick." He wants to be a full-fledged dick. He is, characterologically, a *shmuck*, and he is named Kenneth LePeters. The phallic implications in this contrivance are italicized by his experiences with women, and at the end he has his initiation—although he discovers at the end, in one more turn of the screw, that the state of full genital prepossession is not what it is cracked up to be, wherefore he subsides, withdraws from competition, ambitious now only to plow his own field properly.

The metaphor in each case presumably begins as a device for exploration of a subject, a summary name for a modern situation. What more perfectly apposite a hero than a plumber, for a journey through modern American consciousness?—given the truth that our lives are terribly antiseptic, superficial, timid, callow, glib, and unrooted. Or, given the same general truth, a "dick" will do to introduce us to the problem of self-assertion. In the latter instance, of course, because Freud has long been a public utility, the amount of realization in the metaphor is so evident as to be beyond analysis. But in each case the metaphor is utterly insistent, for the reason that its availability is virtually the sum of its properties. It is also to the point that Friedman and Wallant are emphatically Jewish novelists of this moment—Jews, that is to say, for whom Judaism is a kind of strawberry mark, something that must mean something because it is celebrated in literature. As has been said, the Jew, with his prior claims to persecution and urban exile, is the hero of our time. It follows that the postulate of Jewish characters with Jewish tracings by authors with Jewish names in itself touches upon an exemplification, and perhaps hints at the revelation of the lost dauphin. Within Joe Berman, as Wallant's story makes clear, there is the tale of Job, that earlier Jewish plumber. Joe Berman is not only an outcast but he is designed to be a mythical outcast. Kenneth LePeters has changed his name from "Sussman." This act implies: (1) that a Jew in America is prevented from thinking that he is a real man, (2) that those social forces which would convert him to the faith of the Gentiles demand that he be faithless to himself, (3) that before society corrupted him, in the past and within himself, he was sweet and self-sufficient, (4) that the lust and aggression of real manhood are characteristic of contemporary American society while Judaism means innocence, and the act also implies (5) that every LePeters is suspect because every LePeters contains a Sussman. Indeed, every LePeters contains a "Lapidus," that celebrated, tortured comedian. It is the Jewish joke: *He changed his name!*, and at the same time it is the national dream of the resource of innocence lurking guiltily within. The Jew, driven by contemporary pressures to disingenuousness but vaguely, guiltily, shyly, always remembering himself, is everybody.

Joe Berman and Kenneth LePeters have in common the fact that they are emblems, existing together in the area midway between myth and stereotype. Though they yearn in different directions, they identify that area.

In the time-present of his novel, Berman is a fifty-nine-year-old man. His wife has just died. His mourning is the occasion for the novel. His children are by now either dead or fled, he is at once too old to start a new life and too young to lapse into easy grandfatherliness, and his house—and life—are now reverberatingly empty. Much of the novel consists of Berman's memories of the ordinary but rich life which he has had—his *shtetl* childhood, his arrival in the United States, his family, his work as a ditchdigger and his fight with the Irish foreman, his marriage, the birth of his children and the death of one of them. This now is his season for metaphysics, because in the past, even in times of grief, his life has presented to him patterns of sustaining meaning. So, during his childhood, when his father had died, he had been struck in the midst of his suffering by the beauty of the ongoingness of life. When his son had been killed, during the war, he had searched for and discovered answers:

> To know why . . . why . . . Such pain, such pain. He had never dreamed there could be pain like that. It crushed him, wrenched his bones, trod on his brain. And he knew what made the pain so much worse, so unimaginably worse. No one else knew, only he, only he. He had sinned, he had been guilty. He had loved his son less than his daughters. . . . Now he would pay, how he would pay. For eternity he would suffer remorse along with his grief. (p. 56)

The answer to the pain, that is to say, had been the remorse; death had not been arbitrary. In this time nothing sustains him, nothing makes sense, and for much of the novel he moves laterally back and forth between lethean numbness and rage against God. It is Joe Berman's necessity, obviously, to find a new basis for living.

Kenneth LePeters, in his novel, is a man nearing forty, come to the point of what might be expected ordinarily to be maximum relationship with the world. He has a wife, a ten-year-old daughter, a mother somewhere, a house in the suburbs, a job which represents a significant promotion, colleagues and neighbors who are almost friends. But every gain in relationship is, of course, an actual or potential loss. His wife has been distant from him for years, and she has an affair with one of the real dicks. His love for his daughter verges on incest. He has already betrayed his mother and the memory of his father. The house in the suburbs turns out to be in the black school district, and that is an eventuality which is not ironic but rather another cause for uncertainty. LePeters appears to be mysteriously persecuted, all normal expectations turning backside to him, but in fact the root of his problem is a dilemma of proprieties. All seeming securities are really contingencies, on closer inspection, waiting for the right attitude, and he cannot manage to be resolute about his attitudes. As a suburban aspirer and as a doting father, he is horrified in the matter of the black school district; but then he is not horrified, or rather his horror is sabotaged, because he is not comfortable in the suburbs anyway, because his love for his daughter has sexual implications and so does blackness, because blackness is alluring as well as frightening, because he is liberal, and because he himself is guilty of ethnic faithlessness. No act will fully sanction him. And so he temporizes.

At the end both of these protagonists find the resolution that was waiting all along. Berman goes to live with his married daughter. LePeters takes training and becomes a full dick, and then he turns in his badge. Having proved himself, he can abandon his nervous ambitions. The resolution in each instance is, however, a matter of a few terminal pages. The real subject in each instance is the exemplary situation which will justify the emblematic hero. And despite all apparent differences, the processes of justification are remarkably similar. Each instance begins with an assumption that a man is sustained and identified by his conventional relationships which prove, however, to be untrustworthy and inessential. The rule of these novels, that is to say, is the arbitrary dissolution of domestic life. So the main point in Joe Berman's previous religious feeling has been that it was unquestioned, and he had not questioned because the circumstances of his life had supported his feeling. The motion of the novel is created by his realization now of the illusory nature of those circumstances. At the end it does happen that he will give some new credit to his old illusions, but that again is a function of his finding a way out. And the main point in LePeters' quest for potency is the failure of domestic circumstances to certify his potency. He is not a victim. Rather, everything goes wrong and he does not know how to act. Were these novels constructed in another fashion, the drama might go toward exploration of existential consciousness, or were these novels of another time, they might have gone toward expression of ethical disillusions. They are in truth far more terrifying, in good part because of the modesty of their range and despite the salvation registered in the one and the comedy of the other. They are novels about the giving way of the minimal institutions in a time when—it goes without saying—nothing else sustains a man. And despite their certain glibness and apparent lack of realization of their own materials, Wallant and Friedman are novelists who locate an authentic desperation. Their glibness and the something second-hand about them is a part of the measure.

EDWARD LEWIS WALLANT

Wallant died in 1962, at the age of thirty-six. His four completed novels were published almost all at one time—within a period of four years—two of the novels being published posthumously. His early death necessarily made his fiction seem the more intensely poignant, but so did the fact of the rapid successiveness of the novels. The circumstances of the publication were peculiarly appropriate. They implied Wallant's sincerity, indeed the obsessive unitariness of his purpose. In each of the novels he had posited on the one side protagonists who were self-protectively aloof, emotionally numb, and cynical, and on the other side an emphatically ordinary and also offensive humanity. The novels were one novel which seemed a single extravagant and hopeless attempt to leap the distance between the solitary individual and the humanity outside, thereby to provide the protagonist with a basis for life.

But there were differences in the novels, which testify further to the authentic desperation which Wallant had discovered. In terms of tone and plot, the novels strangely became more sanguine; they became more sanguine as they became more and more emblematic, and less informed by a persuasive accumulation of experience. For one thing, the protagonists came to be successively both younger and less encumbered. Berman, in the first novel, is fifty-nine and he is surrounded, now, by his personal losses. Sol Nazerman in *The Pawnbroker*[4] is forty-five years old, but he has already survived his losses. He had been in the concentration camps. His wife and children had been murdered. He has for years now practiced living beyond his nightmare memories, building a bastion around his spirit, although with incomplete success. During the term of the novel, his memories press on him. In the next novel, *The Tenants of Moonbloom* (1963), the hero, Norman Moonbloom, is thirty-three. He is feckless, a perpetual student, and pastless. By the momentary chance that makes the occasion of the novel, he has come to be the rent agent for his brother's apartment buildings, and the tenants eventually constitute his teeming humanity, but that development is less than an imperative of his situation. Indeed, the tenants can work upon his consciousness because Moonbloom is provided with little else to worry about. And finally in *The Children at the Gate*,[5] the protagonist, Angelo DeMarco, is a boy of nineteen who keeps furiously to himself largely for intellectual reasons: as a reader of books on science, he cannot abide his family's pietism. As the protagonists become younger, they have fewer vital disillusions with which to frustrate new experience, they become more vulnerable, and they necessarily postulate greater hope for the communion in humanity which is the climax of each of the novels.

On the other hand, Wallant's manipulation becomes progressively more wilful. In *The Pawnbroker* the agent of the climax is Nazerman's assistant in the pawn shop, a Puerto Rican youth significantly named Jesus. The relationship between the two—the two Nazarenes—is plausibly filial, and therefore there is pointedness in Nazerman's refusal of feeling. In a terminal episode, during an attempted robbery, the boy dies for Nazerman. Nazerman is thereby enabled to discover love:

Something was breaking out of him. His body felt full of the
flow of some great wound. A rush and a torment burned him.
He felt naked and flayed and he hung over the dying youth like
a frayed canopy. . . . And then the dry retching sound of weeping, growing louder and louder and louder, filling the Pawnbroker's ears, flooding him, drowning him, dragging him back
to that sea of tears he had thought to have escaped. . . . All his
anesthetic numbness left him. He became terrified of the touch
of air on the raw wounds. What was this great, agonizing sensitivity and what was it for? Good God, what was all this? *Love?*
Could this be *love?* (pp. 271–72)

All of this is sudden enough, but it very well could be love. There
is such a sufficient complexity in the motion between Nazerman's
burdens and his motives as to make it so. The accompanying
religious symbolism is, meanwhile, for the most part subservient.
In *Moonbloom,* however, there is scarcely any complexity within
the given situation, and therefore eventualities and symbols are
made to do the work of a plot. It is a given that the protagonist
is a contented melancholic. As a rental agent he is presented with
a dozen-odd "characters" who stand conspicuously for the dross
and common condition of humanity, but the novel does not present him with any reason for making his dealings urgent. They
do become so, of course, but only according to plan. The novel
realizes a theme rather than an action; the essential action is over
almost before it begins, and the rest is elaboration. On an occasion, and early on in the novel, the affectless Moonbloom takes
a fever, and with that much arbitrariness he is sensitized. Now he
can begin to see the implications residing in his agentry, and for
the rest of the novel he takes upon himself the sufferings and the
filth of his tenants. The preliminary idea gives way to frenzy, and
the frenzy to joy. And, finally, in *The Children at the Gate* there is
at least an equal lack of persuasive connection between the
protagonist and his metaphysical destiny. Angelo is made to be
a druggist's clerk. It is one of his duties to solicit orders at the

Sacred Heart Hospital. Whereas Moonbloom was initially disen-
chanted to the point of mildness, Angelo is fierce—we are told
that he has the dedicated look of a worker priest—but once again
the protagonist's career, his movement forward, is available only
within a non-contingent symbology. There is the recalcitrant,
science-minded angel on the one side, and there are those sick
people on the other. The sick are, moreover, mostly children;
having presented himself with that token identification, Wallant
skimped on most other details. The effort of the novel is then to
provide a mediation between the two abstractions, a ritual of
engagement which will act, as it were, as a converting ordinance.
The mediant is a character named Sammy. He is an orderly; he
is Jewish, racy, ironically irreverent, nutty, by designation capable of high mockery and deep pity. He meets the sick, that is to
say, in holy fashion on the human level, thereby offering a
demonstration. And he is nothing if not explicit:

> ". . . I love you all, you hear? Nothing turns *my* stomach. I'll kiss
> your gallstones, your ulcers, your cancers, your bleeding piles
> —and they'll all disappear! It's all psychosomatic anyhow and
> I'm the miracle man. I cure snakebite, dt's, dropsy, broken
> hearts—from angina, of course. Let a laugh be your umbrella
> . . . da, da, da, dee, dee . . . Hey, did you hear this one? He was
> carrying the cross down the street, crowds all around, soldiers
> in front of Him, soldiers behind Him. Two guys were watching,
> and they noticed He was moving His lips, muttering something.
> So they get up close to hear, and what do you think? He was
> singing 'I Love a Parade.' Hah, is that something? You get it,
> hah? Am I a comedian or am I a comedian? Oh, hey, I got a
> million jokes, a billion." (p. 158)

There are some other devices in the novel, but Sammy's sermons
are the important part of Angelo's tutelage. And, as was to be
anticipated, Angelo is persuaded to the message of universal love
in a Godless world.

The formal development of this fiction, in one way of looking at the matter, was toward allegory, or what must have seemed to Wallant to be allegory. Even by the time of the second novel, and certainly thereafter, he had so well established his thematic terms as to make character, action, and conflict largely supererogatory. Wallant's clear purpose, however, involved a realization about the nature of contemporary culture, without which the theme lacked justifying pressure. The making of allegory depends on the abeyance of skepticism and the elimination of problematics, which is to say elimination of the devices by which ordinary reality might be apprehended at first hand. As Wallant doubted less, his elaborations and his tropes, his secular miracles and his fantastic resolutions became the more detached from any necessity. The clarity of his realization had indeed from the beginning been uncertain. Joe Berman speaks a non-language, for instance, which depletes his personal reality as it tends toward deliberated vulgarisms: "Okay, then I take a second mortgage out and do the whole house over, top to bottom. Then we're set, see." (p. 18) . . ."How much can I ask? And I don't want no kitchen privilege, just to sleep. He can sit around at night and look at television. How do I tell them that I don't want no drinkers?" (p. 79) Berman in fact doesn't do much speaking. The greater part of the novel is non-discursive, and it goes toward lyrical inflation:

> Yet in the dark, miraculously, he heard it.
> Heard it in the crevice between day and sleep—the river, singing that one glorious monotony. It left him forever yet always arrived again. He woke to it in the morning, under the blackened wooden ceiling. It was as great as the sound of his father's harsh morning prayers, more and less, too, that that bass voice crying "*Adonoi.*" Yet part of it, too, like the bread smell, was wedded to the river scent.
> "So what, what is it all about?" he asked in his old man's American bed. And he realized that he was not through with it, that he had at least a little of the answer to find. (pp. 172–73)

The rhythms of this prose frustrate inquiry. And in *The Human
Season* Wallant was already substituting epiphanies and iteration
for the logic of motives. In a novel of less than two hundred
pages, a not-inconsiderable ten pages is given over to Berman's
hurling curses at God.

In the succeeding novels these abstract intensities became
more prominent, and therefore presumably Wallant found the
materials of his composition more malleable. A better novelist
would have tested himself more severely. But there can be no
doubting of Wallant's seriousness or his dedication to a vision.
He had an idea which must be called religious. What must be
implied, however, by the progressive ease, indeed the faith, with
which he composed instances of his vision is his inability to have
imagined a salvation more provisional. And in that happenstance
—given a concerned man of obvious intelligence—there is a further implication that is truly terrifying. He created emblemati-
cally ordinary characters who proceeded from a state of hermetic
isolation, also emblematic, to a vast conviction of the human
community based on love, and who proceeded without significant mediation. The validity of the idea is hardly open to question, and of course Wallant never questioned it. But if there is
nothing in between, if Wallant could not conceive of any lesser
likelihood for a character's accomplishment of humane social
identity, then the act of religious vision is a dismissal of culture.
Not even defiance, for one can assume Wallant's good will. Or
the vision might have been its own justification without further
implication had it been religious in the usual sense, but Wallant
did not believe in God except as a convenient illusion. His purpose, to look at the matter another way, was to locate an ordinary,
precisely middling ground of reality, and the best he could see
was an ultimate abstraction. The novels make constant appeals to
density and dirt. Berman, as an artisan, likes cement. Moonbloom
in a climactic moment bathes ecstatically in the detritus flowing
from broken sewage pipes. And the kind and the frequency of

these appeals suggests once again that a day-to-day being of men among men simply was not an imaginative possibility for Wallant. The domestic life in which all of his protagonists are potentially implicated simply and rapidly ceases to exist.

BRUCE JAY FRIEDMAN

The protagonists of Friedman's three novels are ripe, whatever their ages, in the terminal stages of a domestic life which is defined as an assault on personal honor. They are created so as to be unmistakably lacking in the resources of independent identity, and their dependence is at the same time continuously betrayed. Kenneth LePeters as a public-relations man for a homicide bureau is not even marginal to a social enterprise; he is perfectly useless. The protagonist of Friedman's first novel, *Stern*,[6] is by occupation a writer of editorial materials for product labels. Joseph in *A Mother's Kisses*[7] is a seventeen-year-old boy who has just finished high school and is on his way to college for the sole reason that going to college is the next thing to do. He has some information and even some intellectual capabilities, but no personal ambitions. On the other hand, Friedman situates these protagonists in a moment of social transition, when a prior cultural identity has been or is being withdrawn and the new culture seems to be bafflingly malign. Therein is half the basis for the comedy. They are all middle-class New York Jews—the more purely because they are given nothing else to be. They are all upwardly mobile. Joseph goes to college. Stern, like LePeters, moves to the suburbs. What follows among other things is a comedy of manners but seen from the point of view of the ignorant intruder. Upward mobility means for them an environment composed of all of those things that New York Jews are not supposed to know anything about—chiefly, in Friedman, Gentiles and nature. Stern is the only Jew in the neighborhood, and therefore almost as a consequence his shrubbery is half eaten away by caterpillars. Joseph goes to a college named Kansas Land Grant Agricultural—no place, as one knows, for a Jewish boy. When we see these protagonists they are already far gone toward crazed unrelatedness.

They each make some clutching motions toward the past. That is to be expected, but it is also to be expected that they are less than fully committed to their New York City Jewish roots. The plot of each of the novels might easily allow for a return; Friedman takes no particular care to put the past beyond recapturing. The particular past, however—as one is expected once again to know—is of a thinness amounting to hypocrisy. That fact accounts for the movement out of New York City and into the world of the Gentiles, as it accounts for the indistinctness of character which these protagonists bring to the world of the Gentiles. They are not children of the *shtetl.* Their parents before them, as they are given in the novels, have already achieved marginality or, on the maternal side, defensively boisterous pretension. The fathers are dull slaves to insulting non-jobs. (The elder LePeters-Sussman "had worked like a dog in badger pelts" (p. 6) at Frickman Furs. Stern's dad is in shoulder-pads.) The mothers are Jewish mothers, which in these instances means overbearing and theatrical but also, finally, impersonal. The most extensive case is Meg in *A Mother's Kisses.* She prides herself on not being like other mothers, the joke being that she is just like other Jewish mothers and a little more so. She is flauntingly sexual without being seductive. She is protective without being understanding. She is a vulgarian with tokens of sophistication, and at the same time she is wistfully needful. Her main action in the novel, and the main action of the novel as a whole, consists in her refusing to let go of her son. She schemes, virtually whores, and perpetually arranges during the summer of Joseph's anxiety about being admitted to a college, and then she goes to Kansas with him. She is a

standard type, except that the suggestions of Jocasta in the Jewish-mother joke are more blatant in her than is usual. But then
her broadly seeming lustfulness is akin to all of her other exag-
gerations, and is a function of her real poverty. She surrounds
Joseph with madly confused energies, and she is in herself a
woman without apprehensible personality.

The past provides no sustaining inheritance for the various
protagonists, and the present is locked against them. The other
half of Friedman's comedy rests on the fact that all human contact
is likely to be tangential at best. Dramatis personae in the world
of this fiction are "characters," which is to say people defined by
their idiosyncrasies. It is impossible for them to talk to each
other, and indeed one of Friedman's dependable devices is illus-
tration of that fact through a kind of non-discursive dialogue.
The protagonist lives in a world where everyone speaks out of his
own deafness:

> At the airport Joseph's father asked him if he had ever been
> on a plane. "Well, that's something to think about," he said.
> "How do you know you're going to like it?"
> "I don't, Dad," said Joseph.
> "Well, there you are, you've saved this for the last second. A
> lot of people get up there and they find they don't care for
> flying. They get nauseous. What are you going to do then?
> Look, I can't run your life. If that happens, tell your mother,
> and the people on the plane will get you something. They must
> have something for people in that condition. What the hell, the
> airlines are big business today. You act as though you're the
> first person ever flew a plane." (p. 194)

And Stern, with an ulcer, on one occasion is sent to have a
stomach X-ray:

> "Think of delicious dishes. Your favorites."
> Stern was barefooted and wore a thin shift; the light in the
> streets had not yet come up and his eyes were crusted with

sleep. "I may be sick," he said. "How can I think of delicious things? All right, eggs."

"Don't fool around," said the man, squinting into the machine. "I've got to get a lot of people in. Give me your favorite taste temptations; otherwise the pictures will be grainy."

"I really do like eggs," Stern said. "Late at night, when I've been out, I'd rather have them than anything."

"Are you trying to make a monkey out of me?" the man screamed, darting away from the machine. "Do you know how many I have got to get in today? *You give me your favorites.*" He flew at Stern, fat fists clenched, blond curls shaking, like a giant, enraged baby, and Stern, frightened, said, "Soufflés, soufflés."

"That ought to do it," said the man, his eye to the machine again. "I'm not sending out any grainy pictures." (pp. 77–78)

The smaller talk of the novels is a continuous frustration. In moments of what might be confrontation the pitch is raised and communication is the more stubbornly resisted.

Friedman's response to this situation in terms of plot is a series of assertive gestures and rapid defeats, with the end being somewhat hopeful but mostly inconclusive. What is in fact thereby revealed is a subtle and frustrating balancing-off of motives. The action of *Stern* is exemplary. It begins in a moment of hopeless relief from absolute despair:

One day in early summer it seemed, miraculously, that Stern would not have to sell his house and move away. Some small blossoms had appeared on one of the black and mottled trees of what Stern called his Cancer Garden, and there was talk of a child in the neighborhood for his son, a lonely boy who sat each day in the center of Stern's lawn and sucked on blankets. Stern had found a swift new shortcut across the estate which cut his walking time down ten minutes to and from the train, and the giant gray dogs which whistled nightly across a fence and took his wrists in their mouths had grown bored and preferred to hang back and howl coldly at him from a distance. (p. 9)

These reprieves are of course as ironic as the tone suggests. In the next movement forward the neighbor down the way, whose little boy was to be the new companion for Stern's little boy, knocks Stern's wife to the ground, glances incidentally at her uncovered crotch, and calls her kike. The episode should be Stern's opportunity; it focuses his incapacities past and present as a husband, father, neighbor, suburbanite, and a man. His response is prompt, his courage is abortive, he makes several visits to the vicinity of the kike man's house, and he fantasizes. Ultimately he reacts by giving birth to an ulcer, his appropriate agent of vengeance. The novel then turns to the drama of his recovery from his ulcer. He goes to a rest home which is populated by persons still more abrading and grotesquely idiosyncratic than the inhabitants of his normal life. The time at the rest home is another round of parrying unreasonableness. He is seemingly cured, however, when he discovers a fleeting community among the authentically sick, crazy, and dying. But back home the kike man is still waiting, Stern's son is still on the lawn with his blanket, and his wife is perhaps having an affair with her modern dance instructor. He finally has a brief fight with the kike man, who bloodies his ear. Stern now feels better.

It is obviously right that this ending should be so temperate. Triumph for Stern would be an unlikelihood. That is the case, however, not just because he is so purely by nature and nurture a victim, but also because within his circumstances it must be an open question whether he can prefer aggression to impotence. His past will not sustain him. He has left it for good reason. This suburban life as epitomized by the kike man is all he has, and if Stern fails to demonstrate simple manly courage, it is because the necessity of his situation is that he be ingratiating. All of his dreams of revenge on the kike man are accompanied by counter-dreams of brotherhood and camaraderie. He is desperate to prove that he is nice. His very outrage is therefore at the same time the language of surrender.

The grimmer irony within this comedy is, meanwhile, that Stern cannot surrender either. Neither the kike man nor anybody else wants what he might offer, for reasons implicated in the fact that they have nothing to offer him. They are all isolates, living in a happenstance propinquity, as is the case in Friedman's other novels. The comedy altogether is a charade of social efforts played out by a gullible, good, ordinary man in a place and time of cultural collapse. When they are touched, it turns out that the units of ordinary social enterprise—wife and family, a job of work, religious community, neighbors and neighborhood—have no reality, and all that remains is that poor schlemiel trying to find a friend. Friedman is the man who revived (and translated) the term "black humor" for current use. He has meant by the term an ability to comprehend horrors by finding them funny. It happens that discretely horrible things, events, and people are not really constants in his novels. His manner is not brutal; Friedman is no Céline. His subject is a middle range of experience, and the manner of Friedman's concern is rather pleasant. Nonetheless, constantly and beyond any explicitness, he writes out of a feeling for the abyss. Utter social disintegration is the given.

NOTES

1. Edward Lewis Wallant, *The Tenants of Moonbloom.* New York: Harcourt, Brace and World, Inc., 1963.

2. Edward Lewis Wallant, *The Human Season.* New York, Harcourt, Brace and World, Inc., 1960.

3. Bruce Jay Friedman, *The Dick.* New York: Alfred A. Knopf, 1970.

4. Edward Lewis Wallant, *The Pawnbroker.* New York: Harcourt, Brace and World, Inc., 1961.

5. Edward Lewis Wallant, *The Children at the Gate*. New York: Harcourt, Brace and World, Inc., 1964.

6. Bruce Jay Friedman, *Stern*. New York: Simon and Schuster, 1962.

7. Bruce Jay Friedman, *A Mother's Kisses*. New York, Simon and Schuster, 1964.

Dybbukianism: The Meaning of Method in Singer's Short Stories

EDWIN GITTLEMAN

"Who writes it all? God?"
"Not you."
"Where does He get so much paper?"
"Don't let your brains dry up in worrying about that."
—from "In the Poorhouse," in *The Spinoza of Market Street*

Often I said the opposite of what I intended, as if a literary dibbuk
had gotten into me.
—from "Schloimele," in *A Friend of Kafka*

Publication of Isaac Bashevis Singer's fifth collection of stories in English, *A Friend of Kafka* (1970), makes conveniently available twenty-one recent stories by America's most formidable writer of short fiction. Therefore it is a welcome event. But it is a significant one as well. This book amplifies the displacements of consciousness and sensibility which are to be found in Singer's earlier books, and which more than anything else provide the distinctive literary and personal qualities defining him as a writer.

Individually and as a collection, the new stories extend the displacements far beyond the experience of the provincial Jewish village of East Europe (the *shtetl*) and the great East European city (Warsaw) in which they originate. *A Friend of Kafka* is Singer's most American book. Consequently it calls attention not only to itself but also the the fifty-five other impressive stories Singer has published in book form, beginning with *Gimpel the Fool* (1957) and followed by *The Spinoza of Market Street* (1961), *Short Friday* (1964), and *The Séance* (1968). And thus, as never before the reader is forced to confront the baffling literary intelligence responsible for this entire corpus of short fiction.

Non-dramatic narrative is the characteristic mode Isaac Bashevis Singer has developed for his short stories. It was perfected as early as 1933 while he was writing *Satan in Goray*, the proto-novelistic fiction which remains his most impressive single book and the work from which his subsequent art of short story derives. Its usual and most interesting form might well be called that of story-as-information since his narrative strategy requires that stories be a telling of a special fictional kind of fact and for a special fictional purpose. As in *Satan in Goray*, what is told purports to be extracted from memories of the past, understood as communal Yiddish culture of the *shtetl* (even for stories not set in Europe) interacting with private history and psychology, and recoverable by a brooding imagination which swiftly and aggressively structures remembered facts. For this reason the narrative past-tenses in his most powerful writing are not so much conventional or convenient as necessary and accurate. The past itself is a current event. It is alive and accessible, more so than the present moment. For Singer nothing significant is possible in the ill-defined present (or future) except the act of telling; everything significant is possible in the cultural-historical-psychological past.

In these non-dramatic narratives the present has no validity. Nothing actually happens or can happen on the level of present

experience except the act of recall. The process of telling therefore is the primary reality which defines Singer's short fiction.
The authority of the past is such that it either blocks the present
or uses it only as the oral space needed for releasing what has
been internalized in consciousness and therefore stands urgently
in need of utterance. The single function the present can perform
for Singer is thus occasional, providing him with opportunities
for in-formed recitation.

Geographical places mentioned in Singer's stories, for example, are invariably authentic and locatable on appropriate
maps, usually old maps of Poland. These places, which have
no present or future meaning, only a significance which is
past, are not so much depicted as they are casually named
without further identification: Frampol, Krashnik, Yanev, Tur-
bin, Bilgoray, Malopol, or dozens of other such strange-
sounding places turning up in Singer's stories. They are cited
as if the confident act of naming is sufficient to make the
once-known again familiar. By contrast, however, the specific
locale for a story acquires its unique identity in a named town
by being painstakingly enumerated:

> Around Cunegunde's hut, isolated at the edge of the forest,
> weeds grew, brambles, hairy leaves with scales like scabs, poiso-
> nous berries, and thorns that seemed to bite at one's clothing.
> . . . There was an entire apothecary in her hovel: devil's dung
> and snake venom, wormy cabbage and the rope with which a
> man had been hung, adder's meat and elves' hair, leeches and
> amulets, wax and incense.[1]

Incantational enumeration is the characteristic act by which a
Singer story becomes specifically located in the limited geographical space reserved for it. Contained by the past more
than by town limits, the locale too—with its alien vegetation

and morbid household staples—becomes a matter of fact, however outrageous it might otherwise seem. The past can make anything comprehensible, especially if it is unnerving and disquieting.

In such regions of detailed finiteness which Singer's imagination for the past penetrates—where space is marginal, nonessentials crowded out, the air claustrophobic, and the mood ominous—it is fitting that shadings of light and dark are not at all visible to the reader, certainly not as qualities glancing off the surfaces of things. Rather, they are precisely recalled and distinguishable absolutes whose values are psychological and eschatological:

> The setting sun, remarkably large, stared down angrily like a heavenly eye upon the Frampol market place. Never before had Frampol seen such a sunset. Like rivers of burning sulphur, fiery clouds streamed across the heavens, assuming the shapes of elephants, lions, snakes, and monsters. They seemed to be waging a battle in the sky, devouring one another, spitting, breathing fire. It almost seemed to be the River of Fire they watched, where demons tortured the evil-doers amidst glowing coals and heaps of ashes. The moon swelled, became vast, blood-red, spotted, scarred, and gave off little light. The evening grew very dark, dissolving even the stars.[2]

Here light and dark are shocking apocalyptic abstractions, with masses calculable by some mysterious mathematics ritually cognate to enumeration.

Nor are ordinary colors shown; instead, when they occur (which is not often in an essentially chiaroscuro atmosphere), they are specified without subtle gradations of tone: "Although yellow hair does not readily change color, Abba's beard had turned completely white, and the white, staining, had turned yellow again."[3] And consistent with the peculiar nature of space and the erratic conditions of light and color, Singerian time does not elapse or have significant duration:

> A day or two later the news was that Alter was dying. The menfolks gathered; the burial society waited at the door. Well, listen to what happened. When she saw that Alter was at his final gasp, Shifra Leah ran for the doctor. But by the time she got back with the doctor in tow, there was Leizer Godl, the elder of the burial society, holding a feather to her Alter's nostrils. It was all over, they were ready to lift him off the bed, as the custom is. The instant Shifra Leah took it in, she flew into a frenzy; God help us, her screaming and wailing could be heard at the edge of the town.[4]

Within such a system of fictional coordinates—where experience as we know it is absent or else distorted by compression—it is natural that characters do not develop under the pressures of experience; rather, like towns, places, shading, color, and time, they are fixed by the very process of being mentioned:

> My father-in-law's second fault was his uncontrollable anger. He had been able to conquer all his other moral weaknesses, but not that one. If a merchant did not repay a debt on time and to the penny, he called him a swindler and refused to have any further dealings with him. If the town shoemaker made him a pair of boots, and they were a little too tight or too loose, he harangued him heartlessly.[5]

Accordingly, while character is controlled, emotions cannot be expressed:

> When she flew into a rage, she said things that would not even occur to an insane person. Swear words poured from her mouth like worm-eaten peas. She knew every curse in the holy book by heart. She was not beyond throwing rocks. Once, in the middle of winter, she broke a neighbor's windowpane and the neighbor never learned why.[6]

Nor do we. Whatever reality emotions (and motives) may have is a function of the narrative terms in which they are described.

In a fictional system in which experience is structured like this, where the voice telling of the past possesses the only available reality, nothing can happen. Events cannot possibly occur. They can only be reviewed:

> All night long Hindele felt herself lying in blood and pus. The one who had raped her snored, coughed, hissed like an adder. Before dawn a group of hags ran into the room, pulled the sheet from under her, inspected it, sniffed, began to dance. That night never ended. True, the sun rose. It was not really the sun, though, but a bloody sphere which somebody hung in the sky. Women came to coax the bride with smooth talk and cunning but Hindele did not pay any attention to their babble. They spat at her, flattered her, said incantations, but she did not answer them. Later a doctor was brought to her, but Hindele saw that he was a horned buck. No, the black powers could not rule her, and Hindele kept on spiting them.[7]

If human situations are not generated by the interactions between character and circumstance in Singer's fiction, then they are formulated by the act of narration itself:

> The way it looked, there didn't appear to be any reason why Reb Bunim and his family would not live out their days in peace as so often happens with ordinary people who because of their simplicity are spared bad luck and go through life without any real problems. . . . But Reb Bunim also had a daughter, and women, as it is well known, bring misfortune. . . . On more than one occasion, Reb Bunim, who was devoted to her, would say sorrowfully: "It's a shame that she's not a boy. What a man she would have made."[8]

The values of the narrative voice alone determine the directions the story will take.

The world evoked in Singer's short stories is therefore a problematical one. But it was not a world without recurring patterns of fact and circumstance which provide laws natural to it: long-suffering old men who reject Satan's irrefutable arguments against God are miraculously capable of engendering children; ambitious women who undertake work, learning, or forms of piety traditionally reserved for men eventually commit monstrous crimes; yellow-haired men with bulging temples are either simpletons or eunuchs; pretty daughters of wealthy fathers marry unhappily and consort with demons; pious rabbis confirm their faith by temporarily abandoning their faith and their faithful followers; queer old women living alone beyond village limits are malicious daughters of Lilith whose rewards will come in Gehenna; hardworking but impoverished shopkeepers and artisans become saints if they are faithful and uneducated or inept; brilliantly intellectual women acquire sexual passions which prove disastrous; common family tragedies undermine belief in God by those who are most pious; virtuous spinsters who eventually marry risk discovering that their bridegrooms are repulsive demons with webbed feet; scholarly writers and learned rabbis are the men most likely to accept Satan's intellectualized skepticisms; anger may condense into fires literally capable of burning houses; mischievous tricks turn out to have deadly effects; modest women who would repel the sexual advances of ordinary men accept lovers claiming to be demons; superbly efficient servants destroy the happiness of their prosperous masters; and evil spirits, including Satan, frequently commune with Singer's readers because the agents of darkness (and the Wicked One himself) are not only convincingly articulate but magnificent story-tellers as well.

Because of the persistence of the narrative voice, and the responsibilities assigned it by Singer—rendering the past by naming places, enumerating locales, recalling conditions of light and dark, specifying colors, disconnecting time, determining character, describing emotion, reviewing events, and formulating situations—the narrative voice exercises an authority which subordinates all other voices in the stories. It is, after all, the primary means of control in the fiction. Consequently, conversation is never directly heard by the reader, although in his presence it is recollected for him between quotation marks:

> "Rebe," said she, "my husband's taken leave of his senses. He's brought an idle glutton into our home. And if that's not enough, he's turned over all the money to him." The stranger, she said, held the purse, and whenever she, Motiekhe, needed anything, she had to go to him. He was the cashier. . . .
> The rabbi sent for Motie, but the man insisted: "I've carried enough grain sacks. I can permit myself to hire a helper." In the end, the rabbi dismissed them both with the command: "Let there be peace!" What else could he say?[9]

Heard in dialogue are therefore actually skillful modulations of the narrative. Similarly, nonverbal sounds are not uttered, they are offered to the reader as a series of reports:

> In the middle of the night there was a scream and running toward it they caught sight of the animal making for the outskirts of town. A man shouted that he had been bitten in the shoulder. Frightened, some of the men dropped back, but others continued to give chase. One of the hunters saw it and threw his axe. Apparently the animal was hit, for with a ghastly scream it wobbled and fell. A horrible howling filled the air. Then the beast began to curse in Polish and Yiddish and to wail in a high-pitched voice like a woman in labor. Convinced that they had wounded a she-devil, the men ran home.
> All that night the animal groaned and babbled. It even dragged itself to a house and knocked at the shutters. Then it became silent and the dogs began to bark. When day dawned, the bolder people came out of their houses. . . . The hatchet had

buried itself in her back. The dogs had already partaken of her entrails.[10]

The reverberations of the telling effectively drown out even the loudest screams and howls.

Except for the shifting cadences of the narrative voice which determine and sustain the various components of story, actions do not happen in Singer's short fiction; actions there can only be recalled:

> On the other hand, Avigdor's lot grew steadily worse. Peshe tormented him and finally would not give him enough to eat and even refused him a clean shirt. . . . Most of the townspeople sided with Avigdor and blamed Peshe for everything. Avigdor soon began pressing Peshe for a divorce, and, because he did not want to have a child by such a fury, he acted like Onan, or, as the Gemara translates it: he threshed on the inside and cast his seed without.[11]

And gestures do not have the status of motions but function as indications of the controlling intelligence embodied in the narrative:

> Dr. Yaretsky looked up at the sky. The stars shone against the dawn, divinely luminous, filled with unearthly joy. The heavenly spheres appeared festive. But was it truly so?—No, it was a deception. If there was life on other planets, it was the same pattern of gluttony and violence as on earth. Our planet also appeared shining and glorious if viewed from Mars or the Moon. Even the town slaughterhouse looked like a temple from the distance.
> He spat at the sky but the spittle landed on his own knee.[12]

Like actions and gestures, objects are never presented with an authenticity or immediacy equal to those of the narrative itself. The characteristic form in which objects are recalled is that of a self-consciously recited catalogue:

Shoshe scrimped throughout the week, but on the Sabbath she was lavish. Into the heated oven went cakes, cookies, and the Sabbath loaf. In winter, she prepared puddings made of chicken's neck stuffed with dough and rendered fat. In summer she made puddings with rice or noodles, greased with chicken fat and sprinkled with sugar or cinnamon. The main dish consisted of potatoes and buckwheat, or pearl barley with beans, in the midst of which she never failed to set a marrowbone. To insure that the dish would be well cooked, she sealed the oven with loose dough.[13]

The narrative has the capacity to transform foods into recipes.

As a consequence of the force of the narrative voice and its dominant role in the fiction, life in the Singerian village or city is never dramatized or enacted. It is, however, always recorded as data:

The street was full of tumult: wagons rolled by on the cobblestones; horses neighed; coachmen screamed with hoarse voices and cracked their whips; girls laughed and screeched; children cried; women quarreled, called one another names, uttered obscenities. Every once in a while Zeidel stopped murmuring, but only to doze with his head sunken on his chest. He no longer had any earthly desire, but one yearning still plagued him: to know the truth. . . . The sun burned down on him, the rains soaked him, pigeons soiled him with their droppings, but he was impervious to everything. Now that he had lost his only passion, pride, nothing material mattered to him.[14]

Within limits imposed by the manner of telling, the reader may hear (or overhear) Singer's stories, but the lives and experiences with which they concern themselves can never be witnessed or envisioned by the reader. The stories can never transcend their status as verbal constructs. They remain *something told.*

Singer's narrative method is of course anti-mimetic in form and perverse in effect. While the mode of narration increases the formal distance separating the reader-listener from the substance of the narrative, it nevertheless creates an intimacy between narrative voice and reader. Each is engaged in a reciprocal transaction which defines the other's role. But it is a dangerous intimacy. In effect, the narrative voice aggressively invades the consciousness of the reader and struggles to control it. An alien presence whose revelations resist being confirmed by the reader's own experience, the narrative voice nevertheless has succeeded in dramatizing and enacting the one basic experience which makes Singer's aural act of the short story possible: the reader, while reading, is—without understanding it at the time—possessed by a *dybbuk.*

According to Jewish folklore, a dybbuk is an aberrant supernatural being, either a demon (perhaps even Satan himself) or the wicked spirit of a dead person, who wanders about in search of a living human body to inhabit. Finding it, the dybbuk is manifested as a terrible voice speaking what ought not be said and causing its unfortunate victim to act in uncharacteristic ways which others consider shocking.

> The page is too short for a recital of all that the dybbuk did and said that night and the nights that followed—his brazen tricks, his blasphemies against the Lord, the insults he hurled at the townsfolk, the boasts of all the lecheries he had committed, the mockery, the outbursts of laughing and of crying, the stream of quotations from the Torah and wedding jester's jokes, and all of it in singsong and in rhyme.
>
> The dybbuk made himself heard only after dark. During the day, Liebe Yentl [the female host] lay exhausted in bed and evidently did not remember what went on at night.[15]

A perverse spirit compulsive about its perversity, the dybbuk relentlessly disorients the victim harboring it, and threatens the stability of the community to which he belongs. Exorcism, which may result in the death of the host, is the only way for this dangerous phenomenon to be dealt with.

Once in the bedroom, the rabbi, Reb Yeruchim, ordered the Ram's Horn to be blown. He had the beadle pile hot coals into a brazier, then he poured incense on the coals. As the smoke of the herbs filled the room, he commanded the evil one with Holy Oaths from the Zohar, the Book of Creation and other books of the Cabala to leave the body of the woman Liebe Yentl, daughter of Zise Feige. But the unholy spirit defied everyone. Instead of leaving, he played out a succession of dances, marches, hops—just with the lips. He boomed like a bass viol, he jingled like a cymbal, he whistled like a flute, and drummed like a drum. . . .

Since the incantations and the amulets of the Shidlovtse rabbi were of no avail, Reb Sheftel went to seek the advice of the Radzymin rabbi.[16]

Dybbuks, in the short stories of Singer, are as folk tradition describes them: unwilling brides are possessed by them on their wedding night; bright young men studying sacred books abandon their faith because of them; sexual frustrations and domestic tensions are explosively released by them; entire communities are destroyed by them; and, on behalf of God and righteousness, pious old rabbis painfully struggle against them. But for Singer they are much more besides.

In addition to being an alien will seizing control of an innocent body—and thus a convenient means of showing how religious faith is lost, present values repudiated, and sins committed—and an obvious demonstration of schizophrenia and paranoia in a pre-Freudian world, the dybbuk is a convention full of meaning. For Singer, it is a complex variety of revenant which discloses itself in many subtle ways. "I am possessed by my demons," he once said, and they are largely responsible for "my vision and my expression."[17]

The dybbuk is the disembodied past recklessly returning and seeking ways of preserving itself. It is memory intent upon being articulated and gaining validation. It is personal assertiveness in conflict with orthodox styles of behavior. It is history depriving the present of its claim to a secret destiny of its own. It is old guilt confirming new guilt. It is the surfacing of dangerous thoughts during solitary moments. It is consciousness in quest of form. It is the demonic vision-giving spirit which is responsible for fiction. And, not least significantly, because it is all of these it is also the expressive story-telling voice which can tolerate neither its own silence nor the talk of others, and which therefore struggles to take possession of the conciousness of Singer's unwary reader.

The narrative voice heard in Singer's five collections of stories —whether the teller is unidentified, an old woman, a male gossip, the young son of a rabbi, an imp whose power admittedly resides in his tongue, a Hasid or Misnagid, a credulous fool, an infernal demon, a self-confessed dybbuk, or even Satan himself—is constant and dybbukian: nervously energetic, short-breathed, obsessed with detail, colloquial, limited in understanding, unanalytical, reluctant to make any but conventional moral assessments, possessing an orthodox Jewish memory derived from the communal experience of East Europe, and totally committed to telling. This dybbuk-narrator, whoever he purports to be, commands the reader's attention, insistently using inscrutable facts as instruments of his sauntering authority. He is determined to make the reader become a victim of his dybbukian beliefs and knowledge, imposing upon the consciousness of the reader customs and events foreign to the reader's experience and sense of possibilities.

The reader is neither encouraged nor permitted to willingly suspend disbelief; instead he is deprived forcibly of his own original memory. He is under compulsion to adopt strange assumptions and new beliefs—those of the dybbuk-narrator—in miracle-working rabbis, the imminence of the end of the world, the ritual need to wear prayer shawls and phylacteries, the reality of imps twisting with iron pincers the nipples of women condemned to spend a year in Gehenna before entering Heaven, the reverence owed members of certain renowned rabbinic dynasties, observing the Sabbath as a ceremonial act of joy, the efficacies of witch-craft, the practice of ritual bathing for purposes of spiritual purifi-cation, the values of studying Cabala in addition to Pentateuch and Talmud, the usefulness of learning elaborate demonologies, and belief in other such archaisms associated with so-called unen-lightened, pre-modern Jewishness.

The function of the reader-listener is therefore only to receive the detached, self-sustaining will of the dybbuk-narrator. In need of a consciousness to possess which can give it effective form, the voice creates its victim, forcing the reader-listener to surrender his own personality and identity, displacing him and disorienting him, depriving him of the power of choice, causing him to experi-ence (in psychological terms) the control being exercised over him, and forcing him to undergo an abstract equivalent of the suffering which is nearly pervasive in the stories told.

In effect, then, given the values which underlie the fiction—as distinct from those which underlie the telling—this is the means by which the humanity of Singer's audience is directly affirmed. He humanizes his readers. For behind the world of Singer's short stories is the conviction that to be human is to be either possessed by a dybbuk or to be exposed to the threat of such possession. However, to be dybbuk-proof, to be exempt from the risk of being possessed by alien power, is to be de-humanized. It is to *be* a dybbuk. But Singer protects his readers against this possibil-ity. Just as he sees the interactions between victims (realized and potential) and victimizers accounting for all of human history, so he enables his readers to participate as innocents in that universal destiny.

In Singer's short stories characters are functionally defined as victims, conceived for the purpose of being tormented either by men or by demons. Passions move them, madness moves them, custom moves them, obsessions move them, reverence moves them, diabolical urges move them, but never the freedom of their own choosing wills. Says one of the narrators, an old gossip: "It is written somewhere that every man is followed by devils—a thousand on the left and ten thousand on the right."[18] (Singer's readers know where that is written—on the pages of his short stories.) If not all his characters are afflicted, this is not so much a function of special grace as it is of the limitations of art and the measured powers at work in the world. Exemption from suffering, when it occurs, is simply an accident of time. The danger remains. To be human is to risk disaster. Given enough writing space, Singer would eventually, in one story or another as yet unwritten, imaginatively remember one which a dybbuk could tell, of every person's encounter with suffering caused by alien power. In Singer's vision, victimage is the universal human destiny and the narrative voice its agent.

This, after all, is the meaning of Singer's stories, if indeed they have any single meaning: suffering is universal; and when joy exists (as infrequently it does), it exists only by virtue of the belief that suffering—as something endured and experienced as real, even though undeserved—is the ultimate confirmation that God exists; and therefore the memory of it is itself mysteriously meaningful, however irrational.

If to be *possessed* is human, then to be *in possession of* is dybbukian. To be a dybbuk is to appropriate form which is not one's own, and to master it by employing words as instruments of control; it is also to remember so strenuously that repose may be found only by putting the past to present use through force of language. The implications of this are clear: to be a literary artist, and especially a writer of fiction, is morally dangerous.

"When people have extreme power over other people," Singer has said, "it's a terrible thing. I always pray to God . . . don't give me any power over any other human beings. I have always avoided this kind of power like the plague."[19] Therefore the rationale for the mode of non-dramatic narrative: a surrogate voice assumes responsibility for both stories and their effect upon readers. It protects Singer by relieving him of moral responsibility for victimage, while at the same time permitting him to continue exercising the kind of control an artist must. He is possessed by his own demons, Singer has said.[20] Not surprisingly then, since he is a writer of both novels and short stories, he has also been reported to have once said: "In a short work you can concentrate on quality. In a large novel, you give only essentials. In short stories you elaborate. . . . It is true that your control cannot be perfect . . . in a novel, only in a short story."[21] Accordingly, by Singer's own admission, his five collections of stories are the best index of his literary art. There his perfect control is elaborated.

But Isaac Bashevis Singer is not the only one moved by the desire to tell stories and to tell them well. All good stories must end, and by bringing his stories to their necessary conclusions, the dybbuk-narrator repeatedly effects his own exorcism. Since words are the sources of his power, the silence which punctuates the cessation of story-telling devastates him. Or rather, it brings about his release, discharging him to wander without form until Singer's next need to protect himself against his own artistry.

It is not accident that allows terminal silence to drive the dybbuk-narrator out of the reader's consciousness, restoring the reader to a more familiar world. For silence is sacred in Singer's scheme of values. It is sacred because it is understood by him as a Divine quality. God Himself is always silent, remaining outside the limits of narrative (just as He is absent from everyday life) and always invisible. Because it exists, His silence complements human suffering as confirmation of His existence. And Singer, too, creative artist that he also is, remains silent in the stories (as he never does in an everyday life filled with interviews, conferences, and university lectures), standing mute and invisible outside the narrative, while the dybbuk-narrator slowly detaches himself by bringing his story-telling to a reluctant close.

Most, but not all of Singer's stories have distinctive narrative dynamics conforming to the dybbukian *shtetl*-Warsaw model which has been described. The significant variation on these patterns of method and meaning is found in what may be called *new-world* stories, of which fourteen have been collected. Nine are concentrated in *A Friend of Kafka*, giving it special status as a Singer book; the rest are scattered casually in two collections, *Short Friday* and *The Séance*.[22]

Although set in the United States (all but one in New York City) except for one each in Canada, Argentina, and Israel, the new-world stories are formally distinguished less by geographical fact or matters of culture than by a relationship to memory and the past which is different from that in Singer's other stories: in them the terms of non-dramatic narrative and story-as-information break down.

In an important sense, all of Singer's stories are American stories, regardless of setting or form. They are American by virtue of having been written in the United States as a response to experience in America. By emigrating to New York City from Poland in 1935, Singer made his perceptions of Jewish life in East Europe available in the United States. Translated into English from Yiddish under his supervision, and in recent years by himself with assistance from others, Singer's stories have appeared in such magazines as *The New Yorker, Esquire, Harper's, Cosmopolitan, Partisan Review, Commentary,* and *Playboy.* Consequently, all of his stories are literally products of his American experience, and have become part of our own. But only the new-world stories, with their meaningful deviations from the narrative structures found in the other stories, betray formal indications of the severe cultural shocks Singer suffered by being detached from the old-world sources of his memory and imagination. In them the dybbuk has wandered off from his customary narrative position.

Self-consciousness gives form to the new-world stories *qua* stories. They are aware of themselves as something to be read, not heard or overheard, and are aware of the presence of the reader as reader, not as listener or eavesdropping victim. Bound to its audience by literacy, the intelligence purporting to be responsible is *scribal*. It is a writerly sensibility which is prepared and eager to be absorbed by a complementary reading intelligence. Story-writing perspicuity therefore makes a narrative voice superfluous:

> At about three o'clock in the afternoon, Bessie Popkin began to prepare to go down to the street. Going out was connected with many difficulties, especially on a hot summer day: first, forcing her fat body into a corset, squeezing her swollen feet into shoes, and combing her hair, which Bessie dyed at home and which grew wild and was streaked in all colors—yellow, black, gray, red; then making sure that while she was out her neighbors would not break into her apartment and steal linen, clothes, documents, or just disarrange things and make them disappear.[23]

Here, as at times elsewhere in new-world stories, the scribal authority is asserted by being suppressed, the narration trying but failing to conceal the figure of the writer who by inference is responsible for the story-as-writing.

But more often than not, the scribal authority is exposed at the outset, substituting for the dybbuk-narrator, trying to embody itself as a presence which will participate in the action rather than control it:

> Even though I have reached the point where a great part of my earnings is given away in taxes, I still have the habit of eating in cafeterias when I am by myself. I like to take a tray with a tin knife, fork, spoon, and paper napkin and to choose at the counter the food I enjoy. Besides, I meet there the *landsleit* from Poland, as well as all kinds of literary beginners and readers who know Yiddish. The moment I sit down at table, they come over. . . . I cannot spend too long with these Yiddishists, because I am always busy. I am writing a novel, a story, an article. I have to lecture today or tomorrow; my datebook is crowded with all kinds of appointments for weeks and months in ad-

vance. But meanwhile we converse in the mother language and
I hear of intrigues and pettiness about which, from a moral
point of view, it would be better not to be informed. . . . It was
in the fifties that a woman appeared in the group who looked
younger than the rest of us. . . . She was introduced to me.
. . . She told me that she had read my writing while still in
Poland, and later in the camps in Germany after the war. She
said to me, "You are my writer."[24]

And in a sense she did not intend, he is. The scribe usually
functions as a listener to others who are themselves possessed by
the story-telling urge.

Whether hidden or revealed, this scribal intelligence exists on
the same reality-plane as the stories he writes and the situations
he writes about. Of course, only a fictional creation which chroni-
cles versions of whatever purports to be witnessed and heard, the
putative scribe is a sensation-seeking *persona* distilled from Singer's experience in New York, designed to protect Singer's private sense of himself while he publicly reconstructs memories.
Appearing personally interested while actually aloof, inviting
confessions for the sake of possible stories, exposing the emotions of others while restraining his own, the scribe takes form
and comfort in sharing with a reader the superficial reminis-
cences and confidences he has received.

The scribal stories are contrived, diffuse, and theatrical rather
than dramatic. Nevertheless, when characters speak (even in long
operatic monologues), voices are heard. And that is where the
missing dybbuk has concealed himself—not in the inscribed
confessions but in the confessional urges prompting them. Of
this the scribe is seemingly unaware.

They are the as yet unarticulated urges of old-world victims
who have been transported into an alien new world: people
whose endurance continues to be strained by the unfamiliar pressures of the refuge into which they have escaped; crippled people, impoverished people, and demoralized people; people

haunted by recollections of other-worldly experiences; people seeking escape from the past by ignoring the present and imagining the future; extrasensory people convinced that their lives involve astral bodies, telepathy, telekinesis, and other dubious varieties of the supernatural; people scarred by the knowledge of German extermination camps; pathetic old women trying futilely to disguise the past by heavy applications of cosmetic rouge and nail lacquer; hemorrhoidal old men with prostate disorders straining to conceal pain and shame; people who have sacrificed old-world pieties and customs in a feeble attempt to engender new lives; and people so fearful of a strange American culture that they turn inward upon their memories. Singer has identified them all. But the scribal intelligence invariably betrays them.

In them, in their ill-defined consciousness—not in the new-world stories in which they are marginally contained—is located the displaced dybbuk. Too remote from readers to have any humanizing effect upon them, the dybbuk nevertheless continues to work away mysteriously on the old-world victims, outside the stories and independently of the cheap sensationalism of the new-world scribe. But being incapable of honest self-scrutiny, the scribe cannot comprehend this. Instead he reflects:

> This metropolis has all the symptoms of a mind gone berserk.
> But since insanity has not yet taken over altogether, one has to act as though there were still order—according to Vaihinger's principle of "as if." I continued with my scribbling. I delivered manuscripts to the publisher. I lectured. . . . I saw with amazement that all my efforts turned into paper. My apartment was one big wastepaper basket. From day to day, all this paper was getting drier and more parched. I woke up at night fearful that it would ignite. There was not an hour when I did not hear the sirens of fire engines.[25]

His heroism is suspect. This scribe need not fear any cosmic disaster befalling him, only self-deception. Believing himself dybbuk-proof, he is less than human and insensitive to the dybbuks in others.

In a universe of suffering, the new world is a life full of the Mystery which is freedom, a life which remains even after victimization and defeats. This Singer understands. However, *Satan in Gotham* (a hypothetical new-world counterpart to *Satan in Goray*) is as yet unwritten; and the authentic new-world stories, which will derive from it, await its publication. Isaac Bashevis Singer may have become his own translator, but so far he has failed to imaginatively remember the new-world forms and new-world vocabulary into which dybbukianism may be translated.

NOTES

1. "Cunnegunde," in *Short Friday and Other Stories* (New York, 1964), p. 219.
2. "The Gentleman from Cracow," in *Gimpel the Fool and Other Stories*, Avon ed. (New York, 1965), p. 34.
3. "The Little Shoemakers," in *Gimpel the Fool*, p. 92.
4. "The Man Who Came Back," in *The Spinoza of Market Street and Other Stories*, Avon ed. (New York, 1963), p. 111.
5. "A Piece of Advice," in *Spinoza of Market Street*, p. 122.
6. "Hennie Fire," in *The Séance and Other Stories* (New York, 1968), p. 136.
7. "The Black Wedding," in *Spinoza of Market Street*, p. 32.
8. "The Destruction of Kreshev," in *Spinoza of Market Street*, p. 147.
9. "Big and Little," in *Short Friday*, p. 20.
10. "Blood," in *Short Friday*, pp. 45–46.
11. "Yentl the Yeshiva Boy," in *Short Friday*, p. 149.
12. "The Shadow of a Crib," in *Spinoza of Market Street*, p. 78.
13. "Short Friday," in *Short Friday*, p. 232.
14. "Zeidlus the Pope," in *Short Friday*, p. 187.
15. "The Dead Fiddler," in *The Séance*, p. 40.
16. Ibid.
17. "An Interview with Isaac Bashevis Singer," *Commentary*, XXXVI (November, 1963), 371.

18. "The Wife Killer," in *Gimpel the Fool*, p. 50.

19. "An Interview," p. 369.

20. Ibid., p. 371.

21. Quoted by Irving H. Buchen, *Isaac Bashevis Singer and the Eternal Past* (New York, 1968), pp. 26–27.

22. The new-world stories are: "Alone" and "A Wedding in Brownsville" (in *Short Friday*); "The Séance," "The Lecture," and "The Letter Writer" (in *The Séance*); "The Key," "The Cafeteria," "The Mentor," "The Joke," "Schloimele," "The Colony," "The Son," "Fate," and "Power" (in *A Friend of Kafka and Other Stories*). The last part of the six-part "The Little Shoemakers" (in *Gimpel the Fool*) is set in the United States, but its form is that of non-dramatic narrative, not new-world.

23. "The Key," in *A Friend of Kafka and Other Stories* (New York, 1970), p. 38.

24. "The Cafeteria," in *A Friend of Kafka*, pp. 77–80.

25. Ibid., p. 93.

Contemporary American-Jewish Literature: A Selected Checklist of Criticism

JACKSON R. BRYER

This checklist is designed as a supplement to the essays in this volume. It presents a representative sampling of the comment in print on modern American-Jewish literature and on the specific writers discussed in this book. Accordingly, it is divided into two basic sections, one devoted to general studies of modern American-Jewish literature and/or two or more specific American-Jewish writers, the other to studies of the individual authors who are the subjects of the essays in this book.

Within the general section, no attempt at an exhaustive listing has been made. I have included only those items which seemed most relevant to the subject of this book. I have provided brief annotations as an indication usually of which specific writers are covered in many of these general entries. In Part II, before the listings for each specific author, I have provided cross-references to items in Part I which concern that writer.

Within Part II, the selectivity and criteria for inclusion of items vary somewhat. For writers like Saul Bellow, Bernard Malamud, and Norman Mailer, about whom there is abundant material in print, I have listed only major studies and essays which stress the

Jewish element in that author's work. On the other hand, with authors like Wallant, Trilling, Schwartz, and Fiedler, who are the subjects of relatively little commentary, I have tended to include virtually anything I could find, including important reviews of their works (these are annotated Rev.-art.) and even, in a few instances, doctoral dissertations. Books entirely about one of the authors are listed in capital letters.

While this listing does not pretend to completeness, whatever degree of usefulness it does have could not have been reached without the help of Stephen Sirota and Miss Mary Anne Dempsey, especially the latter, who did not have to be there but was.

I. GENERAL

A. Books.

ALDRIDGE, JOHN W. *Time to Murder and Create—The Contemporary Novel in Crisis.* New York: David McKay, 1966. [" 'Nothing Left to Do But Think'—Saul Bellow," pp. 87–94; "The Complacency of *Herzog,*" pp. 133–138; "Norman Mailer: The Energy of New Success," pp. 149–163; *"The Second Stone,"* pp. 225–229.]

ALLEN, WALTER. "War and Post War: American." In his *The Modern Novel in Britain and the United States.* New York: E.P. Dutton, 1964. Pp. 293–332. [Mailer, Salinger, Bellow, H. Gold, Malamud, et al.]

ALTER, ROBERT. *After the Tradition: Essays on Modern Jewish Writing.* New York: E.P. Dutton, 1969. ["Saul Bellow: A Dissent From Modernism," pp. 95–115; "Bernard Malamud: Jewishness as Metaphor," pp. 116–130.]

————. *America and Israel—Literary and Intellectual Trends.* New York: Hadassah Education Series, 1970. [Bellow, P. Roth, Mailer.]

BALAKIAN, NONA, and CHARLES SIMMONS, eds. *The Creative Present: Notes on Contemporary American Fiction.* Garden City, N.Y.: Doubleday, 1963. [Robert Gorham Davis, "The American Individualist Tradition: Bellow and Styron," pp. 111–141; Diana Trilling, "The Radical Moralism of Norman Mailer," pp. 145–171; Granville Hicks,

"Generations of the Fifties: Malamud, Gold, and Updike," pp. 217–237.]

BAUMBACH, JONATHAN. *The Landscape of Nightmare: Studies in the Contemporary American Novel.* New York: New York University Press, 1965. ["The Double Vision: *The Victim* by Saul Bellow," pp. 35–54; "All Men Are Jews: *The Assistant* by Bernard Malamud," pp. 101–122; "The Illusion of Indifference: *The Pawnbroker* by Edward Lewis Wallant," pp. 138–151.]

BRYANT, JERRY H. *The Open Decision—The Contemporary American Novel and Its Intellectual Background.* New York: Free Press, 1970. Pp. 156–164 (Heller); 236–240 (Salinger); 324–340 (Malamud); 341–369 (Bellow); 369–394 (Mailer).

BURGESS, ANTHONY. *The Novel Now—A Student's Guide to Contemporary Fiction.* London: Faber & Faber, 1967. Pp. 49–52, 59 (Mailer); 195–196, 201 (Bellow); 197–198, 202 (Malamud).

DETWEILER, ROBERT. *Four Spiritual Crises in Mid-Century American Fiction.* Gainesville: University of Florida Press, 1964. ["Religion in Postwar American Fiction," pp. 1–5; "Philip Roth and the Test of Dialogic Life," pp. 25–35.]

EISINGER, CHESTER E. *Fiction of the Forties.* Chicago: University of Chicago Press, 1963. ["Lionel Trilling and the Crisis in Our Culture," pp. 135–144; "Saul Bellow: Man Alive, Sustained By Love," pp. 341–362; see also pp. 33–38 (Mailer).]

FIEDLER, LESLIE A. "Adolescence and Maturity in the American Novel." In his *An End to Innocence: Essays on Culture and Politics.* Boston: Beacon Press, 1955. Pp. 191–210. [Bellow, Trilling, Schwartz, et al.]

————. *The Jew in the American Novel.* New York: Herzl Press, 1959.

————. *No! In Thunder—Essays on Myth and Literature.* Boston: Beacon Press, 1960. ["Malamud: The Commonplace as Absurd," pp. 101–110; "Negro and Jew: Encounter in America," pp. 231–250; see also pp. 14–17 (Bellow).]

————. *Waiting for the End.* New York: Stein and Day, 1964. ["Zion as Main Street," pp. 65–88; "Jewish-Americans, Go Home!" pp. 89–103 (Bellow, Salinger, Mailer, Malamud, P. Roth, Shapiro, Trilling, et al.)]

FINKELSTEIN, SIDNEY. *Existentialism and Alienation in American Literature.* New York: International Publishers, 1965. ["Lost Social Convictions and Existentialism: Arthur Miller and Saul Bellow," pp. 252–269; "Existentialism and Social Demands: Norman Mailer and James Baldwin," pp. 269–284.]

FRENCH, WARREN, ed. *The Fifties: Fiction, Poetry, Drama.* Deland, Fla.: Everett/Edwards, 1971. [Warren French, "The Age of Salinger," pp. 1–39; William Hoffa, "Norman Mailer: *Advertisements for Myself,*" pp. 73–82; David R. Jones, "The Disappointments of Maturity: Bellow's *The Adventures of Augie March,*" pp. 83–92; William Freedman, "From Bernard Malamud, With Discipline and With Love," pp. 133–143.]

GEISMAR, MAXWELL. *American Moderns—From Rebellion to Conformity.* New York: Hill and Wang, 1958. ["Norman Mailer: The Bohemian of the National Letters," pp. 171–179; "Saul Bellow: Novelist of the Intellectuals," pp. 210–224.]

GROSS, THEODORE L. *The Heroic Ideal in American Literature.* New York: The Free Press, 1971. ["Saul Bellow: The Victim and the Hero," pp. 243–261; "Norman Mailer: The Quest for Heroism," pp. 272–295.]

GUHA, NARESH. "Notes on the Importance of Jewish-American Literature." In Sujit Mukherjee and D.V.K. Raghavacharyulu, eds. *Indian Essays in American Literature: Papers in Honour of Robert E. Spiller.* Bombay: Popular Prakashan, 1969. Pp. 247–259.

GUTTMANN, ALLEN. *The Jewish Writer in America—Assimilation and the Crisis of Identity.* New York: Oxford University Press, 1971. [Includes sections on Bellow, P. Roth, Mailer, Malamud, Kazin, Goodman, Shapiro, Ginsberg, et al.]

HARPER, HOWARD M., JR. *Desperate Faith: A Study of Bellow, Salinger, Mailer, Baldwin and Updike.* Chapel Hill: University of North Carolina Press, 1967. ["Saul Bellow—The Heart's Ultimate Need," pp. 7–64; "Norman Mailer—A Revolution in the Consciousness of Our Time," pp. 96–136.]

HASSAN, IHAB. *Radical Innocence: Studies in the Contemporary American Novel.* Princeton, N.J.: Princeton University Press, 1961. ["Encounter With Necessity: Styron, Swados, Mailer," pp. 124–152; "The Qualified Encounter: Three Novels By Buechner, Malamud, and Ellison," pp. 153–179; "Saul Bellow: The Quest and Affirmation of Reality," pp. 290–324.]

HICKS, GRANVILLE. *Literary Horizons—A Quarter Century of American Fiction.* New York: New York University Press, 1970. ["Saul Bellow," pp. 49–63; "Bernard Malamud," pp. 65–83; "Philip Roth," pp. 245–255; "Norman Mailer," pp. 273–290.]

HOFFMAN, FREDERICK J. "The Last Ten Years." In his *The Modern Novel in America.* Chicago: Henry Regnery, 1956. Pp. 188–224. [Shaw, Mailer, Hersey, Bellow, Trilling, et al.]

HYMAN, STANLEY EDGAR. *Standards: A Chronicle of Books for Our Time.* New York: Horizon Press, 1966. ["A New Life for a Good Man" (Malamud), pp. 33–37; "A Novelist of Great Promise" (Roth), pp. 73–77; "The Yiddish Hawthorne" (Singer), pp. 83–87; "An Exceptional First Novel" (Friedman), pp. 98–102; "Norman Mailer's Yummy Rump," pp. 274–278.]

KAZIN, ALFRED. *Contemporaries.* Boston: Little, Brown, 1962. ["Bernard Malamud: The Magic and the Dread," pp. 202–207; "The World of Saul Bellow," pp. 217–223; "How Good Is Norman Mailer," pp. 246–250; "Tough-minded Mr. Roth," pp. 258–262; "The Saint as Schlemiel" (Singer), pp. 283–288.]

KLEIN, MARCUS. *After Alienation: American Novels in Mid-Century.* Cleveland: Meridian, 1965. ["Saul Bellow: A Discipline of Nobility," pp. 33–70; "Bernard Malamud: The Sadness of Goodness," pp. 247–293.]

KOSTELANETZ, RICHARD, ed. *On Contemporary Literature.* New York: Avon Books, 1964. [Harris Dienstfrey, "The Fiction of Norman Mailer," pp. 422–436; plus reprinted material on Bellow, Malamud, P. Roth, and Singer.]

LEWIS, R.W.B. "Recent Fiction: Pícaro and Pilgrim." In Robert E. Spiller, ed. *A Time of Harvest—American Literature 1910–1960.* New York: Hill and Wang, 1962. Pp. 144–153. [Bellow, Mailer, Salinger.]

LIPTZIN, SOLOMON. *The Jew in American Literature.* New York: Bloch, 1966. Pp. 194–195 (Bellow); 198–199 (Kazin); 230–231 (Mailer); 226–228 (Malamud); 228–229 (P. Roth); 216–217 (Shapiro).

LUDWIG, JACK. *Recent American Novelists.* Minneapolis: University of Minnesota Press, 1962. Pp. 7–18 (Bellow); 24–28 (Mailer); 28–30 (Salinger); 39–41 (Malamud).

MALIN, IRVING. *Jews and Americans.* Carbondale: Southern Illinois University Press, 1965. [Bellow, Fiedler, Malamud, P. Roth, Schwartz, Shapiro, et al.]

———, and Irwin Stark. "Introduction." In their ed. *Breakthrough—A Treasury of Contemporary American-Jewish Literature.* New York: McGraw-Hill, 1964. Pp. 1–24. [Bellow, P. Roth, Shapiro, Trilling, H. Gold, Fiedler, Nemerov, Schwartz, Mailer, Goodman, Malamud, Howe, Kazin, et al.]

MATTHIESSEN, F. O. *Responsibilities of the Critic,* ed. John Rackliffe. New York: Oxford University Press, 1952. ["A New York Childhood" (Schwartz), pp. 112–115; "Four American Poets, 1944," (Shapiro), pp. 116–128.]

MEETER, GLENN. *Bernard Malamud and Philip Roth—A Critical Essay.* Grand Rapids, Mich.: W.B. Eerdmans, 1968.

MERSAND, JOSEPH. *Traditions in American Literature—A Study of Jewish Characters and Authors.* Port Washington, N.Y.: Kennikat Press, 1968. [Originally published in 1939.]

MOORE, HARRY T., ed. *Contemporary American Novelists.* Carbondale: Southern Illinois University Press, 1964. [Charles Alva Hoyt, "Bernard Malamud and the New Romanticism," pp. 65–79; Frederick J. Hoffman, "The Fool of Experience: Saul Bellow's Fiction," pp. 80–94; Edmond L. Volpe, "James Jones-Norman Mailer," pp. 106–119.]

PINSKER, SANFORD. *The Schlemiel as Metaphor—Studies in the Yiddish and American Jewish Novel.* Carbondale: Southern Illinois University Press, 1971. ["The Isolated Schlemiels of Isaac Bashevis Singer," pp. 55–86; "The Schlemiel as Moral Bungler—Bernard Malamud's Ironic Heroes," pp. 87–124; "The Psychological Schlemiels of Saul Bellow," pp. 125–157.]

PODHORETZ, NORMAN. *Doings and Undoings—The Fifties and After in American Writing.* New York: Noonday Press, 1964. ["Jewish Culture and the Intellectuals," pp. 112–125; "Norman Mailer: The Embattled Vision," pp. 179–204; "The Adventures of Saul Bellow," pp. 205–227; "The Gloom of Philip Roth," pp. 236–243.]

RIBALOW, HAROLD U. "Introduction—The Jewish Short Story in America." In his ed. *This Land, These People.* New York: Beechhurst Press, 1950. Pp. 1–10. [Schwartz, A. Miller, Levin, Lewisohn, Shaw, et al.]

ROSENFELD, ISAAC. "The Situation of the Jewish Writer." In his *An Age of Enormity—Life and Writing in the Forties and Fifties.* Cleveland: World, 1962. Pp. 67–69.

RUPP, RICHARD H. *Celebration in Postwar American Fiction—1945–1967.* Coral Gables, Fla.: University of Miami Press, 1970. ["Bernard Malamud: A Party of One," pp. 165–188; "Saul Bellow: Belonging to the World in General," pp. 189–208.]

SCHULZ, MAX F. *Radical Sophistication: Studies in Contemporary Jewish-American Novelists.* Athens: Ohio University Press, 1969. [Sections on Singer, West, Malamud, Mailer, Bellow, Fiedler, Wallant, Friedman, and Salinger.]

SCOTT, NATHAN A., JR., ed. *Adversity and Grace—Studies in Recent American Literature.* Chicago: University of Chicago Press, 1968. [Nathan A. Scott, Jr., "*Sola Gratia*—The Principle of Bellow's Fiction," pp. 27–57; Giles B. Gunn, "Bernard Malamud and the High Cost of Liv-

ing," pp. 59–85; David Hesla, "The Two Roles of Norman Mailer,"
pp. 211–238.]

SHERMAN, BERNARD. *The Invention of the Jew—Jewish-American Education
Novels (1916–1964).* New York: Thomas Yoseloff, 1969. [Bellow,
Kazin, et al.]

SYRKIN, MARIE. "Jewish Awareness in American Literature." In Oscar I.
Janowsky, ed. *The American Jew: A Reappraisal.* Philadelphia: Jewish
Publication Society of America, 1964. Pp. 211–233. [Levin, Halper,
H. Roth, Lewisohn, Shaw, Mailer, Wouk, Bellow, Malamud, P. Roth,
Friedman, Salinger, Schwartz, Shapiro, et al.]

TANNER, TONY. *City of Words—American Fiction 1950–1970.* New York:
Harper & Row, 1971. ["A Mode of Motion" (Bellow, Heller), pp.
64–84; "Fictionalized Recall—or 'The Settling of Scores! The Pursuit of Dreams!' " (Bellow, P. Roth, Conroy), pp. 295–321; "A New
Life" (Malamud), pp. 322–343; "On the Parapet" (Mailer), pp. 344–
371.]

TELLER, JUDD L. "From Yiddish to Neo-Brahmin." In his *Strangers and
Natives—The Evolution of the American Jew from 1921 to the Present.* New
York: Delacorte Press, 1968. Pp. 251–272. [Singer, Bellow, Mailer,
Malamud, P. Roth, Fiedler, Shapiro.]

WEINBERG, HELEN. *The New Novel in America: The Kafkan Mode in Contemporary Fiction:* Ithaca, N.Y.: Cornell University Press, 1970. ["Kafka
and Bellow: Comparisons and Further Definitions," pp. 29–54;
"The Heroes of Saul Bellow's Novels," pp. 55–107; "The Heroes
of Norman Mailer's Novels," pp. 108–140; see also pp. 168–178
(Malamud).]

Writers at Work—The "Paris Review" Interviews. Third Series. New York:
Viking Press, 1967. [Gordon Lloyd Harper, "Saul Bellow," pp. 175–
196; Steven Marcus, "Norman Mailer," pp. 251–278.]

B. Articles

AARON, DANIEL. "Some Reflections on Communism and the Jewish
Writer," *Salmagundi,* I (Fall 1965), 23–36.

ADLER, SIDNEY. "The Image of the Jew in the American Novel," *Bulletin
of Bibliography,* XXIII (September–December 1962), 211–213.
[Unannotated checklist.]

ALTER, ROBERT. "Sentimentalizing the Jews," *Commentary,* XL (September 1965), 71–75. [Faust, Fiedler, Rovit, Wallant, Charyn, Nissenson.]

ANGOFF, CHARLES. "Jewish-American Imaginative Writings in the Last Twenty-Five Years," *Jewish Book Annual*, XXV (1967), 129–139. [Trilling, Mailer, Wouk, Malamud, et al.]

BELLMAN, SAMUEL IRVING. "Fathers and Sons in Jewish Fiction," *Congress Bi-Weekly*, XXXIV (May 22, 1967), 18–20. [Malamud, P. Roth, H. Gold, Friedman, Harris, et al.]

———. "The 'Jewish Mother' Syndrome," *Congress Bi-Weekly*, XXXII (December 27, 1965), 3–5.

BOROWITZ, EUGENE B. "Believing Jews and Jewish Writers: Is Dialogue Possible?" *Judaism*, XIV (Spring 1965), 172–186.

BUCHEN, IRVING H. "Jewish-American Writers as a Literary Group," *Renascence*, XIX (Spring 1967), 142–150.

CHAMETZKY, JULES. "Notes on the Assimilation of the American-Jewish Writer: Abraham Cahan to Saul Bellow," *Jahrbuch für Amerikastudien*, IX (1964), 173–180. [Cahan, M. Gold, Odets, Bellow.]

CHARLES, GERDA. "Elizabethan Age of Modern Jewish Literature— 1950–1960: Decade of the Great Break-Through," *World Jewry*, IV (September 1961), 15–17. [Bellow, Salinger, Malamud, Wouk, A. Miller, Chayevsky.]

CLAY, GEORGE R. "The Jewish Hero in American Fiction," *The Reporter*, XVII (September 19, 1957), 43–46.

"Comments by Jewish Writers on 'What Happens to Jewish Writing?' " *Congress Weekly*, XVI (March 28, 1949), 15. [Comments by Ludwig Lewisohn, Meyer Levin, Karl Shapiro, and Paul Goodman, on Ribalow article (see below).]

"The Creative Writer As a Jew," *Congress Bi-Weekly*, XXX (September 16, 1963), 42–59. [Fiedler, et al.]

DE MOTT, BENJAMIN. "Jewish Writers in America," *Commentary*, XXXI (February 1961), 127–134.

ELLIOTT, GEORGE P. "A Surfeit of Talk," *Commentary*, XXXIX (June 1965), 97–100. [Rev.-art.]

FEINSTEIN, HERBERT. "Contemporary American Fiction: Harvey Swados and Leslie Fiedler," *Wisconsin Studies in Contemporary Literature*, II (Winter 1961), 79–98. [Two interviews which include discussions of Mailer, Bellow, H. Roth, Fiedler, West, and P. Roth.]

FIEDLER, LESLIE A. "The Breakthrough: The American Jewish Novelist and the Fictional Image of the Jew," *Midstream*, IV (Winter 1958), 15–35. [Fuchs, West, H. Roth, Mailer, Shaw, Schulberg, Wouk, Salinger, Malamud, Schwartz, Trilling, Bellow, et al.]

————. "The Jew as Mythic American," *Ramparts*, II (Autumn 1963), 32–48. [Malamud, Mailer, Wouk, Bellow, et al.]

FINEMAN, IRVING. "The Image of the Jew in Fiction of the Future," *National Jewish Monthly*, LXXXII (December 1967), 48–51. [Cahan, Lewisohn, Mailer, Wouk, Bellow, Malamud, P. Roth, Potok.]

————. "The Image of the Jew in Our Fiction," *Tradition*, IX (Winter 1966), 19–47. [Cahan, Lewisohn, H. Roth, M. Gold, Mailer, Wouk, Bellow, Malamud.]

FLEISCHMANN, WOLFGANG BERNARD. "The Contemporary 'Jewish Novel' in America," *Jahrbuch für Amerikastudien*, XII (1967), 159–166. [Bellow, Malamud, Salinger, P. Roth.]

FREEDMAN, WILLIAM. "American Jewish Fiction: So What's the Big Deal?" *Chicago Review*, XIX (No. 1, 1966), 90–107. [P. Roth, Howe, Friedman, Malamud, Wallant, Bellow, Singer, Mailer.]

GEISMAR, MAXWELL. "The Jewish Heritage in Contemporary American Fiction," *Ramparts*, II (Autumn 1963), 5–13. [P. Roth, Jones, Salinger, Bellow, Malamud.]

GLANVILLE, BRIAN. "Speaking of Books: Anglo-Jewish Writers," *New York Times Book Review*, April 17, 1966, pp. 2, 40. [Bellow, Malamud, Singer, P. Roth, Charles, et al.]

GLICKSBERG, CHARLES I. "A Jewish American Literature?" *Southwest Review*, LIII (Spring 1968), 196–205. [Lewisohn, Shapiro, Malamud, Wallant, Fiedler, Mailer.]

————. "The Jewish Element in American Drama," *Chicago Jewish Forum*, X (Winter 1951–52), 110–115. [Rice, Anderson, Odets, Miller.]

————. "The Theme of Alienation in the American Jewish Novel," *The Reconstructionist*, XXIII (November 29, 1957), 8–13. [Bellow, Rosenfeld, Lewisohn, Hecht.]

GOLDBERG, MARK F. "Books: The Jew as Lover," *National Jewish Monthly*, LXXXIV (November 1969), 64. [Bellow, Cahan, P. Roth.]

GUTTMANN, ALLEN. "The Conversions of the Jews," *Wisconsin Studies in Contemporary Literature*, VI (Summer 1965), 161–176. See above pp. 39–57.

————. "Jewish Radicals, Jewish Writers," *American Scholar*, XXXII (Autumn 1963), 563–575.

HICKS, GRANVILLE. "A Matter of Critical Opinion," *Saturday Review*, XLVIII (August 7, 1965), 19–20. [Mailer and Bellow.]

HOWE, IRVING. "Mass Society and Post-Modern Fiction," *Partisan Review*, XXVI (Summer 1959), 420–436. [Mailer, Malamud, Salinger, Bellow, et al.]

HURWITZ, RUTH SAPIN. "American-Jewish Writing," *Times Literary Supplement*, December 4, 1959, p. 709. [Letter to the Editor.]

HYMAN, FREIDA CLARK. "Jewish Themes in Recent Fiction," *Jewish Spectator*, XXVII (October 1962), 24–28. [Rev.-art.: Singer and Schwartz.]

"The Jewish Intellectual and Jewish Identity," *Congress Bi-Weekly*, XXX (September 16, 1963), 19–41. [Fiedler, P. Roth.]

"Jewishness and the Creative Process," *Congress Bi-Weekly*, XXX (September 16, 1963), 60–85. [Fiedler, P. Roth.]

"Jewishness & the Younger Intellectuals," *Commentary*, XXXI (April 1961), 306–359. [P. Roth et al.]

KAHN, LOTHAR. "The American Jewish Novel Today," *Congress Bi-Weekly*, XXXVI (December 5, 1969), 3–4.

KAMINSKY, ALICE R. "The American Jew in the Academic Novel," *Midwest Quarterly*, III (Summer 1962), 305–318. [Nemerov, Malamud, et al.]

KAUFFMANN, STANLEY. "Some of Our Best Writers," *New York Times Book Review*, May 30, 1965, pp. 1, 16–17. [Rev.-art.]

KAZIN, Alfred. "The Jew as Modern Writer," *Commentary*, XLI (April 1966), 37–41.

KOSTELANETZ, RICHARD. "Militant Minorities," *Hudson Review*, XVIII (Autumn 1965), 472–480. [Rev.-art.]

LAINOFF, SEYMOUR. "American Jewish Fiction Before the First World War," *Chicago Jewish Forum*, XXIV (Spring 1966), 207–217.

LANDIS, JOSEPH C. "Reflections on American Jewish Writers," *Jewish Book Annual*, XXV (1967), 140–147. [Bellow, Malamud, et al.]

MAILER, NORMAN. "Norman Mailer vs. Styron, Jones, Baldwin, Bellow, Heller, Updike, Burroughs, Salinger, Roth," *Esquire*, LX (July 1963), 64–69. [Rev.-art.]

MUDRICK, MARVIN. "Who Killed Herzog? or, Three American Novelists," *University of Denver Quarterly*, I (Spring 1966), 61–97. [Malamud, Bellow, P. Roth.]

PINSKER, SANFORD. "The 'Hassid' in Modern American Literature," *The Reconstructionist*, XXX (March 6, 1970), 7–15. [Cahan, M. Gold, P. Roth, Wallant, Malamud, Singer.]

_____. "Salinger, Malamud and Wallant: The Jewish Novelist's Quest," *The Reconstructionist*, XXXII (November 25, 1966), 7–14.

_____. "The Schlemiel in Yiddish and American Literature," *Chicago Jewish Forum*, XXV (Spring 1967), 191–195.

PODHORETZ, NORMAN. "The New Nihilism in the American Novel," *Parti-*

san Review, XXV (Fall 1958), 576–590. [Rev.-art.: Bellow and Malamud.]

RIBALOW, HAROLD U. "American Jewish Writers and Their Judaism,"
Judaism, III (Fall 1954), 418–426.

———. "Fifty Basic Works of American-Jewish Fiction," *Chicago Jewish
Forum*, X (Spring 1952), 193–198. [Annotated checklist.]

———. "From 'Hungry Hearts' to 'Marjorie Morningstar'—The Progress of an American Minority Told in Fiction," *Saturday Review*, XL
(September 14, 1957), 46–48.

———. "The Jewish Side of American Life," *Ramparts*, II (Autumn
1963), 24–31. [Bellow, P. Roth, Fiedler, Kazin, Mailer, A. Miller, et
al.]

———. "What Happens to Jewish Writing?" *Congress Weekly*, XVI (March
28, 1949), 10–12.

———. "What's This Jewish Book Craze All About?" *National Jewish
Monthly*, LXXXI (November 1966), 50, 52. [Bellow, Malamud, et al.]

RIDEOUT, WALTER B. " 'O Workers' Revolution . . . The True Messiah':
The Jew as Author and Subject in the American Radical Novel,"
American Jewish Archives, XI (October 1959), 157–175. [Cahan, H.
Roth, Mailer, Wolfert, Fast, et al.]

ROSENTHAL, T.G. "The Jewish Writer in America," *The Listener*, LXVII
(April 12, 1962), 635. [Kazin, Malamud, Schulberg, Rosten, et al.]

ROTH, PHILIP. "The New Jewish Stereotypes," *American Judaism*, XI
(Winter 1961), 10–11. 49–51.

———. "Writing American Fiction," *Commentary*, XXXI (March 1961),
223–233. [Bellow, H. Gold, Salinger, et al.]

RUBIN, LOUIS D., JR. "Southerners and Jews," *Southern Review*, n.s. II
(July 1966), 697–713. [Rev.-art.: Wallant, Bellow, et al.]

SANES, IRVING A., and HARVEY SWADOS. "Certain Jewish Writers—Notes
on Their Stereotype," *Menorah Journal*, XXXVII (Spring 1949),
186–204. [Rosenfeld, Howe, Bellow.]

SCHAPPES, M.U. "Anglo-Jewish and Yiddish-Jewish Literature in America," *Yidishe Kultur*, XXIX (April 1967), 41–45. [In Yiddish.]

SCHULMAN, ELIAS. "Notes on Anglo-Jewish Writers," *Chicago Jewish
Forum*, XXIV (Summer 1966), 276–280. [Fiedler, Singer, Bellow.]

SHERMAN, BERNARD A. "The Jewish-American Initiation Novel," *Chicago
Jewish Forum*, XXIV (Fall 1965), 10–14.

STEVENSON, DAVID L. "The Activists," *Daedalus*, XCII (Spring 1963),
238–249. [Bellow, H. Gold, Malamud, Mailer, Engel, P. Roth, et al.]

THOMPSON, JOHN. "The Fiction Machine," *Commentary*, XLVI (October 1968), 67–71. [Mailer, Bellow, et al.]

"Under Forty: A Symposium on American Literature and the Younger Generation of American Jews," *Contemporary Jewish Record*, VII (February 1944), 3–36. [Participants: Muriel Rukeyser, Alfred Kazin, Delmore Schwartz, Lionel Trilling, Ben Field, Louis Kronenberger, Albert Halper, Howard Fast, David Daiches, Clement Greenberg, and Isaac Rosenfeld.]

"A Vocal Group—The Jewish Part in American Letters," *Times Literary Supplement*, November 6, 1959, pp. xxxv–xxxvi. [Fiedler, Bellow, Trilling, Howe, Malamud, Kazin.]

WALDMEIR, JOSEPH J. "Only an Occasional Rutabaga: American Fiction Since 1945," *Modern Fiction Studies*, XV (Winter 1969–1970), 467–481. [Mailer, Bellow, Malamud, Friedman, et al.]

WEBER, BROM. "Some American Jewish Novelists," *Chicago Jewish Forum*, IV (Spring 1946), 177–184. [West, Levin, Maltz, Lewisohn, Halper.]

WEBER, RONALD. "Jewish Writing in America: Jewish or American?" *Ball State University Forum*, X (Spring 1969), 40–46.

WHITE, ROBERT L. "The English Instructor as Hero: Two Novels by Roth and Malamud," *Forum* (Houston), IV (Winter 1963), 16–22. [*Letting Go* and *A New Life.*]

YEDWAB, STANLEY. "The Jew as Portrayed in American Jewish Novels of the 1930's," *American Jewish Archives*, XI (1959), 148–154.

II. INDIVIDUAL WRITERS

Saul Bellow

(Under General, see Aldridge; Allen; Alter, *After the Tradition;* Alter, *America and Israel;* Balakian and Simmons; Baumbach; Bryant; Burgess; Eisinger; Fiedler, "Adolescence and Maturity . . ."; Fiedler, *No! In Thunder;* Fiedler, *Waiting for the End;* Finkelstein; French; Geismar; Gross; Guttmann; Harper; Hassan; Hicks; Hoffman; Kazin; Klein; Kostelanetz; Lewis; Liptzin; Ludwig; Malin; Malin and Stark; Moore; Pinsker; Podhoretz; Rupp; Schulz; Scott; Sherman; Syrkin; Tanner; Teller; Weinberg; *Writers at Work;* Chametzky; Charles; Feinstein; Fiedler, "The Breakthrough"; Fiedler, "The Jew . . ."; Fineman, "The Image of the Jew in Fiction of the Future";

Fineman, "The Image of the Jew in Our Fiction"; Fleischmann; Freedman; Geismar; Glanville; Glicksberg, "The Theme of Alienation . . ."; Goldberg; Hicks; Howe; Landis; Mailer; Mudrick; Podhoretz; Ribalow, "The Jewish Side . . ."; Ribalow, "What's This Jewish Book Craze All About?"; Roth, "Writing American Fiction"; Rubin; Sanes and Swados; Schulman; Stevenson; Thompson; "A Vocal Group"; Waldmeir.)

ALLEN, MICHAEL. "Idiomatic Language in Two Novels by Saul Bellow," *Journal of American Studies,* I (October 1967), 275–280. [*Augie March* and *Henderson.*]

ATKINS, ANSELM. "The Moderate Optimism of Saul Bellow's *Herzog,*" *The Personalist,* L (Winter 1969), 117–129.

AXTHELM, PETER M. "The Full Perception: Bellow." In his *The Modern Confessional Novel.* New Haven, Conn.: Yale University Press, 1967. Pp. 128–177.

BAIM, JOSEPH. "Escape From Intellection: Saul Bellow's *Dangling Man,*" *University Review,* XXXVII (Autumn 1970), 28–34.

BAKER, SHERIDAN. "Saul Bellow's Bout With Chivalry," *Criticism,* IX (Spring 1967), 109–122.

BARUCH, FRANKLIN R. "Bellow and Milton: Professor Herzog in His Garden," *Critique,* IX (No. 3, 1967), 74–83.

BEZANKER, ABRAHAM. "The Odyssey of Saul Bellow," *Yale Review,* LVIII (Spring 1969), 359–371.

BRADBURY, MALCOLM. "Saul Bellow and the Naturalist Tradition," *Review of English Literature* (Leeds), IV (October 1963), 80–92.

———. "Saul Bellow's *Herzog,*" *Critical Quarterly,* VII (Autumn 1965), 269–278.

———. "Saul Bellow's *The Victim,*" *Critical Quarterly,* V (Summer 1963), 119–128.

CAMPBELL, JEFF H. "Bellow's Intimations of Immortality: *Henderson the Rain King,*" *Studies in the Novel,* I (Fall 1969), 323–333.

CHAPMAN, ABRAHAM. "The Image of Man as Portrayed by Saul Bellow," *College Language Association Journal,* X (June 1967), 285–298.

CHASE, RICHARD. "The Adventures of Saul Bellow: Progress of a Novelist," *Commentary,* XXVII (April 1959), 323–330. [Rev.-art.]

CIANCIO, RALPH. "The Achievement of Saul Bellow's *Seize the Day.*" In Thomas F. Staley and Lester F. Zimmerman, eds. *Literature and Theology.* Tulsa, Okla.: University of Tulsa, 1969. Pp. 49–80.

CLAYTON, JOHN JACOB. SAUL BELLOW—IN DEFENSE OF MAN. Bloomington: Indiana University Press, 1968.

COOK, BRUCE. "Saul Bellow: A Mood of Protest," *Perspective on Ideas and the Arts*, XII (February 1963), 46–50.

CROZIER, ROBERT D. "Theme in *Augie March*," *Critique*, VII (Spring–Summer 1965), 18–32.

DEMAREST, DAVID P., JR. "The Theme of Discontinuity in Saul Bellow's Fiction: 'Looking for Mr. Green' and 'A Father-to-Be,' " *Studies in Short Fiction*, VI (Winter 1969), 175–186.

DETWEILER, ROBERT. "Patterns of Rebirth in *Henderson the Rain King*," *Modern Fiction Studies*, XII (Winter 1966–1967), 405–414.

———. SAUL BELLOW—A CRITICAL ESSAY. Grand Rapids, Mich.: W.B. Eerdmans, 1967.

DONOGHUE, DENIS. "Commitment and the Dangling Man," *Studies*, LIII (Summer 1964), 174–187.

DUTTON, ROBERT R. SAUL BELLOW. New York: Twayne, 1971.

[ENCK, JOHN J.] "Saul Bellow: An Interview," *Wisconsin Studies in Contemporary Literature*, VI (Summer 1965), 156–160.

FIEDLER, LESLIE. "Saul Bellow," *Prairie Schooner*, XXXI (Summer 1957), 103–110.

FISCH, HAROLD. "The Hero as Jew: Reflections on *Herzog*," *Judaism*, XVII (Winter 1968), 42–54.

FLAMM, DUDLEY. "Herzog—Victim and Hero," *Zeitschrift für Anglistik und Amerikanistik*, XVII (No. 2, 1969), 174–188.

FOSSUM, ROBERT H. "The Devil and Saul Bellow," *Comparative Literature Studies*, III (No. 2, 1966), 197–206.

FREEDMAN, RALPH. "Saul Bellow: The Illusion of Environment," *Wisconsin Studies in Contemporary Literature*, I (Winter 1960), 50–65.

FROHOCK, W.M. "Saul Bellow and His Penitent Picaro," *Southwest Review*, LIII (Winter 1968), 36–44.

GALLOWAY, DAVID D. "Moses-Bloom-Herzog: Bellow's Everyman," *Southern Review*, n.s. II (January 1966), 61–76.

GARRETT, GEORGE, "To Do Right in a Bad World: Saul Bellow's *Herzog*," *Hollins Critic*, II (April 1965), 1–12. [Rev.-art.]

GOLDBERG, GERALD JAY. "Life's Customer: Augie March," *Critique*, III (Summer 1960), 15–27.

GOLDFINCH, MICHAEL A. "A Journey to the Interior," *English Studies*, XLIII (October 1962), 439–443. [*Henderson.*]

GUERARD, ALBERT J. "Saul Bellow and the Activists: On *The Adventures of Augie March*," *Southern Review*, n.s. III (July 1967), 582–596.

HABER, LEO. "Saul Bellow's Discourse," *Jewish Frontier*, XXXVII (June 1970), 24–26. [Rev.-art.]

HALL, JAMES. "Portrait of the Artist as a Self-Creating, Self-Vindicating, High Energy Man: Saul Bellow." In his *The Lunatic Giant in the Drawing Room—The British and American Novel Since 1930*. Blooming-ton: Indiana University Press, 1968. Pp. 127–180.

HANDY, WILLIAM J. "Saul Bellow and the Naturalistic Hero," *Texas Studies in Literature and Language*, V (Winter 1964), 538–545.

HOFFMAN, MICHAEL J. "From Cohn to Herzog," *Yale Review*, LVIII (Spring 1969), 342–358.

HOWARD, JANE. "Mr. Bellow Considers His Planet," *Life*, LXVIII (April 3, 1970), 57–60.

HUGHES, DANIEL J. "Reality and the Hero: *Lolita* and *Henderson the Rain King*," *Modern Fiction Studies*, VI (Winter 1960–1961), 345–364.

KAZIN, ALFRED. "My Friend Saul Bellow," *The Atlantic*, CCXV (January 1965), 51–54.

KNIPP, THOMAS R. "The Cost of Henderson's Quest," *Ball State University Forum*, X (Spring 1969), 37–39.

LEACH, ELSIE. "From Ritual to Romance Again: *Henderson the Rain King*," *Western Humanities Review*, XIV (Spring 1960), 223–224.

LEVENSON, J.C. "Bellow's Dangling Men," *Critique*, III (Summer 1960), 3–14.

LEVINE, PAUL. "Saul Bellow: The Affirmation of the Philosophical Fool," *Perspective*, X (Winter 1959), 163–176.

LUDWIG, JACK. "The Wayward Reader," *Holiday*, XXXVII (February 1965), 16, 18–19, [Rev.-art.]

MALIN, IRVING. SAUL BELLOW'S FICTION. Carbondale: Southern Illinois University Press, 1969.

———, ed. SAUL BELLOW AND THE CRITICS. New York: New York University Press, 1967. [Reprinted essays and reviews by Fiedler, Geismar, Chase, Levenson, Freedman, Hughes, Klein, Weiss, Malin, Rovit, Read, Aldridge, and Bellow.]

MATHIS, JAMES C. "The Theme of *Seize the Day*," *Critique*, VII (Spring–Summer 1965), 43–45.

MORROW, PATRICK. "Threat and Accommodation: The Novels of Saul Bellow," *Midwest Quarterly*, VIII (Summer 1967), 389–411.

OPDAHL, KEITH MICHAEL. THE NOVELS OF SAUL BELLOW—AN INTRO-DUCTION. University Park: Pennsylvania State University Press, 1967.

OVERBECK, PAT T. "The Women in *Augie March*," *Texas Studies in Literature and Language*, X (Fall 1968), 471–484.

POIRIER, RICHARD. "Bellows to Herzog," *Partisan Review,* XXXII (Spring 1965), 264–271. [Rev.-art.]

PORTER, M. GILBERT. *"Herzog:* A Transcendental Solution to an Existential Problem," *Forum* (Houston), VII (Spring 1969), 32–36.

QUINTON, ANTHONY. "The Adventures of Saul Bellow," *London Magazine,* VI (December 1959), 55–59. [Rev.-art.]

RANS, GEOFFREY. "The Novels of Saul Bellow," *Review of English Literature* (Leeds), IV (October 1963), 18–30.

ROSS, THEODORE J. "Notes on Saul Bellow," *Chicago Jewish Forum,* XVIII (Fall 1959), 21–27.

ROVIT, EARL. SAUL BELLOW. Minneapolis: University of Minnesota Press, 1967.

RUBENSTEIN, RICHARD L. "The Philosophy of Saul Bellow," *The Reconstructionist,* XXX (January 22, 1965), 7–12. [*Herzog.*]

SCHNEIDER, HAROLD W. "Two Bibliographies: Saul Bellow, William Styron," *Critique,* III (Summer 1960), 71–91.

SHULMAN, ROBERT. "The Style of Bellow's Comedy," *PMLA,* LXXXIII (March 1968), 109–117.

STOCK, IRVIN. "The Novels of Saul Bellow," *Southern Review,* n.s. III (Winter 1967), 13–42.

TANNER, TONY, SAUL BELLOW. Edinburgh: Oliver and Boyd, 1965.

TRACHTENBERG, STANLEY. "Saul Bellow's *Luftmenschen:* The Compromise With Reality," *Critique,* IX (No. 3, 1967), 37–61.

TROWBRIDGE, CLINTON W. "Water Imagery in *Seize the Day,*" *Critique,* IX (No. 3, 1967), 62–73.

UPHAUS, SUZANNE HENNING. "From Innocence to Experience: A Study of *Herzog,*" *Dalhousie Review,* XLVI (Spring 1966), 67–78.

VOGEL, DAN. "Saul Bellow's Vision Beyond Absurdity: Jewishness in *Herog,*" *Tradition,* IX (Spring 1968), 65–79.

WAY, BRIAN. "Character and Society in *The Adventures of Augie March,*" *British Association for American Studies Bulletin,* No. 8 (June 1964), 36–44.

WEBER, RONALD. "Bellow's Thinkers," *Western Humanities Review,* XXII (Autumn 1968), 305–313.

WEISS, DANIEL. "Caliban on Prospero: A Psychoanalytic Study on the Novel *Seize the Day,* by Saul Bellow," *American Imago,* XIX (Fall 1962), 277–306.

YOUNG, JAMES DEAN. "Bellow's View of the Heart," *Critique,* VII (Spring–Summer 1965), 5–17. [*Herzog.*]

Leslie Fiedler

(Under General, see Aldridge; Malin; Malin and Stark; Schulz; Teller; Alter; "The Creative Writer As a Jew"; Feinstein; Glicksberg, "A Jewish American Literature?"; "The Jewish Intellectual and Jewish Identity"; "Jewishness and the Creative Process"; Ribalow, "The Jewish Side . . ."; Schulman; "A Vocal Group.")

ALTER, ROBERT. "Jewish Dreams and Nightmares," *Commentary*, XLV (January 1968), 48–54.

BELLMAN, SAMUEL IRVING. "The American Artist as European Frontiersman: Leslie Fiedler's *The Second Stone*," *Critique*, VI (Winter 1963), 131–143. [Rev.-art.]

————. "The Frontiers of Leslie Fiedler," *Southwest Review*, XLVIII (Winter 1963), 86–89. [Rev.-art.]

————. "Leslie A. Fiedler: Lazarus or Prophet?" *Congress Bi-Weekly*, XXXI (December 21, 1964), 10–12.

CHASE, RICHARD. "Leslie Fiedler and American Culture," *Chicago Review*, XIV (Autumn–Winter 1960), 8–18. [Rev.-art.]

DAVIS, ROBERT GORHAM. "Leslie Fiedler's Fictions," *Commentary*, XLIII (January 1967), 73–77. [Rev.-art.]

Bruce Jay Friedman

(Under General, see Hyman; Schulz; Syrkin; Bellman, "Fathers and Sons . . ."; Freedman; Waldmeir.)

KAPLAN, CHARLES. "Escape Into Hell: Friedman's *Stern*," *California English Journal*, I (1965), 25–30.

Irving Howe

(Under General, see Malin and Stark; Freedman; Sanes and Swados; "A Vocal Group.")

CAPOUYA, EMILE. "Howe Now," *Studies on the Left*, IV (Spring 1964), 63–67. [Rev.-art.]

KOSTELANETZ, RICHARD. "On Irving Howe: The Perils and Paucities of 'Democratic Radicalism,'" *Salmagundi*, II (Spring 1967), 44–60.

Alfred Kazin

(Under General, see Guttmann; Liptzin; Malin and Stark; Sherman; Ribalow, "The Jewish Side"; Rosenthal; "Under Forty"; "A Vocal Group.")

FREEDMAN, MORRIS. "The Jewish Artist as a Young American," *Chicago Jewish Forum*, X (Spring 1952), 212–214. [Rev.-art.]

Norman Mailer

(Under General, see Adridge; Allen; Alter, *America and Israel;* Balakian and Simmons; Bryant; Burgess; Eisinger, Fiedler, *Waiting for the End;* Finkelstein; French; Geismar; Gross; Guttmann; Harper; Hassan; Hicks; Hoffman; Hyman; Kazin; Kostelanetz; Lewis; Liptzin; Ludwig; Malin and Stark; Moore; Podhoretz; Schulz; Scott; Syrkin; Tanner; Teller; Weinberg; *Writers at Work;* Angoff; Feinstein; Fiedler, "The Breakthrough"; Fiedler, "The Jew . . ."; Fineman, "The Image of the Jew in Fiction of the Future"; Fineman, "The Image of the Jew in Our Fiction"; Freedman; Glicksberg, "A Jewish American Literature?"; Hicks; Howe; Ribalow, "The Jewish Side . . ."; Rideout; Stevenson; Thompson; Waldmeir.)

ALDRIDGE, JOHN W. "Mailer, Burns, and Shaw: *The Naked Zero."* In his *After the Lost Generation—A Critical Study of the Writers of Two Wars.* New York: Noonday Press, 1958. Pp. 133–156.

———. "The Perfect Absurd Figure of a Mighty, Absurd Crusade," *Saturday Review*, LIV (November 13, 1971), 45–49, 72.

ALTER, ROBERT. "The Real and Imaginary World of Norman Mailer," *Midstream*, XV (January 1969), 24–35.

AUCHINCLOSS, EVE, and NANCY LYNCH. "An Interview With Norman Mailer," *Mademoiselle*, LII (February 1961), 76–77, 160–163.

BALDWIN, JAMES. "The Black Boy Looks at the White Boy: Norman Mailer," *Esquire*, LV (May 1961), 102–106.

BERSANI, LEO. "The Interpretation of Dreams," *Partisan Review*, XXXII (Fall 1965), 603–608.

BREIT, HARVEY. "Talk With Norman Mailer," *New York Times Book Review*, June 3, 1951, p. 20.

COOK, BRUCE A. "Norman Mailer: The Temptation to Power," *Renascence*, XIV (Summer 1962), 206–215, 222.

DUPEE, F.W. "The American Norman Mailer," *Commentary*, XXIX (February 1960), 128–132.

FOSTER, RICHARD. "Mailer and the Fitzgerald Tradition," *Novel*, I (Spring 1968), 219–230.

———. NORMAN MAILER. Minneapolis: University of Minnesota Press, 1968.

GLICKSBERG, CHARLES I. "Norman Mailer: The Angry Young Novelist in

America," *Wisconsin Studies in Contemporary Literature*, I (Winter 1960), 25–34.

————. "Sex in Contemporary Literature," *Colorado Quarterly*, IX (Winter 1961), 277–287.

GOLDSTONE, HERBERT. "The Novels of Norman Mailer," *English Journal*, XLV (March 1956), 113–121.

GORDON, ANDREW. "*The Naked and the Dead:* The Triumph of Impotence," *Literature & Psychology*, XIX (Number 3–4, 1969), 3–13.

HOFFMAN, FREDERICK J. "Norman Mailer and the Revolt of the Ego: Some Observations on Recent American Literature," *Wisconsin Studies in Contemporary Literature*, I (Fall 1960), 5–12.

HOWE, IRVING. "A Quest for Peril: Norman Mailer." In his *A World More Attractive—A View of Modern Literature and Politics.* New York: Horizon Press, 1963. Pp. 123–129.

HUX, SAMUEL. "Mailer's Dream of Violence," *Minnesota Review*, VIII (No. 2, 1968), 152–157.

KAHN, LOTHAR. "The Jewish Soldier in Modern Fiction," *American Judaism*, IX (No. 3, 1960), 12–13, 30–31.

KAUFMANN, DONALD L. NORMAN MAILER: THE COUNTDOWN (THE FIRST TWENTY YEARS). Carbondale: Southern Illinois University Press, 1969.

LAKIN, R.D. "D.W.'s: The Displaced Writer in America," *Midwest Quarterly*, IV (Summer 1963), 295–303.

LEEDS, BARRY H. THE STRUCTURED VISION OF NORMAN MAILER. New York: New York University Press, 1969.

LUCID, ROBERT F., ed. NORMAN MAILER: THE MAN AND HIS WORK. Boston: Little, Brown, 1971. [Reprinted essays and reviews by Podhoretz, Vidal, Macdonald, Kazin, Poirier, Diana Trilling, Foster, et al.]

MACDONALD, DWIGHT. "Massachusetts vs. Mailer," *New Yorker*, XXXVI (October 8, 1960), 154–166.

MUDRICK, MARVIN. "Mailer and Styron: Guests of the Establishment," *Hudson Review*, XVII (Autumn 1964), 346–366.

NEWMAN, PAUL B. "Mailer: The Jew as Existentialist," *North American Review*, n.s. II (July 1965), 48–55.

RICHLER, MORDECAI. "Norman Mailer," *Encounter*, XXV (July 1965), 61–64.

SCHRADER, GEORGE A. "Norman Mailer and the Despair of Defiance," *Yale Review*, LI (Winter 1961–62), 267–280.

SCHROTH, RAYMOND A. "Mailer and His Gods," *Commonweal*, XC (May 9, 1969), 226–229.

SOKOLOFF, B.A. A COMPREHENSIVE BIBLIOGRAPHY OF NORMAN MAILER. Folcroft, Penna.: Folcroft Press, 1970.

SOLOTAROFF, ROBERT. "Down Mailer's Way," *Chicago Review,* XIX (No. 3, 1967), 11–25.

STEINER, GEORGE. "Naked But Not Dead," *Encounter,* XVII (December 1961), 67–70. [Rev.-art.]

STERN, RICHARD G. "Hip, Hell, and the Navigator: An Interview With Norman Mailer," *Western Review,* XXIII (Winter 1959), 101–109.

SWADOS, HARVEY. "Must Writers Be Characters?" *Saturday Review,* XLIII (October 1, 1960), 12–14, 50.

TOBACK, JAMES. "Norman Mailer Today," *Commentary,* XLIV (October 1967), 68–76. [Rev.-art.]

VIDAL, GORE. "The Norman Mailer Syndrome," *The Nation,* CXC (January 2, 1960), 13–16.

WAGENHEIM, ALLAN J. "Square's Progress: *An American Dream,*" *Critique,* X (No. 1, 1968), 45–68.

WEBER, BROM. "A Fear of Dying: Norman Mailer's *An American Dream,*" *Hollins Critic,* II (June 1965), 1–11. [Rev.-art.]

WILLINGHAM, CALDER. "The Way It Isn't Done: Notes on the Distress of Norman Mailer," *Esquire,* LX (December 1963), 306–308.

WINEGARTEN, RENEE. "Norman Mailer—Genuine or Counterfeit?" *Midstream,* XI (September 1965), 91–95.

WITT, GRACE. "The Bad Man as Hipster: Norman Mailer's Use of Frontier Metaphor," *Western American Literature,* IV (Fall 1969), 203–217.

WOOD, MARGERY. "Norman Mailer and Nathalie Sarraute: A Comparison of Existential Novels," *Minnesota Review,* VI (No. 1, 1966), 67–72.

Bernard Malamud

(Under General, see Allen; Alter, *After the Tradition;* Balakian and Simmons; Baumbach; Bryant; Burgess; Fiedler, *No! In Thunder;* Fiedler, *Waiting for the End;* French; Guttmann; Hassan; Hicks; Hyman; Kazin; Klein; Kostelanetz; Liptzin; Ludwig; Malin; Malin and Stark; Meeter; Moore; Pinsker; Rupp; Schulz; Scott; Syrkin; Tanner; Teller; Weinberg; Angoff; Bellman, "Fathers and Sons . . ."; Charles Fiedler, "The Breakthrough"; Fiedler, "The Jew . . ."; Fineman, "The Image of the Jew in Fiction of the Future"; Fineman, "The Image of the Jew in Our Fiction"; Fleischmann; Freedman; Geismar; Glanville; Glicksberg, "A Jewish American Literature?";

Howe; Kaminsky; Landis; Mudrick; Pinsker, "The 'Hassid' . . .";
Pinsker, "Salinger, Malamud and Wallant"; Podhoretz; Ribalow,
"What's This Jewish Book Craze All About?"; Rosenthal; Ste-
venson; "A Vocal Group"; Waldmeir; White.)

ALLEY, ALVIN D., and HUGH AGEE. "Existential Heroes: Frank Alpine
and Rabbit Angstrom," *Ball State University Forum*, IX (Winter 1968),
3–5.

BARSNESS, JOHN A. *"A New Life*—The Frontier Myth in Perspective,"
Western American Literature, III (Winter 1969), 297–302.

BAUMBACH, JONATHAN. "Malamud's Heroes: The Fate of Fixers," *Commonweal*, LXXXV (October 28, 1966), 97–99. [Rev.-art.]

BELLMAN, SAMUEL IRVING. "Women, Children, and Idiots First: The
Transformation Psychology of Bernard Malamud," *Critique*, VII
(Winter 1964–1965), 123–138.

BLUEFARB, SAM. "Bernard Malamud: The Scope of Caricature," *English
Journal*, LIII (May 1964), 319–326, 335.

CHARLES, GERDA. "Bernard Malamud—The 'Natural' Writer," *Jewish
Quarterly*, IX (Spring 1962), 5–6.

DUPEE, F.W. "Malamud: The Uses and Abuses of Commitment." In his
"The King of the Cats" and Other Remarks on Writers and Writing. New
York: Farrar, Straus and Giroux, 1965. Pp. 156–163.

EIGNER, EDWIN M. "Malamud's Use of the Quest Romance," *Genre*, I
(January 1968), 55–75.

ELMAN, RICHARD M. "Malamud on Campus," *Commonweal*, LXXV (October 27, 1961), 114–115. [Rev.-art.]

FEATHERSTONE, JOSEPH. "Bernard Malamud," *The Atlantic*, CCXIX
(March 1967), 95–98.

FIELD, LESLIE A., and JOYCE W. FIELD, eds. BERNARD MALAMUD AND THE
CRITICS. New York: New York University Press, 1970. [Reprinted
essays and reviews.]

FRANKEL, HASKEL. "Interview With Bernard Malamud," *Saturday Review*,
IX (September 10, 1966), 39–40.

FRIEDMAN, ALAN WARREN. "Bernard Malamud: The Hero as Schnook,"
Southern Review, n.s. IV (October 1968), 927–944.

GOLDMAN, MARK. "Bernard Malamud's Comic Vision and the Theme of
Identity," *Critique*, VII (Winter 1964–65), 92–109.

GOODMAN, OSCAR B. "There Are Jews Everywhere," *Judaism*, XIX (Summer 1970), 283–294.

GREIFF, LOUIS K. "Quest and Defeat in *The Natural*," *Thoth*, VIII (Winter
1967), 23–34.

HAYS, PETER L. "The Complex Pattern of Redemption in *The Assistant*," *Centennial Review*, XIII (Spring 1969), 200–214.

HILL, JOHN S. "Malamud's 'The Lady of the Lake'—A Lesson in Rejection," *University Review*, XXXVI (Winter 1969), 149–150.

KOSOFSKY, RITA N. BERNARD MALAMUD—AN ANNOTATED CHECKLIST. Kent, Ohio: Kent State University Press, 1969.

LEER, NORMAN. "Three American Novels and Contemporary Society: A Search for Commitment," *Wisconsin Studies in Contemporary Literature*, III (Fall 1962), 67–86.

LEFCOWITZ, BARBARA F. "The *Hybris* of Neurosis: Malamud's *Pictures of Fidelman*," *Literature & Psychology*, XX (Number 3, 1970), 115–120.

MANDEL, RUTH B. "Bernard Malamud's *The Assistant* and *A New Life*: Ironic Affirmation," *Critique*, VII (Winter 1964–1965), 110–121.

MAY, CHARLES E. "The Bread of Tears: Malamud's 'The Loan,'" *Studies in Short Fiction*, VII (Fall 1970), 652–654.

MELLARD, JAMES M. "Malamud's Novels: Four Versions of Pastoral," *Critique*, IX (No. 2, 1967), 5–19.

———. "Malamud's *The Assistant*: The City Novel as Pastoral," *Studies in Short Fiction*, V (Fall 1967), 1–11.

PERRINE, LAURENCE. "Malamud's 'Take Pity,'" *Studies in Short Fiction*, II (Fall 1964), 84–86.

PINSKER, SANFORD. "The Achievement of Bernard Malamud," *Midwest Quarterly*, X (Summer 1969), 379–389.

———. "A Note on Bernard Malamud's 'Take Pity,'" *Studies in Short Fiction*, VI (Winter 1969), 212–213.

RATNER, MARC L. "Style and Humanity in Malamud's Fiction," *Massachusetts Review*, V (Summer 1964), 663–683.

RIBALOW, HAROLD U. "Bernard Malamud: 'The Suffering of the Jews . . . ,'" *The Reconstructionist*, XXXIII (June 9, 1967), 12–16.

RICHMAN, SIDNEY. BERNARD MALAMUD. New York: Twayne, 1966.

ROVIT, EARL H. "Bernard Malamud and the Jewish Literary Tradition," *Critique*, III (Winter–Spring 1960), 3–10.

SHEAR, WALTER. "Culture Conflict in *The Assistant*," *Midwest Quarterly*, VII (Summer 1966), 367–380.

SHULMAN, ROBERT. "Myth, Mr. Eliot, and the Comic Novel," *Modern Fiction Studies*, XII (Winter 1966–1967), 395–403.

SIEGEL, BEN. "Victims in Motion: Bernard Malamud's Sad and Bitter Clowns," *Northwest Review*, V (Spring 1962), 69–80.

SOLOTAROFF, THEODORE. "Bernard Malamud's Fiction: The Old Life and the New," *Commentary*, XXXIII (March 1962), 197–204. [Rev.-art.]

"A Talk With B. Malamud," *New York Times Book Review,* October 8, 1961, p. 28.

TURNER, FREDERICK W., III. "Myth Inside and Out: Malamud's *The Natural,*" *Novel,* I (Winter 1968), 133–139.

WASSERMAN, EARL R. *"The Natural:* Malamud's World Ceres," *Centennial Review,* IX (Fall 1965), 438–460.

WEISS, SAMUEL A. "Notes on Bernard Malamud," *Chicago Jewish Forum,* XXI (Winter 1962–1963), 155–158.

————. "Passion and Purgation in Bernard Malamud," *University of Windsor Review,* II (Fall 1966), 93–99.

Philip Roth

(Under General, see Alter, *America and Israel;* Detweiler; Fiedler, *Waiting for the End;* Guttmann; Hicks; Hyman; Kazin; Kostelanetz; Liptzin; Malin; Malin and Stark; Meeter; Podhoretz; Syrkin; Tanner; Teller; Bellman, "Fathers and Sons . . ."; Feinstein; Fineman, "The Image of the Jew in Fiction of the Future"; Fineman, "The Image of the Jew in Our Fiction"; Fleischmann; Freedman; Geismar; Glanville; Goldberg; "The Jewish Intellectual and Jewish Identity"; "Jewishness and the Creative Process"; "Jewishness & the Younger Intellectuals"; Mailer; Mudrick; Pinsker, " 'The Hassid' . . ."; Ribalow, "The Jewish Side . . ."; Stevenson; White.)

CHEUSE, ALAN. "A World Without Realists," *Studies on the Left,* IV (Spring 1964), 68–82.

DEER, IRVING and HARRIET. "Philip Roth and the Crisis in American Fiction," *Minnesota Review,* VI (No. 4, 1966), 353–360.

DITSKY, JOHN. "Roth, Updike, and the High Expense of Spirit," *University of Windsor Review,* V (Fall 1969), 111–120. [Rev.-art.]

DONALDSON, SCOTT. "Philip Roth: The Meanings of *Letting Go,*" *Contemporary Literature,* XI (Winter 1970), 21–35.

GORDON, LOIS G. " 'Portnoy's Complaint': Coming of Age in Jersey City," *Literature & Psychology,* XIX (Nos. 3 & 4, 1969), 57–60. [Rev.-art.]

GROSS, JOHN. "Marjorie Morningstar PhD.," *New Statesman,* LXIV (November 30, 1962), 784. [Rev.-art.]

HOCHMAN, BARUCH. "Child and Man in Philip Roth," *Midstream,* XIII (December 1967), 68–76.

ISAAC, DAN. "In Defense of Philip Roth," *Chicago Review,* XVII (Nos. 2 & 3, 1964), 84–96.

KOCH, ERIC. "Roth's 'Goodbye Columbus,'" *Tamarack Review*, No. 13 (Autumn 1959), 129–132. [Rev.-art.]

LANDIS, JOSEPH C. "The Sadness of Philip Roth: An Interim Report," *Massachusetts Review*, III (Winter 1962), 259–268.

LEER, NORMAN. "Escape and Confrontation in the Short Stories of Philip Roth," *Christian Scholar*, XLIX (Summer 1966), 132–146.

LEVINE, MORDECAI H. "Philip Roth and American Judaism," *College Language Association Journal*, XIV (December 1970), 163–170.

SHAW, PETER. "Portnoy and His Creator," *Commentary*, XLVII (May 1969), 77–79. [Rev.-art.]

SOLOTAROFF, THEODORE. "Philip Roth and the Jewish Moralists," *Chicago Review*, XIII (Winter 1959), 87–99. See above pp. 13–29.

WOHLGELERNTER, MAURICE. "Mama and Papa and All the Complaints," *Tradition*, X (Fall 1969), 70–87. [Rev.-art.]

Delmore Schwartz

(Under General, see Fiedler, "Adolescence and Maturity . . ."; Malin; Malin and Stark; Matthiessen; Ribalow; Syrkin; Fiedler, "The Breakthrough"; Hyman; "Under Forty.")

ALSTERLUND, B. "Two Young Poets—George Barker and Delmore Schwartz," *Wilson Library Bulletin*, XVI (June 1942), 790, 792.

BONHAM, SISTER M. HILDA, I.H.M. "Delmore Schwartz: An Idea of the World," *Renascence*, XIII (Spring 1961), 132–135.

CHAPIN, KATHERINE GARRISON. "The Man He Chose to Be," *New Republic*, CXLI (November 9, 1959), 24–26. [Rev.-art.]

CHOGUILL, FRANCINE O. Delmore Schwartz: The Moral Responsibility of the Writer, unpublished doctoral dissertation, Syracuse University, 1968. [Abstract in *Dissertation Abstracts*, XXIX (May 1969), 4000A.]

DEUTSCH, R[OBERT]. H. "Delmore Schwartz: Middle Poems," *Concerning Poetry*, II (Fall 1969), 19–28.

———. "Poetry and Belief in Delmore Schwartz," *Sewanee Review*, LXXIV (October–December 1966), 915–924.

———. The Poetry of Delmore Schwartz, unpublished doctoral dissertation, University of Southern California, 1968. [Abstract in *Dissertation Abstracts*, XXIX (March 1969), 3131A–3132A.]

FISK, WINIFRED. "Among the Younger Poets," *Saturday Review*, XXV (April 11, 1942), 34.

FLINT, ROBERT W. "The Stories of Delmore Schwartz," *Commentary*, XXXIII (April 1962), 336–339. [Rev.-art.]

HALIO, JAY L. "Delmore Schwartz's Felt Abstractions," *Southern Review*, n.s. I (October 1965), 803–819.

KAZIN, ALFRED. "Delmore Schwartz, 1913–1966," *Book Week* (New York *World Journal Tribune*), October 9, 1966, pp. 1, 17–18.

KENNER, HUGH. "Bearded Ladies & The Abundant Goat," *Poetry*, LXXIX (October 1951), 50–53. [Rev.-art.]

KNAPP, JAMES F. "Delmore Schwartz: Poet of the Orphic Journey," *Sewanee Review*, LXXVIII (Summer 1970), 506–516.

KRIEGER, ROBERT. "Speaking at Twilight, Singing in the Morning," *Prairie Schooner*, XXXIV (Summer 1960), 123–127.

MACDONALD, DWIGHT. "Delmore Schwartz (1913–1966)," *New York Review of Books*, September 8, 1966, pp. 14–16.

O'CONNOR, WILLIAM VAN. "The Albatross Was Intended to Fly," *Poetry*, LXXIX (October 1951), 55–59. [Rev.-art.]

O'DONNELL, GEORGE MARION. "Delmore Schwartz's Achievement," *Poetry*, LIV (May 1939), 105–108. [Rev.-art.]

POLITZER, HEINZ. "The Two Worlds of Delmore Schwartz—Lucifer in Brooklyn," *Commentary*, X (December 1950), 561–568.

POSS, STANLEY. "Low Skies, Some Clearing, Local Frost," *New England Quarterly*, XLI (September 1968), 438–442. [Schwartz's "A Dog Named Ego" and Frost's "Stopping by Woods."]

ROSENTHAL, M.L. "Deep in the Unfriendly City," *The Nation*, CXC (June 11, 1960), 515–516. [Rev.-art.]

SEIF, MORTON. "Fallen David and Goliath America: The Battle Report of Delmore Schwartz," *Jewish Social Studies*, XIII (October 1951), 311–320.

STRICKHAUSEN, HARRY. "Extensions in Language," *Poetry*, XCV (February 1960), 300–303. [Rev.-art.]

Karl Shapiro

(Under General, see Fiedler, *Waiting for the End;* Guttmann; Liptzin; Malin; Malin and Stark; Matthiessen; Syrkin; Teller; "Comments by Jewish Writers . . ."; Glicksberg, "A Jewish American Literature?")

BRADLEY, SAM. "Shapiro Strikes at the Establishment," *University of Kansas City Review*, XXIX (Summer 1963), 275–279.

COLEMAN, ALICE. " 'Doors Leap Open,' " *English Journal*, LIII (November 1964), 631–633. [On Shapiro's "Auto Wreck."]

CONQUEST, ROBERT. "Mistah Eliot—He Dead?" *Audit*, I (March 28, 1960), 12–17.

DAICHES, DAVID. "The Poetry of Karl Shapiro," *Poetry*, LXVI (August 1945), 266–273.

DE VRIES, PETER. "Poetry and the War," *College English*, V (December 1943), 113–120.

ENGLE, PAUL. "Five Years of Pulitzer Poets," *English Journal*, XXXVIII (February 1949), 59–66.

FITTS, DUDLEY. "Mr. Shapiro's Ars Poetica," *Poetry*, LXVIII (April 1946), 39–44. [Rev.-art.]

KOHLER, DAYTON. "Karl Shapiro: Poet in Uniform," *College English*, VII (February 1946), 243–249.

O'CONNOR, WILLIAM VAN. "Karl Shapiro: The Development of a Talent," *College English*, X (November 1948), 71–77.

————. "Shapiro's Southwest Pacific Poems," *Poetry*, LXIV (September 1944), 326–334.

RICHMAN, ROBERT. "Alchemy or Poetry," *Sewanee Review*, LIV (Autumn 1946), 684–690.

RUBIN, LOUIS D., JR. "The Search for Lost Innocence: Karl Shapiro's *The Bourgeois Poet*," *Hollins Critic*, I (December 1964), 1–16. [Rev.-art.]

SHAFTER, TOBY. "Karl Shapiro, Poet in Khaki," *National Jewish Monthly*, LXII (April 1948), 288–291.

SLOTKIN, RICHARD. "The Contextual Symbol: Karl Shapiro's Image of 'The Jew,'" *American Quarterly*, XVIII (Summer 1966), 220–226.

SMITH, HAMMETT W. "Karl Jay Shapiro: A Poet of Human Relations," *College Language Association Journal*, I (March 1958), 97–100.

SOUTHWORTH, JAMES G. "The Poetry of Karl Shapiro," *English Journal*, LI (March 1962), 159–166.

VAN DE WATER, CHARLOTTE. "A Soldier Poet—Karl Jay Shapiro," *Senior Scholastic*, XLVII (October 1, 1945), 19.

WHITE, WILLIAM. KARL SHAPIRO: A BIBLIOGRAPHY. Detroit: Wayne State University Press, 1960.

Isaac Bashevis Singer

(Under General, see Hyman; Kazin; Kostelanetz; Pinsker; Schulz; Teller; Freedman; Glanville; Hyman; Pinsker, " 'The Hassid' . . ."; Schulman.)

ALLENTUCK, MARCIA, ed. THE ACHIEVEMENT OF ISAAC BASHEVIS SINGER. Carbondale: Southern Illinois University Press, 1969, [William H.

Gass, "The Shut-In," Eli Katz, "Isaac Bashevis Singer and the Classical Yiddish Tradition," Morris Golden, "Dr. Fischelson's Miracle: Duality and Vision in Singer's Fiction," Maximillian E. Novak, "Moral Grotesque and Decorative Grotesque in Singer's Fiction," Edwin Gittleman, "Singer's Apocalyptic Town: *Satan in Goray,"* Max F. Schulz, "The Family Chronicle as Paradigm of History: *The Brothers Ashkenazi* and *The Family Moskat,"* Cyrena N. Pondrom, "Conjuring Reality: I.B. Singer's *The Magician of Lublin,"* Frederick R. Karl, "Jacob Reborn, Zion Regained: I.B. Singer's *The Slave"* Mary Ellmann, "The Piety of Things in *The Manor,"* H.R. Wolf, "Singer's Children's Stories and *In My Father's Court:* Universalism and the Rankian Hero," Paul N. Siegel, "Gimpel and the Archetype of the Wise Fool."]

BUCHEN, IRVING H. "The Art and Gifts of Isaac Bashevis Singer," *Chicago Jewish Forum,* XXIV (Summer 1966), 308–312.

————. *Isaac Bashevis Singer and the Eternal Past.* New York: New York University Press, 1968.

CHRISTENSEN, BONNIEJEAN McGUIRE. "Isaac Bashevis Singer: A Bibliography," *Bulletin of Bibliography,* XXVI (January–March 1969), 3–6.

EISENBERG, J.A. "Isaac Bashevis Singer—Passionate Primitive or Pious Puritan?" *Judaism,* XI (Fall 1962), 345–356.

ELMAN, RICHARD M. "The Spinoza of Canal Street," *Holiday,* XXXVIII (August 1965), 83–87.

————, and Joel Blocker. "An Interview With Isaac Bashevis Singer," *Commentary,* XXXVI (November 1963), 364–372.

FIXLER, MICHAEL. "The Redeemers: Themes in the Fiction of Isaac Bashevis Singer," *Kenyon Review,* XXVI (Spring 1964), 371–386.

FLENDER, HAROLD. "An Interview With Isaac Bashevis Singer," *National Jewish Monthly,* LXXXII (March 1968), 18–19, 78–79; LXXXII (April 1968), 14–16.

GLATSTEIN, JACOB. "The Fame of Bashevis Singer," *Congress Bi-Weekly,* XXXII (December 27, 1965), 17–19.

GOODHEART, EUGENE. "The Demonic Charm of Bashevis Singer," *Midstream,* VI (Summer 1960), 88–93.

GOTTLIEB, ELAINE. "A Talk With Isaac Bashevis Singer," *The Reconstructionist,* XXV (March 6, 1959), 7–11.

HEMLEY, CECIL. "Isaac Bashevis Singer." In Elaine Gottlieb, ed. *Dimen-*

sions of Midnight—Poetry and Prose. Athens: Ohio University Press, 1968. Pp. 217–233.

HINDUS, MILTON. "Isaac Bashevis Singer," *Jewish Heritage*, V (Fall 1962), 44–52.

HOCHMAN, BARUCH. "I.B. Singer's Vision of Good and Evil," *Midstream*, XIII (March 1967), 66–73.

HOWE, IRVING. "I.B. Singer," *Encounter*, XXVI (March 1966), 60–70.

———. "Introduction." In his ed. *Selected Short Stories of Isaac Bashevis Singer.* New York: Modern Library, 1966. Pp. v–xxiv.

JACOBSON, DAN. "The Problem of Isaac Bashevis Singer," *Commentary*, XXXIX (February 1965), 48–52.

KAHN, LOTHAR. "A World of Spirits and Imps—Isaac Bashevis Singer," *Commonweal*, LXXXI (January 22, 1965), 538–540.

LEVIANT, CURT. "The Phenomenon of Isaac Bashevis Singer," *Congress Bi-Weekly*, XXXIV (December 18, 1967), 9–12.

LEVIN, BEATRICE. "Isaac Bashevis Singer," *Jewish Spectator*, XXX (May 1965), 20–22. [Interview.]

LIEBER, DOLORES. "A Conversation With Isaac Bashevis Singer," *Congress Bi-Weekly*, XXXVI (December 5, 1969), 13–15.

MADISON, CHARLES A. "I. Bashevis Singer—Novelist of Hasidic Gothicism." In his *Yiddish Literature—Its Scope and Major Writers.* New York: Frederick Ungar, 1968. Pp. 479–499.

MALIN, IRVING, ed. CRITICAL VIEWS OF ISAAC BASHEVIS SINGER. New York: New York University Press, 1969. [Reprinted material by Eisenberg, Fixler, Howe, Wolkenfeld, Hochman, Schulz, and Malin plus: Ruth Whitman, "Translating With Isaac Bashevis Singer," Karl Malkoff, "Demonology and Dualism: The Supernatural in Isaac Singer and Muriel Spark," Jules Chametzky, "History in I.B. Singer's Novels," Melvin J. Friedman, "Isaac Bashevis Singer: The Appeal of Numbers," Edwin Gittleman, "Isaac's Nominal Case: *In My Father's Court*," Samuel I. Mintz, "Spinoza and Spinozism in Singer's Shorter Fiction," Jackson R. Bryer and Paul E. Rockwell, "Isaac Bashevis Singer in English: A Bibliography."]

MUCKE, EDITH. "Isaac B. Singer and Hassidic Philosophy," *Minnesota Review*, VII (No. 3, 1967), 214–221.

NEWMAN, RICHARD A. "Isaac Bashevis Singer," *Hibbert Journal*, LXV (Autumn 1966), 27–28.

PINSKER, SANFORD. "The Fictive Worlds of Isaac Bashevis Singer," *Critique*, XI (No. 2, 1969), 26–39.

————. "Isaac Bashevis Singer: An Interview," *Critique*, XI (No. 2, 1969), 16–25.

PONDROM, CYRENA N. "Isaac Bashevis Singer: An Interview and a Biographical Sketch," *Contemporary Literature*, X (Winter 1969), 1–38; X (Summer 1969), 332–351.

RIBALOW, REENA SARA. "A Visit to Isaac Bashevis Singer," *The Reconstructionist*, XXX (May 29, 1964), 19–26.

SIEGEL, BEN. ISAAC BASHEVIS SINGER. Minneapolis: University of Minnesota Press, 1969.

————. "Sacred and Profane: Isaac Bashevis Singer's Embattled Spirits," *Critique*, VI (Spring 1963), 24–47.

SLOAN, JACOB. "I.B. Singer and His Yiddish Critics," *Congress Bi-Weekly*, XXXIII (March 7, 1966), 4–5.

SLOMAN, JUDITH. "Existentialism in Pär Lagerkvist and Isaac Bashevis Singer," *Minnesota Review*, V (August–October 1965), 206–212.

WOLKENFELD, J.S. "Isaac Bashevis Singer: The Faith of His Devils and Magicians," *Criticism*, V (Fall 1963), 349–359.

ZATLIN, LINDA G. "The Themes of Isaac Bashevis Singer's Short Fiction," *Critique*, XI (No. 2, 1969), 40–46.

Lionel Trilling

(Under General, see Eisinger; Fiedler, "Adolescence and Maturity . . ."; Fiedler, *Waiting for the End;* Hoffman; Malin and Stark; Angoff; Fiedler, "The Breakthrough"; "Under Forty"; "A Vocal Group.")

BOYERS, ROBERT. *"The Middle of the Journey* and Beyond: Observations on Modernity and Commitment," *Salmagundi*, I (No. 4, 1966–1967), 8–18.

FRAIBERG, LOUIS. "Lionel Trilling's Creative Extension of Freudian Concepts." In his *Psychoanalysis and American Literary Criticism.* Detroit: Wayne State University Press, 1960. Pp. 202–224.

FRANK, JOSEPH. "Lionel Trilling and the Conservative Imagination," *Sewanee Review*, LXIV (Spring 1956), 296–310. [Rev.-art.]

FREEDMAN, WILLIAM. *"The Middle of the Journey:* Lionel Trilling and the Novel of Ideas." In Warren French, ed. *The Forties: Fiction, Poetry, Drama.* Deland, Fla.: Everett/Edwards, 1969. Pp. 239–248.

FROHOCK, W.M. "Lionel Trilling and the American Reality," *Southwest Review*, XLV (Summer 1960), 224–232.

HAGOPIAN, JOHN V. "The Technique and Meaning of Lionel Trilling's

The Other Margaret," *Etudes Anglaises,* XVI (July–September 1963), 225–229.

KEECH, JAMES M. "Trilling's 'Of This Time, Of That Place,' " *The Explicator,* XXIII (April 1965), Item 66.

KENDLE, BURTON S. "Trilling's 'Of This Time, Of that Place,' " *The Explicator,* XXII (April 1964), Item 61.

KUBAL, DAVID L. "Trilling's *The Middle of the Journey:* An American Dialectic," *Bucknell Review,* XIV (March 1966), 60–73.

TANNER, TONY. "Lionel Trilling's Uncertainties," *Encounter,* XXVII (August 1966), 72–77. [Rev.-art.]

WEST, PAUL. "Romantic Identity in the Open Society—Anguished Self-Scrutiny Among the Writers," *Queen's Quarterly,* LXV (Winter 1959), 578–585.

Edward Lewis Wallant

(Under General, see Baumbach; Schulz; Alter; Freedman; Glicksberg, "A Jewish American Literature?"; Pinsker, " 'The Hassid' . . ."; Pinsker, "Salinger, Malamud and Wallant"; Rubin.)

AYO, NICHOLAS. "The Secular Heart: The Achievement of Edward Lewis Wallant," *Critique,* XII (No. 2, 1970), 86–94.

DAVIS, WILLIAM V. Sleep Like the Living: A Study of the Novels of Edward Lewis Wallant, unpublished doctoral dissertation, Ohio University, 1967. [Abstract in *Dissertation Abstracts,* XXVIII (February 1968), 3177A.]

_____. "The Sound of Silence: Edward Lewis Wallant's *The Children at the Gate,*" *Cithara,* VIII (November 1968), 3–25.

_____. "A Synthesis in the Contemporary Jewish Novel: Edward Lewis Wallant," *Cresset,* XXXI (May 1968), 8–12.

EPSTEIN, SEYMOUR. "Edward Wallant's Literary Legacy," *Congress Bi-Weekly,* XXXII (May 10, 1965), 8–10.

FEIN, RICHARD J. "Homage to Edward Lewis Wallant," *Midstream,* XV (May 1969), 70–75.

HOYT, CHARLES ALVA. "The Sudden Hunger—An Essay on the Novels of Edward Lewis Wallant." In his ed. *Minor American Novelists.* Carbondale: Southern Illinois University Press, 1970. Pp. 118–137.

LORCH, THOMAS M. "The Novels of Edward Lewis Wallant," *Chicago Review,* XIX (No. 2, 1967), 78–91.

LYONS, JOSEPH. *"The Pawnbroker:* Flashback in the Novel and Film," *Western Humanities Review,* XX (Summer 1966), 243–248.

RIBALOW, HAROLD U. "The Legacy of Edward L. Wallant," *Chicago Jewish Forum*, XXII (Summer 1964), 325–327.

ROVIT, EARL. "A Miracle of Moral Animation," *Shenandoah*, XVI (Winter 1965), 59–62. [Rev.-art.]

STANFORD, RANEY. "The Novels of Edward Wallant," *Colorado Quarterly*, XVII (Spring 1969), 393–405.

Notes on Contributors

Robert Alter teaches at the University of California at Berkeley. He is the author of *After the Tradition, Rogue's Progress,* and *Fielding and the Nature of the Novel.*

Jackson R. Bryer teaches at the University of Maryland. He has compiled the definitive bibliography on F. Scott Fitzgerald's critical reputation and edited *Fifteen Modern American Writers.*

David Daiches teaches at the University of Sussex. He is the author of many distinguished works of literary criticism and the autobiographical *Two Worlds.*

L. S. Dembo teaches at the University of Wisconsin. He is the editor of *Contemporary Literature.* His books on modern American poetry are well known.

Melvin J. Friedman teaches at the University of Wisconsin at Milwaukee. He is the editor of books on Beckett, Styron, Flannery O'Connor, and Roman Catholic novelists.

Edwin Gittleman teaches at the University of Massachusetts. He is the author of *Jones Very: The Effective Years, 1833–1840.*

Sheldon Norman Grebstein teaches at the State University of New York at Binghamton. He is the author of books on Sinclair Lewis and John O'Hara.

Allen Guttmann teaches at Amherst College. He is the author of *The Wound in the Heart* and *The Conservative Tradition in America.*

Marcus Klein teaches at the State University of New York at Buffalo. He is the author of *After Alienation,* a study of contemporary American novelists.

Karl Malkoff teaches at the City College of New York. He is the author of *Theodore Roethke: An Introduction to the Poetry* and a pamphlet on Muriel Spark.

Sanford Pinsker teaches at Franklin and Marshall College. He has recently published a book on modern Jewish writers, *The Schlemiel as Metaphor.*

Max F. Schulz teaches at the University of Southern California. He is the author of *The Poetic Voices of Coleridge* and *Radical Sophistication: Studies in Contemporary Jewish-American Novelists.*

Theodore Solotaroff is the editor of *New American Review.* His collection of essays, *The Red Hot Vacuum,* was published recently.

Helen Weinberg teaches at the Cleveland Institute of Art. Her book, *The New Novel in America,* was published recently.